Saving Grace

KYM FORREST

Trilogy Christian Publishers
A Wholly Owned Subsidary of Trinity Broadcasting Network
2442 Michelle Drive
Tustin, CA 92780

Library of Congress Cataloging-in-Publication Data is available.

ISBN 978-1-64088-939-2 (Print Book)
ISBN 978-1-64088-940-8 (ebook)

Dedication

....

To my dad, David Stinson, who was always my number one fan no matter what I was into at the time. I can't wait to see you again.

Contents

Acknowledgments

THANK YOU TO NORIKO WARNES for your input and editing expertise. Who knew with Japanese as your first language that you would have such mad English skills? Thank you to Pastor Larry Briney for reading the rough copy and giving your support and feedback. Your opinion means so much to me. Thank you to my husband, Robert, and my kids, Danielle and Dason, who recognized my dream for this work and have been so supportive. Thank you to Kayla Ridley for the cover design concept and Sheryl Ridley for the author headshot and forever friendship. And Kerri King whose financial support made the process possible.

1

JULIAN AND NATALIA DEPPROVOUE HAD been married for ten years and had no children. Natalia never wanted children; Julian wanted them badly. Julian found that Natalia had a secret stash of birth control pills in her dresser drawer.

"How could you deceive me this way, Natalia?" asked Julian. Natalia knew his anger was boiling just beneath the surface because he used her full given name. He usually called her Talia for short.

"I have never wanted to have children, Julian. You knew that before we got married."

"But we agreed to try to have just one, and all along over these past ten years, you have been secretly taking birth control. No wonder we haven't been able to conceive. Now I understand why you refused to see a fertility specialist. We agreed, Natalia!"

"I had no choice but to agree. You want children, but I don't. You decided that we would have one! That is not a compromise! That is you getting your way."

"But you agreed to try to have one baby, Natalia."

"I only agreed because your threatened to take your need to have a child elsewhere. I figured as long as you believed we were really trying, that time would go by, and you would eventually change your mind or simply accept that we weren't able to conceive."

"But all the while you were lying to me!"

"I never lied to you! Not once!" Natalia retorted in anger.

"You lied by leading me to believe that we were actually trying to conceive. You knew we would never conceive while you were taking those pills!" Julian's anger was mounting.

"So I allowed you to believe something that wasn't probably ever going to happen. That is not technically lying."

"Okay, then using your logic, I will go out and find a surrogate to carry a child for me, and when the baby is born, you and I will raise the child as our own."

"Julian, you wouldn't dare."

"I would. And technically, it won't be cheating because you are fully aware of my intentions in advance."

Fury was flying back and forth between the couple. Julian loved Natalia, but right, now he could choke her for the years of deception. During all the hours of consoling him as to why they weren't conceiving, she knew all along why they weren't successful in having a baby. And all along, she was lying to him, saying it would happen soon, maybe next month. Damn her!

Natalia's anger was in retaliation. She had gotten what she wanted. She was thirty-four and had avoided having a baby. The longer she could hold Jules off, the harder it would actually be to conceive. He wouldn't dare use another woman. She knew he was bluffing.

After a couple of weeks Jules anger would blow over, and things would go back to normal. They had a very healthy sex life, and they enjoyed each other in and out of the bedroom. Natalia was sure she had won this battle. They would not be having children.

Julian's anger subsided far more quickly than Natalia imagined it would. He was calm and back to normal in a couple of days. He never brought their argument up. She continued to use the birth control pills, and Julian never mentioned it again.

Three months later, Julian announced that he had found a suitable surrogate and that she was pregnant. They would be having a child in their lives in a few months.

"You've got to be kidding me! You actually went out and bedded another woman?"

"Yes, that is exactly what I have done. I found one who was willing to conceive naturally and give up all rights to the child once it is born. The child will be ours completely. We will move to Le Havre, and as long as you keep your mouth shut, no one has to know that the baby isn't ours together."

"I won't go along with this, Julian! It's not just that I didn't want to ruin my body by carrying and giving birth to a baby, I don't want to have to raise one either!"

"What's done is done! When the baby is born, it will be ours, and we will raise it as our own. You will be a mother, and I will be a father. It is no longer open to discussion. You lied to me, you betrayed me, and I was very clear as to what I intended to do."

"What? You can't be serious! I will not be a mother to your whore's child."

Whack. The back of Julian's hand slapped across Natalia's face knocking her to the ground.

"If you love me like you say you do, then you will. I will never look at another woman as long as I live. You have my word."

"I have no choice?"

"You have a choice, me and the baby or divorce."

"Julian!"

"And another thing, the child is never to know that you are not its real mother. So you better play the dutiful wife and mother role like your life depends on it."

* * * * *

Seven months later.

"Talia, meet our daughters."

"Daughters? Plural?"

"Yes, twins." Julian held both girls beaming like the new father he was.

"No! No! Julian, you said one child, not two."

"But they came as a pair. I didn't plan on two. It just happened that way. Nothing has changed except there will be two instead of one? Look at it this way, they will always have each other to play with. They will be less in your hair or a bother because they will be together!"

"You mean two times the work and two times the diapers and laundry, and everything else will come in twos."

Julian stood there holding the twin baby girls in his arms. "Only at the beginning, soon they will be crawling then walking and playing together, and you won't have to entertain them so much."

"Once they are crawling and walking, I will be running all over behind them, and life will morph from one phase to another. Just wait until they're both menstruating at the same time."

"Natalia, as soon as they become sixteen and can be emancipated as adults, I promise we will sell everything and buy the boat of our dreams and sail the world, just you and me."

"It seems that I have no other choice in the matter. But I will never let you forget your promise. As soon as they are sixteen, we will do exactly what you said and sell everything and sail the world."

"In the meantime, the girls need names. I was thinking Kaelynn and Jaelynn. What do you think?"

"I don't actually care what you call them. I will probably just call them the girls anyway."

"Natalia, you have to at least try to love them."

"Do I? I don't recall that ever being part of the deal!"

And so the girls, Kaelynn and Jaelynn, started off with a very rocky beginning. A father who doted on them and a mother who never wanted them.

For the past twenty years, Jules worked at a shipyard in La Havre, France, restoring and maintaining expensive yachts. The best yachts docked for weeks just to have the magic touch of Julian DepProvoue in making everything look brand new and in perfect working order. He made a decent wage and loved the work.

Something about working with his hands made him happy. He felt like he was doing honest work. Sure, it was hard and sometimes difficult, but he never gave up on a challenge, working on it until he could resolve the issue with perfect results. It was the reason so many yacht owners were willing to wait for Julian DepProvoue to work on their boats.

Natalia DepProvoue worked at a local bistro as their chef. She was really a short-order cook with the skills of a chef. But it was work, and it helped pay the bills. After a long day of work, she would arrive home wanting only to put up her feet and rest, but there was a house to clean and clothes to wash and dinner to make and those girls.

Most days, she felt like a maid and cook for the girls! They were sweet and cute and didn't cause much trouble, but they were a lot of work. Julian adored them, and for some reason, that bothered Talia. She felt a sense of jealousy toward them.

Jules came home from work and tossed everything aside to tussle and play with Jaelynn and Kaelynn. Oh, how they squealed as he tossed them high into the air only to catch them and tickle them. The girls adored him as well. As a result, Talia felt like all the discipline fell on her. She was always the parent who made them pick up their clothes, brush their teeth, comb their hair, and any other tasks that normal children would rather not do.

Julian was the fun parent, Natalia was the mean one. She was sure that was how the girls saw it, and it bothered her deeply. She didn't really want to play with the girls; honestly, she wouldn't have the faintest idea what to do with them. Julian kept throwing ideas at her whenever she brought the "good parent, bad parent" subject up.

"Natalia, you should teach them to cook and bake. You are a professional at that, and the girls will need to have those skills when they are grown and on their own. Hey, teach them now, and in a couple of years, they will be doing all the cooking and take that load off of you."

"Julian, the cooking is the one thing I actually enjoy doing. But I'll teach them laundry and cleaning first. Then maybe I won't be so exhausted to teach them cooking later."

And by the time Kaelynn and Jaelynn became ten, that's what life became—school, homework, laundry, and cleaning. There were no complaints when bedtime came. The girls were tired but took a sense of pride in their duties, most days.

By Kaelynn and Jaelynn's thirteenth birthday, pride in the housework was gone; they didn't like all the chores. There was never time to play with friends or go to the park or any of the things other kids their age were doing. Resentment began to set in.

Just before their fourteenth birthdays, Julian came home with a big announcement.

"Come here, my girls! Come on, I have some big news today!"

"What is it, Julian?" Natalia asked.

"What's the news, Papa?" Kaelynn and Jaelynn asked also.

"Today I got a very big increase in pay."

"Oh, Jules, that is wonderful news. Is it enough that I don't need to work anymore?"

"Papa, how much did they give you?" asked Kaelynn

"Yes, it's enough that you don't have to work anymore, Talia. And, Kaelynn, it's enough that we can have a small pool."

Excited whoops rang out in the family living room. Everyone felt like celebrating, so they all went out to dinner at their favorite restaurant, La Tablee, in La Havre. The girls both ordered shrimp scampi, and Julian and Natalia ordered lobster. The food was fabulous and the view spectacular.

A couple of months later, Natalia began teaching the girls how to cook and bake. By the end of the year, the girls were doing practically all the cooking for the household. They both enjoyed it. Cooking didn't seem much like a chore because there was so much variety with different meal selections and baking options.

Natalia was thankful that the girls took to cooking, but she found that she missed the restaurant environment. She talked with Juliane about it, and they agreed the girls were old enough that Natalia could look for a chef opening at a restaurant nearby. Before the week was up, Natalia had a job as a head chef at Jean-Luc Tartarin, a posh French restaurant near their neighborhood. The girls were thrilled. They hoped they would be able to eat out at least once a week.

Juliane's work was growing so much that his boss at the marina suggested that Jules consider opening his own restoration and repair business. The marina owner wasn't excited about this part of the business anyway. He offered Julian the current building and all the tools at a rate well below market value if he would take over that part of the business. He would be able to hire anyone he chose but would take on all the liability and responsibility of ownership. After a discussion with Natalia, Juliane bought the business and put his name on the company ownership papers and buildings, Juliane DepProvoue Repair and Restoration.

Business was booming at the new boat shop, and Natalia was making excellent money at the restaurant. The DepProvoues were putting every penny they could into saving up for their retirement dream, a yacht of their own and the ability to sail around the world.

Clothes were needed for the coming school year. Natalia woke the girls early one morning to conquer the task by the time she was to start work at the restaurant. She had authorized her assistant to purchase the produce, meat, and fish needed for the day's menu.

The girls' birthday was coming in just a few weeks. Natalia intended to get ideas of what they were interested in for gifts. At fifteen, almost sixteen, the girls were naturally fashion conscious. Natalia intended to get them functional clothes at a reasonable price. She had no intentions of hitting any of the high fashion district shops.

After the third thrift store, the girls were restless.

"How many more thrift stores are we going to, Mum?" asked Jaelynn.

"As many as it takes, girls," replied Natalia.

"Let's go closer into downtown, Mum. I'm sure we'll find good items there," chimed Kaelynn

But they continued shopping at thrift stores all morning. When they arrived home looking depressed with their items, Natalia admonished them, "You girls should be thankful. I intended to buy only three outfits each. But we hit a good day, and you each have five. And you can mix and match them with each other like you do so well." She called after them as they slinked off to the room they shared. It wasn't a large room, but it wasn't too small either. The room contained a double bed they shared and a decent-sized closet.

School started two weeks later. The girls were less than excited about their wardrobe but happy they would be seeing their friends again soon.

The girl's birthday was in September. They hurried home from school as instructed that morning by their parents. They had something big for them. They hoped it was a car! Maybe that's why their clothes and school things had all been secondhand and out of style the past few years.

When they rounded the curve leading to their driveway, they saw a large moving truck. A little further down, they could see their father talking with a man beside their family car. As the girls got closer, they entered the house. It was completely empty! Not a stick of furniture, no books, no sofa or fireplace tools. They turned to the kitchen, no table or chairs. They opened cabinets, no dishes, no pots, or pans. Next, they went into their bedroom. Everything was gone except for two suitcases sitting in the middle of the floor. What was going on? Mama had already gone to work, and Papa was still talking to the man outside. Soon the large truck started up and drove away.

Thirty minutes later, they heard the car start. They ran to the front window in time to see their family car driving away down the driveway while their father stood in the driveway waving good-bye. What was Papa thinking? How would he get to work and them to school?

Papa entered the house and tried to look excited. He was a horrible actor.

"Well, that's it, girls! We are about to start a brand-new adventure!" said Julian. "Happy birthday. You are sixteen and officially on your own as of today."

"Where is everything?" asked Kaelynn.

"Where did our car go, Papa?" asked Jaelynn.

"We moved most of the furniture and kitchen things to your new flat where you two will be living. Since you have reached the age of emancipation, you are ready to live on your own. We sold everything else. We bought a beautiful yacht this morning. Everything is paid for two years until you finish school. After that, you're on your own."

The girls looked so confused, then worried.

Kaelynn asked Papa, "What are you talking about? We still have two years of school to finish."

Jaelynn continued, "Who will be there with us to be in charge, who's gonna make sure we eat and go to bed on time?"

Kaelynn chimed in, "Or make sure we do our chores correctly?"

"Now, girls," said Julian, "why do you think you've been learning to do all these things for yourselves these past years?"

"But where are you and Mama going to live?" asked Jaelynn.

"We are going to live on the yacht." Julian cleared his throat and said, "As you know, your mum and I have always had this dream of sailing the world. Now that you girls are old enough, we can retire and fulfill that dream."

"But I thought we were going with you!" exclaimed Kaelynn. "Not dumped off to live on our own."

"We're only sixteen!" barked Jaelynn. "Hardly old enough to live on our own!"

"You're not completely on your own. We arranged for the building manager to look in on you now and then. And besides, there is enough money for food and utilities and medications if necessary, and your lease is paid for two years. We're not dumping you off," cajoled Julian. "You make it sound like we're abandoning you girls. You've known this day was coming since you were very small. On a brighter note," said Julian, "I'm taking you girls out to Jean-Luc Tartarin tonight to celebrate your birthday."

"To celebrate our birthday or finally being rid of us!" blurted Kaelynn, her face growing red.

Jaelynn elbowed Kaelynn in the rib then jumped in, "For our birthday? Our favorite restaurant?"

"Yes," replied Julian.

After dinner, they walked the few blocks to the new flat. It was spacious, with only one bedroom. No matter, the girls were used to sharing a room; they had shared practically everything for their whole lives.

The kitchen was small but functional. The sitting area and living room were combined but large enough to accommodate a small table and chairs and a sleeper sofa. These items were brought over from their house. Everything was handled, and Julian and Natalia would leave as planned on their new yacht tomorrow.

The girls prepared for bed, brushing their teeth and each other's hair. Talia came in from work. The parents hugged the girls good night like they had a thousand times before.

They all spent the night at the new flat, the girls on the pull-out sofa bed in the living area and Julian and Natalia in the girls' bedroom.

Once in bed, neither of the girls could sleep. Their minds were racing about what it would be like living in a flat of their own, with no parents to tell them what to do or where they could and could not go or when to be home. No one would ride them to get their schoolwork done. Freedom was beginning to sound quite awesome.

There was another side to this newfound freedom: responsibility. bills to pay, groceries to buy, all the cooking and cleaning would be theirs. Most of these tasks, they had already been doing for the past two years, so it wouldn't be a huge adjustment. The prospect of budgeting themselves was gnawing at their stomachs. They lay in the sofa bed well past 2:00 a.m. discussing the possibilities.

In the bedroom, no one was sleeping either. Excitement about setting sail at last consumed Natalia's mind. Leaving the girls on their own consumed Julian's.

Julian could not believe after all these years that Natalia was able to walk away from the girls so easily. It didn't seem to weigh on her at all. Julian knew full well it was an agreement made before the girls were born, but he had hoped Natalia would grow to love them as he did. But she hadn't. He wondered if after a week or two she would miss them like he knew he would.

At 4:00 a.m., Julian gave up trying to sleep and got up. Natalia was sleeping soundly. He went to check on the girls; they too were asleep, but their bedding was strewn every which way as if they had been tossing and turning all night. They probably had.

Julian went to the kitchen and put on some strong coffee. As he sipped, his gut told him not to leave the girls just yet. They should wait at least another year, but he had made a promise, and it was not likely that Natalia would go along with any delays at this point.

He was pouring a fresh cup when he heard the newspaper land on the floor outside the flat door. He opened the door and stooped to retrieve it. He quietly walked past the sleeping girls and stepped out onto the small balcony. He settled into a bistro chair just as the sun peaked over the horizon. It was going to be a beautiful day if not for leaving the girls behind.

An idea struck him. He mulled it over and over for several minutes. Yes, it just might work.

"Good morning," murmured Natalia into his ear as she brushed his cheek with a kiss.

"Good morning," he replied.

"Couldn't sleep?"

"No, my head is spinning with all that's happening. I'm just not sure the girls are emotionally ready for this. I mean, they're barely sixteen, Talia."

"Now, Jules, you are not going to back out on our agreement. Besides we've sold everything and don't even have a place to live!"

"I've been mulling over an idea. What if we took the girls with us…"

"No! Jules! No! You made me a promise—"

"Now hear me out, Talia…what if we homeschooled the girls for one year while we sailed, then brought them back here for their last year of schooling? We would be sailing as we've planned. The girls would develop a greater sense of independence as we travel. The only difference would be that the they would be with the us for a few months."

"Julian!" He knew he was in for it when she used his full given name. "You and I made a deal, and I have kept my end of it."

"I know you have, Talia. But I have a very bad feeling about leaving the girls so soon."

"And you'll have a bad feeling about leaving them at seventeen too!"

"No, I won't, I promise."

"You've already made a promise, and I am holding you to it!"

"I'll do all the schooling. The girls won't be a bother at all. You'll see."

Suddenly the girls rushed to the balcony all excited about the idea of sailing with their parents and homeschooling on board.

"No!" shouted Natalia. "We've made a plan, leased the flat, sold all our other belongings. We are not changing it now!" Her face was red and her entire body shaking.

Julian new there would be no changing her mind or their plans. That was that. When Natalia reached this level of anger, she dug in her heels and refused to budge on principle alone. He had never won an argument with her once she reached this level of agitation and anger. He knew he wouldn't win this one either.

2

···

THE FAMILY ALL WENT OUT to the marina to see the new yacht. It was a 16.5-meter (54-foot) vessel with four large cabins and four small cabins for crew. There was a spacious salon with large windows on either side of the boat to give guests an amazing view while sailing. The dining area could easily seat twelve.

The yacht boasted a game room and theater on the upper deck and a full outdoor barbeque kitchen area on the top. All but the master suite were on the bottom deck. The master suite was on the middle deck at the rear of the vessel. It had massive windows that took up three walls with an en suite to die for—large walk in-shower, a soaker tub, double sinks, and his and hers walk-in closets.

After the tour of the boat, the girls tried again to talk their parents into taking them along for the first year. Natalia looked at Julian and said, "We've had this conversation already. You deal with it." Once again, Julian explained that arrangements had already been made. A two-year lease had been paid in advance, and things were what they were. So the girls would not be sailing with them.

At 3:00 p.m., *The DepProvoue* officially set sail. Julian was on the bridge while their captain guided the small yacht smoothly out of the harbor toward open seas. Natalia, in her swimsuit and large-brimmed hat reclined on a deck chair and watched the scenery as they sailed by.

Julian looked back over his shoulder more than once to wave to the girls standing on the dock, both with tears trickling down their cheeks. Julian was misty-eyed himself.

Natalia never even looked back after hugging the girls on the dock. When Julian mentioned it to her later, she said, "We had said good-bye at least ten times, Jules. I'm confident they knew by then that we were really doing this. There was no point in prolonging the inevitable by waving to them repeatedly."

"You're a coldhearted woman," Julian breathed under his breath.

The sea was quiet and calm this afternoon. The forecast for the next two weeks was perfect for sailing.

The girls waived until the boat was out of sight. Then they called an Uber and headed for their new home, a flat in the heart of Le Havre. Practically everything was within walking distance: shops, food markets, bistros, everything they could want or need. Papa had set up a bank account in their joint names and showed them how to use the electronic payment system on their phones.

Jaelynn and Kaelynn were struggling with mixed feelings—on the one hand they were free and independent, which felt quite powerful. On the other, they were alone, feeling vulnerable and a little scared too.

"Let's stop at the bistro and get a coffee," Jaelynn suggested. She was the maverick of the two girls.

Kaelynn agreed, and so they went, for the first time by themselves, to an outdoor café and ordered coffees. Their new normal had just begun. The girls were exhilarated by the power of making their own decisions with no one to object or guide them.

After their coffees, they each ordered a sandwich for an early dinner. When they were finished eating, they paid their bill and went upstairs to their flat. Kaelynn flipped the TV on as they both flopped down on the comfortable sofa. Kaelynn chose a movie and clicked on it to watch. Jaelynn let out a little giggle because no one was there to tell them they couldn't watch an R-rated movie; then, they were both laughing out loud. This was going to be great!

Saturday and Sunday passed with ease as the girls slept in and did whatever they wanted to do. Sunday evening, they decided they should make a sensible schedule and help each other be responsible. So they set out to plan their week with time set aside for school and homework, a day and time for shopping for the week's food, and time for cleaning the flat and laundry. They each agreed to specific chores and duties around the flat. They posted their new schedule on the refrigerator and went to bed.

School days came and went the same as they always had. The only difference was there were only two people to cook and clean for instead of four, and Papa was not there to tease and joke with them. Mama wasn't there to tell them to do a chore they were nearly finished with already or to complain that they hadn't done it good enough and require them to do it again.

The girls followed their schedule, for the most part, occasionally throwing a small party with pizza and sodas. They never had more than four friends over at a time and were careful not to break any of the rules posted by the building owner. They did not want to lose their lease, their home or the money paid for the two years. The building manager described Kaelynn and Jaelynn as "good girls, quiet, clean, never had a problem with them."

As the end of the school year approached, the girls attended a career festival where potential career companies were present to answer questions and recruit new workers. Kaelynn and Jaelynn attended with the anticipation of deciding on some career path to pursue during their last year of school before college.

The forum was packed with potential companies: chef schools, automotive repair, law firms offering to pay for legal secretary or paralegal schooling with a promise of working for them upon completion, and modeling agencies to name a few. Kaelynn and Jaelynn walked the aisles overwhelmed at the prospects, many they had never thought of before.

The girls turned into yet another aisle when a man stepped forward to greet them.

"Hello, ladies, my name is John Stewart. Have you ever considered modeling for a career? You both have the perfect body shape and looks for it."

The girls' mouths gaped, "We have another year of school to complete."

"That is not a problem. We work with students all the time," said John.

"We work around your class schedules and make sure you have time to complete your schoolwork." He grinned and continued, "Plus you will be making thousands of euro each month while you're still in school. Just think of the money you could save for college or clothes and shoes, whatever you want!" he cooed. "We would love to have you join our modeling agency."

The booth was one of the largest they had seen all day. There were posters of well-known supermodels all over the walls and all wearing the latest fashions available.

Both the girls' eyes lit up at the prospect of having money to choose and buy their own clothes and shoes. There would be no more thrift shops for them.

"Where are your parents?" asked John.

"Oh, we are both emancipated," said Kaelynn "What would we have to do?"

Jaelynn added, "We've never modeled before."

John's eyes danced with delight. These girls were not only gorgeous but easily impressed too.

"That is not a problem in any way, ladies. We will teach you everything you need to know."

John directed the girls toward a table and chairs set up toward the back of the booth and off to the side. "Just take a seat here, ladies." John sat down and pulled some papers out of a brief case and prepared to fill in their information.

Kaelynn asked, "What would a typical modeling job entail?"

"That is a most excellent question," John responded.

"Most of our modeling jobs are for magazines. They call us for a certain number of models for clothing or other merchandise photo shoots. You would be working in a group usually and model clothing or jewelry, sometimes with cars or vacation destinations."

"My associate, Megan, works closely with all the models. She travels with our younger models along with a security team to ensure you travel and work safely. You see, you'll be traveling all over the world!"

"All over the world?" asked Jaelynn, her eyes wide and sparkling.

"What about our classes?" ask Kaelynn

"You will have all your assignments and books with you whenever you travel. You will complete all your schoolwork on downtime and turn everything in when we get back to Paris. You won't be traveling more than a day away except for rare occasions when we may be on location for a week or more," said John.

"Trust me, ladies, we have many students in our employ, and the schedule works well for them all. Think about it, how often have you daydreamed through class lectures and still been able to complete the homework without any problems?"

He had a point. The girls sat through boring lectures all day long and often caught themselves dreaming of far-off places. They were both A students.

"You said Paris? We live here in Le Havre. Would we have to move to Paris?" asked Kaelynn.

"Yes, you would be living in a student dorm with all the other young girls of school age."

"What do we have to do to get started?" asked Jaelynn.

"Fantastic!" said John. "I like that spirit!" He called for his associate who appeared from behind a curtain. This is Chris Bouemont. She will help you with the paperwork to sign up with the Farini modeling agency and complete the contract. It's a one-year contract. After that, you can decide if you want to continue modeling with us or try something different."

Kaelynn asked, "What if we get started and it's just not going to work for us?"

John Stewart responded sweetly, "Ladies, we've never had a single problem with any of our models. We make sure the modeling schedule is balanced with your schoolwork. You'll even have time set aside for fun things too. *And* almost everything is paid for by the agency, your travel expense, your food, and any fun excursion we take to revive you on a day off." John's expression was full of excitement, and his voice made everything sound so fun. "You ladies are in for the time of your life."

It took thirty minutes to complete the paperwork and sign a one-year contract with the Farini modeling agency of Paris, France. Forms were in place to put the girls on independent studies for their schoolwork, assigning Megan Stewart as the homeschool liaison. The girls were officially professional models.

3

MATTHEW WILSON CHECKED HIS LIGHT metering one more time before he started snapping shots. Australia in summer was fun and sunny but also hot. Lighting was key to good photography, and Matt was a professional when it came to good lighting. That's why he always had work.

Matt was only twenty-four with dark-brown hair that curled at the ends. His blue eyes sparkled as he set up each shot. At five feet, eleven inches, he wasn't considered tall, but he wasn't short either. He had a muscular build. His hobby was bicycling; it helped him stay in shape and clear his head after long days of photo shoots.

Matt liked his work but sometimes hated his job. Photography was his passion, but working with models was no picnic. Models tended to be self-absorbed, demanding, and whiny when it got hot and sticky.

Matt had worked for the Farini fashion modeling agency for four years now. He knew very well there was a dual business going on; the modeling agency in the foreground and something sleazy in the background. He also knew better than to say a word or even let on that he knew anything about the background business. The money was excellent as long as you kept to yourself and did your job; otherwise, you disappeared.

Not all the girls were involved in the background business. Some were strictly models. Matt's heart went out to the ones who got sucked into the sex trafficking. It usually happened after the girl finished a one- or two-year contract; then, they were offered an insane amount of money to sign a five-year exclusive contract.

All of them signed without reading the fine print or having the contract reviewed by legal counsel. Four years ago, shortly after Matt started working for the Farinis, two models tried to contest their contracts. They hired a lawyer and even had a court date set. Both of them, along with one of the photographers, died in a bizarre plane crash a week before their day in court.

There was an investigation of course, but there was nothing definitive determined. The official reason entered on the report was a probable bird strike in the single engine plane. Everyone who had worked for the agency longer than two years new better. They all knew it was a profound warning to keep their mouths shut.

Most of the girls involved in the trafficking went along because they were too self-absorbed to realize that their money wasn't going into their bank accounts at all. All modeling and hosting expenses were paid for by the company so there wasn't much reason to monitor a bank account.

One model caught Matt's eye early on. There used to be two of them, twins, but one had moved on to another agency. It wasn't so much that she was beautiful; they were all beautiful, but there was something else about this girl. Jaelynn DepProvoue wasn't a prima donna or one of the whiny types. She held her own. She worked hard and long and seldom showed any fatigue or boredom. She was a real pro. Matt guessed she was about his age. She carried herself with excellent poise and grace. He was stunned when he learned that Jaelynn was part of the background business. He had thought she was too smart to fall for that scam. But it was true.

Over the past year, Matt had watched Jaelynn's demeanor change. Depression had set in, and dark circles appeared under her eyes. She was thinner; it looked like she had lost fifteen to twenty pounds in the last eight months. It didn't suit her; she was too thin.

Occasionally Matt was allowed to take one or two of the girls out for dinner after a shoot. He had earned the respect and trust of Mrs. Megan Stewart. She watched over the girls and knew that Matt had a protective eye as well. He had never spoken out of turn or acted in any way inappropriate toward the girls or the agency personnel.

Matt was a solid guy who knew how to keep his mouth shut and the models safe. He could be trusted.

"Mrs Stewart," called Matt, "I was wondering if I might take Ms. DepProvoue to dinner tonight?"

"Let me check the schedule." She looked over her clipboard. "Yes, she is clear for tonight. Maybe you can get her to eat. Lord knows I can't. She hardly eats anything."

"I'll do my best, Mrs. Stewart."

* * * * *

Jaelynn felt lost without Kaelynn, but Kae had decided to go with a different agency when their first year contract was up for renewal.

"Jaelynn, I'm telling you something isn't right. We were worth twenty thousand euro last year, but this renewal is for seventy thousand? Something is not right," said Kaelynn

"What's wrong is you're looking a gift horse in the mouth. Look, we did a great job, they recognize it, and we are reaping the reward now. Why is that so hard to see?"

"Forty thousand euro would be an astounding increase. Seventy-thousand sounds like some unknown expectations are around the corner. Last year's contract was very specific. This new contract has too many vague clauses and contingencies."

"Well, it's sign it or lose it. That's what Mrs. Stewart said. It's not open to negotiation."

Kaelynn bit her lip. "I'm only asking for forty-eight hours. I might want to have a lawyer look it over first."

"I don't think that's gonna happen. What's the big problem, Kae?" asked Jaelynn.

"I just have a bad feeling about this, Jae. It's too good to be so cut and dry. My gut says they're hiding something that's not gonna be good for us."

"I say we sign it. Then have a lawyer look it over later. If it is illegal, we can get out of it."

"I don't think so, Jaelynn. I don't trust the Farinis. Besides, we would have to move to London. You and I are Paris girls. I've gotta go with my gut. I'm not signing."

Jaelynn grabbed her contract and penned her name at the bottom. "Well, I'm taking the deal before it disappears, and you'll see it's legit."

Kaelynn picked up her contract and tore it in half and dropped it on the desk. "I'm out! I've still got the offer from Johansen and Associates. I'm going to sign with them."

Kaelynn walked out the front office door as Megan Stewart walked in the back door.

Kaelynn didn't trust Megan Stewart either. She had traveled with the girls over the past year, and there was something seedy about her. For one, Megan was sickeningly sweet until you crossed a line; then, look out. Two, she had an explosive temper, sometimes yelling at the girls until they were in tears. Then, of course, she would switch back to her sickeningly sweet side again.

Jaelynn was usually the one who had the better business sense for a woman of eighteen. She was the one who was wiser and more mature at handling things. Kaelynn felt like she was the younger twin even though she was the eldest by two minutes.

Jaelynn had a way of holding herself together. When she was mad or upset, you didn't see it on the surface. They say "still waters run deep," well, Jaelynn's water was calm on the surface, but there could be an angry riptide underneath, and you'd never see it. When Jae lost her temper, it was not pretty. But the thing was that Jae could rationally resolve any situation. She was a born diplomat. Not Kaelynn, she was "what you see is what you get."

Kaelynn could take a lot, but you could also see her anger rising and beginning to boil. For those who knew her well, they knew when to back off. Others who weren't that close to her learned fast. But after Kae lost her temper, she too was quick to try to resolve the issue. She was also a very good judge of character. In this area, she had Jae beat. Jae was far too trusting and could get herself into hot water; whereas, Kae would take a step back and evaluate the person first.

As a pair, the twins were unbeatable when they each relied on the other's strengths. But they could also be their own worst enemies. If Jae got something stuck in her head and Kae opposed it out of hand, Jae could dig in her heels on a matter of principle. Kae was the twin that would back off first when they were at odds with each other. Kae thrived on unity.

It felt very odd walking out of Megan's office without Jaelynn. Kae hoped this wasn't one of those times Jae dug her heels in just to prove her sister wrong. Kae had a very bad feeling about this contract. Something was wrong, but it wasn't spelled out. Maybe that was it—all the things that weren't spelled out like they were in last year's contract.

Kaelynn and Jaelynn had already passed their eighteenth birthday. Last year, even though they were past the age of consent in France, they were still internationally considered minors—thus, the ever-present chaperones. But this year, they were internationally recognized as adults, their passports and travel documents updated.

Kae worried about Jae signing this contract. Johansen and Associates was offering forty thousand euros a year with 10 percent increases annually. This deal sounded reasonable. Also this contract was very clear. Kaelynn had fourteen days to review it, and Mr. Johansen encouraged her to have her lawyers look it over. Kae didn't have lawyers, but she intended to get one.

"Where's Kaelynn going?" Megan asked.

"I guess she's out," responded Jaelynn. "I'm in, here's my contract." She handed her document to Megan. It was a five-year contract, and true to what Kaelynn had said, Jaelynn had some questions.

"I have some questions about the contract, some things that weren't very clear," started Jaelynn.

"Kaelynn is a fool," retorted Megan. "Let her go. Come on, Jaelynn, we're going shopping. You're getting a whole new wardrobe." And just like that, the allure of having twins to tempt and please their clients was gone.

Megan and Jaelynn spent the rest of the week shopping for clothes, shoes, swimsuits, everything imaginable for the beach, the mountains, and the desert. Jaelynn found herself with bags and bags of old clothes she would donate to a homeless shelter in her neighborhood.

Megan insisted that Jaelynn would need a flat of her own in London where she would be moving soon. No more sharing in the dorm where the other models lived. Jaelynn thought this was a bit much, but Megan assured her that she would be doing a lot more entertaining under her new contract, and besides, she could afford it because the company would pay for the flat and all utilities as long as Jaelynn worked for them.

"That reminds me," chimed Jaelynn. "I still have some questions about the contract—"

"Not right now, sugar, we're here." Megan pulled into a new car lot. "You're getting a new car!" exclaimed Megan.

Jaelynn's mouth dropped open. "I don't know how to drive," she stated.

Megan said, "You'll learn," as she shut the car door and headed for the showroom.

They settled on a Mercedes AMG C63 S Cabriolet automatic, because that would be easier for Jaelynn to learn to drive.

4

....

KAELYNN SAT ACROSS THE DESK from her new attorney, Josh Freeburg. He was an American attorney practicing in a Paris law firm. He looked to be about thirty. He was dressed in the latest Paris business style, smart but not formal, suit jacket off, shirt sleeves rolled up with a neat bow tie. He was easy to look at too.

Josh reviewed the contract several times making a few notes on his legal tablet. At last he began, "This is a pretty standard modeling contract. You could sign it just like it is and be fine. But I do have a couple of recommendations for you to consider. If they are acceptable, I can draft an addendum to this contract that you can present to Johansen and Associates.

"First, I recommend that you add a clause that you have the option to purchase anything you model, at cost. That way, you keep your personal wardrobe sharp and classy. Lord knows how difficult it can be to find time to shop for clothing in Paris, especially for a supermodel.

"Secondly, after the first year of the contract, you could ask for private transportation to and from your locations. That means limo service in town, business class or better for airline travel. Just a couple of options to make life a little better as you set yourself apart from the other models."

Kaelynn thanked Mr. Freeburg for his insight and asked him to draw up the proposed addendum with a couple of modifications. She would accept the contract as written for the first year. If Johansen and Associates were agreeable to her first year work ethic and extended the contract to the second through fifth years, then the addendum would go into effect.

Josh was quite impressed with Kaelynn's ethical choice of proving herself to Johansen first, then, at their discretion, writing in the addendum. Kaelynn DepProvoue had some class. The addendum was drawn up according to Kaelynn's instructions and legalized for use.

Kae left the law firm with the addendum tucked into her handbag and ready to meet with Mr. Johansen on Monday. It was Friday afternoon, and Kae had a date with a handsome photographer she had met while working a freelance job with Johansen. His name was Jon-Pierre Laurent.

Jon-Pierre was a Frenchman who worked in Australia for Five for Five, an advertising and marketing agency. He liked the variety of work they provided. In addition to shooting for magazines, he got to shoot photos for vacation location brochures, websites, posters, and television advertisements.

For now, Jon-Pierre kept his home base in Paris, France, where he grew up. Jon-Pierre loved to surf and ride his long skateboard. Usually on weekends, he would drive over to La Havre to surf. If he couldn't get away from Paris, he would skateboard at Espace Glisse de Paris, an indoor park.

He had recently met a model that had been consuming his mind. Her name was Kaelynn, and she was drop-dead gorgeous. He hoped she liked him as well. But since he met Kaelynn, all he wanted to do was spend time with her. She didn't skateboard or surf.

Kaelynn opted for a casual outfit for the evening. Jon-Pierre had asked her to go to a bistro he enjoyed and then to catch an outdoor movie together. She wore a faded pair of jeans with a button-down plaid shirt of which she rolled up the sleeves and her favorite pair of black Toms shoes.

Jon-Pierre picked Kaelynn up right at 7:30 p.m. The little bistro wasn't far, and they sat at an outdoor table. Kae ordered bouillabaisse, a classic French seafood stew, while Jon-Pierre ordered boeuf bourguignon. They enjoyed their meal while watching the sun set. Kaelynn commented on the unique positioning of the bistro to enjoy a sunset or sunrise. Jon-Pierre said that is exactly why it is his favorite bistro in Paris.

The movie was set to start at 9:00 p.m. at a nearby park to which they walked. The evening was cool, and as the sun went completely down, a breeze picked up. Kaelynn felt a little shiver run down her spine. Jon-Pierre noticed and took his sport coat off and wrapped it around Kae's shoulders. She thanked him just as they found a large tree limb to sit on.

The movie tonight was a 1936 French classic *The Crime of Monsieur Lange*, about a man and a woman who arrived in a cafe-hotel near the Belgian frontier. The customers recognize the man from the police description. His name is Amedee Lange, and he murdered Batala in Paris. His lady friend Valentine tells the whole story. Both Kaelynn and Jon-Pierre enjoyed the evening even though it turned out a bit chilly.

Jon-Pierre brought Kaelynn home about 11:30 p.m. and kissed her very gentlemanly-like at her building door. Kae went upstairs to her flat almost floating on a cloud. She couldn't wait to tell Jaelynn about her evening. She dialed Jae's number.

A sleepy voice answered, "Hello?"

"I'm so sorry, Jae. Did I wake you? It's barely 11:30."

"Sorry, Kae, I had a very full day. I was modeling until 7:00 p.m. and then shopping with Megan until 10:00 p.m. I think Megan would have kept going until midnight if she could get the shops to stay open. I'm exhausted. What's up?"

"I'll call you tomorrow and tell you."

"No, I'm awake now. Tell me now."

"I just had the most amazing date!"

"Date, you didn't tell me you had a date?" Jaelynn was now fully awake.

"You've been kind of unreachable lately."

"I know, I'm sorry."

"It's fine. I went out with that photographer I was telling you about that reminds me a bit of Matt Wilson?"

"Oh, yah. How was it?"

"Fabulous! He is such a gentleman. We had the best time. We went to Café des Musées."

"I've always wanted to eat there."

"The food was amazing."

"What did you have?"

"I ordered the bouillabaisse and Jon-Pierre ordered boeuf bourguignon. They were both amazing. Then we walked to Parc de la Villette and watched *The Crime of Monsieur Lange*. It was so romantic and fun!"

Jaelynn yawned. "It sounds like you had a great time. Are you planning to see him again?"

"Yes, hopefully next weekend if we don't end up working over in London."

"Yeah, are you coming to London next week? We have to get together!"

"I know, right? It's been too long already."

"Agreed. I don't have my schedule for next week yet, but I'll text you, and we can catch dinner or something."

"Sounds good. I'll let you get back to sleep. Sorry I woke you up. I couldn't wait to tell you about tonight."

"No problem, I'm glad to hear your voice. I love you, sis. Good night."

"Love you too. Good night." And Kaelynn hung up.

She flopped onto her back on her bed and couldn't stop smiling. She really liked Jon-Pierre, and she hopped their relationship would grow to be a long and happy one. Kae laughed; that sounded cheesy even to herself.

5

MEGAN ARRANGED FOR DRIVING LESSONS for Jaelynn, and soon enough, she was cruising around London in her new car. Her first stop when she was properly licensed and driving on her own was to see Kaelynn who was in town for a photo shoot. It had been several weeks since their conversation over the contract. They talked daily over the phone but hadn't seen each other in person.

Kaelynn was dumbfounded when she got into the brand-new car with her sister driving.

"Are you sure you know how to drive this thing?" asked Kaelynn.

"Yep!" replied Jaelynn. "And I've got a license to prove it." She flashed her shiny new license at her sister.

"Let me see that!" Kaelynn grabbed the license from Jae and examined it. It looked real enough.

"Come on," said Jaelynn, "I'm taking you to dinner tonight."

They selected Core by Clare Smyth, a chic little restaurant in London. As soon as they got seated, they perused the menu for what to order.

"So, how are things over at Johansen?" Jaelynn asked.

"Great," replied Kaelynn. "I mean I don't have a new flat and wardrobe, and I certainly don't have a new car, but I am happy with my contract, and the people are great to work with."

"What numbers did you settle on?"

"Forty thousand for the first year. Then a 10 percent increase each consecutive year thereafter."

"Not bad."

"Did you ever get your questions answered about the contract?"

"Not yet, we've been too busy getting everything else going."

"I can see. I love the new clothes, very nice."

"Thank you." Jaelynn was wearing a stylish red jumpsuit with a black belt, matching shoes and handbag.

Their meals arrived, and they spent the rest of the evening catching up and dreaming about the future. Here they were barely eighteen and living the high life. They wondered what Papa would think of them. They had received two postcards from their father over the past year and a half, but that was all—no phone calls or letters, just quickly scribbled postcards.

Kaelynn and Jaelynn ended the evening with coffee and eclairs at 10:00. They both had early mornings.

* * * * *

It had been a whirlwind couple of months, getting settled in the new penthouse flat in London, getting used to driving the new car and parking it in the garage under the flat, plus juggling shoots in Australia, Los Angeles, Prague, and Mexico. Megan invited herself over when they got back into London. She plopped down at the dining room table and helped Jaelynn shuffle through the mail that had piled up. Megan took all the bills and tucked them in her handbag.

"Jaelynn, it's time for us to talk about some of the expectations that are coming with your new contract. You have all new clothes, a new place to live, a fancy new car, and well, all your expenses are paid. This doesn't come without certain expectations in return."

Jaelynn sipped her coffee. "What expectations are you talking about? There wasn't anything specific in the contract."

Megan arched her brows and said, "There wasn't a car, a flat, and a new wardrobe in the contract either." She watched Jaelynn to see if there was any hint of understanding her meaning.

"I didn't ask for any of those things," Jaelynn said softly.

"No, but you have accepted them, and with enthusiasm, I might add."

"I don't think I like the sound of this. You can take all of it back. I don't need any of it."

Megan half sneered, half laughed. "It doesn't work that way, sugar. The fact that you've accepted these, shall we call them perks, implies that you will reciprocate in kind."

"In what kind?" asked Jaelynn, her palms beginning to sweat and the hair on the back of her neck standing at attention.

Oh for heaven's sake, Megan thought, *I'm going to have to spell this out.* "Sugar, you're gonna be expected to host some company parties. Thus, the nice new flat. You're also going to host some company clients and guests."

"Define hosting clients and guests?"

"Some of our biggest clients like *High Fashion Magazine*, for example, will fly in company executives to oversee layout shoots. You'll be expected to wine and dine them when you're not shooting and show them a very good time."

"Define a very good time."

"Oh, Jaelynn, don't be so naïve, sugar. Your job includes making sure they leave Paris wanting to always use Farini for their model needs. If the gentleman wants a nightcap, you bring him up here for a nightcap and anything else he wants. *And* you make sure he's satisfied when he leaves the next morning. In fact, you treat him so good that he regrets even having to leave in the morning. Have I made myself clear?"

"Unfortunately, yes. But I'm afraid there's been a misunderstanding. I didn't sign up for any of this extra…stuff."

"Are you driving a new car? Are you wearing an all-new wardrobe to die for? Are you living in this beautiful penthouse flat all-expenses paid? Why yes, yes you are. And now I believe we understand each other clearly."

"If that's what having all this means"—she waived her hand around the flat—"I don't want it."

"Sugar, you signed a five-year contract. You either play the part this way, or you opt for plan B, and I promise you, you do not want plan B."

"What's plan B?"

"Trust me, you don't want plan B, sugar. It's dirtier, and it doesn't include the flat, the car, or the clothes, but all the other stuff is still required. It's just, well, like I said, dirtier."

"You're telling me that I'm basically a model by day and a prostitute by night?"

"Oh, Jaelynn, don't use such crude terms. You're handsomely paid, and the executives are very nice people. You can do this. You *will* do this."

"I want out of my contract! None of this was even hinted at. I will take the contract to a lawyer, and I will get out of it!"

"I wouldn't advise that." Megan pulled a small manila envelope from her bag and laid eight photos on the table. These two girls tried exactly what you just suggested, and you can see how that worked out for them."

Jaelynn felt sick to her stomach; the photos were of burned dead bodies tangled up in a crashed plane. She sunk into a chair at the table and began to shake. Kaelynn was right; there was something horribly wrong here. If she contested the contract, she was dead. If she went along with plan A, that was unthinkable, but plan B sounded even worse. She had no choice but to accept the consequences of playing right into their hands.

"Oh, and do I even need to tell you what will happen to anyone you tell about this arrangement? Especially your sister, you wouldn't want to have to worry about her every time she steps on a plane, now, would you?"

Jaelynn couldn't sleep that night. She was sick to her stomach all through the next day. When would her nightmare begin? Her boss was about to answer that question.

6

. . . .

KAELYNN CAME BACK FROM LONDON on Sunday afternoon looking down and depressed. Jon-Pierre thought he would take her out of town over to the beach. He would take his surfboard just in case the surf was good. Otherwise, he would walk the boardwalk with Kaelynn and look through the shops there. Maybe some coastal air was just what she needed.

The set out the following Friday afternoon. Jon-Pierre made reservations for them at Spa Hôtel du Pasino, Le Havre. He secured two adjoining rooms because he didn't want to rush the relationship with Kaelynn.

They arrived in Le Havre around 4:00 p.m. and went straight to the hotel. Kaelynn was relieved that Jon-Pierre had gotten two rooms. She felt some pressure lift to know that his expectations were at least pure on the outset. Whether they actually stayed in separate rooms remained to be seen.

Jon-Pierre drove into downtown Le Havre to a small, quaint little bistro where they had an early dinner.

When their food arrived, Jon-Pierre asked, "You looked really down last week when I picked you up from the airport. Did something happen in London?"

"It's more like what didn't happen."

"How so?"

"When I got to the shoot location, I just knew that my sister, Jaelynn, was there. I could feel her, you know? But her agency has her so busy she can't take a crap unless it's on the schedule. I was hoping we would have the evenings to have dinner and catch up.

But the Farinis have her scheduled to host executives for parties and stuff all the time. We didn't even get to have lunch together. It was ridiculous."

"Is this the sister that makes seventy thousand euros a year?"

"Yes, my twin, my only sibling. I don't expect you to understand this, but as twins, we have this connection, you know?"

"No, not exactly. I've heard of it but never knew any twins that have it."

"We have it. It's like we know, we just know. I walked into the studio where the shoot was, and I knew she was there. I could feel her presence. And as I was looking around for her, she was looking around for me. When we saw each other, we both knew we were feeling the other one."

"I can't even imagine what that would be like. It sounds a little creepy."

"No, we've been that way our whole lives. You should've seen us try to play hide-and-seek."

"Oh, yeah," he chuckled. "How did that work?"

"Not too well. We had to focus on blocking the other one out. Now that was hard."

"Do you think that's what she is doing now, shutting you out?"

"No, I could sense her fatigue and frustration. I think she honestly wanted to hang out, but her schedule wouldn't allow it."

After dinner, they went for a walk on the pier. Kaelynn remembered to bring a jacket along, but that didn't stop Jon-Pierre from putting his arms protectively around her.

Back at the hotel, Kaelynn told Jon-Pierre that she wanted to take a shower and went on to her room while he went into his. Kae let the hot water wash away much of her anxiety about Jaelynn. Even though she could feel that Jae was not telling her everything about her big contract, she did her best to push those feelings away. She wanted to spend a nice weekend relaxing and not rushing about. She wanted to have a good time with Jon-Pierre.

When she got out of the shower and toweled off, she stepped out of the bathroom to find a note had been pushed underneath the adjoining door between hers and Jon-Pierre's rooms. She picked it up. It read: *Knock if you want to enjoy the star-studded night and some champagne.*

Kaelynn smiled to herself. Jon-Pierre was so sweet, and a romantic too. She knew he wasn't doing this to get her into bed; he was doing it because it was an enjoyable way to spend an evening. He was so sweet.

Kaelynn dressed in her sweats and socks, then knocked on the adjoining door. Jon-Pierre opened the door. He too was in his sock feet. He was wearing his jeans from the day and a plain white T-shirt. He was looking casual and very sexy to Kaelynn. They stepped out on the balcony of the hotel room, and Jon-Pierre opened the champagne. He filled two flutes half full and handed one to Kaelynn.

"You're awfully confident that I am of drinking age, aren't you?"

"Oh my gosh, I'm sorry. It never even occurred to me that you were under eighteen."

"Relax, I am eighteen. It's fine. I'm just having fun with you."

"Whew, you scared me for a minute. I mean I know the age of consent is fourteen, but I still like to make sure my dates are at least eighteen. I assumed you were about twenty-three or twenty-four honestly. You're very mature for your age."

"Thank you. You learn quickly how to handle yourself as a model. So I understand."

They sipped their champagne and leaned back to enjoy the evening sky. Just then, a star shot across the sky right in front of them.

"Quick, make a wish," said Kaelynn as she grabbed Jon-Pierre's hand.

They held hands, and each made a wish.

"What did you wish for?" asked Jon-Pierre

"I can't tell you, or it won't come true!" said Kaelynn.

They continued to hold hands and drink champagne until half the bottle was gone. Kaelynn was feeling very relaxed. Jon-Pierre seemed hardly affected by the alcohol. It started to get chilly, so they moved inside the room and closed the sliding door. Jon-Pierre took Kaelynn into his arms and kissed her softly. Kaelynn felt her knees weaken and kissed him back.

After a few minutes, they were on the bed, and Jon-Pierre was unbuttoning Kae's shirt. He stopped asked, "Are you sure this is what you want?"

"Yes," she said. "But to be honest, I've never done this before."

"You're a virgin? Tonight will be your first time?" he asked.

"Yes," she said. "Is that okay?"

"Perfectly fine," he said as he lowered his mouth to hers again. After they made love, they fell asleep in each other's arms and slept together all night. It was a wonderful first time for Kaelynn.

* * * * *

Back in London, the first party Jaelynn hosted was for the executives of the Farini modeling agency. It was a simple dinner party. Jaelynn didn't have to do anything really; the food was catered, and there were hired servers who set everything up and people who cleaned everything afterward. At the end of the party, everyone left except Megan and Germain Farini. Jaelynn suddenly knew who her first client would be. Megan gathered her things and hugged Jaelynn.

"I put something on the counter for you in your bathroom. Be sure to use it before you go to bed."

And with that, Megan breezed out the door and was gone.

"Come here, Jaelynn," Germain commanded. He pulled her into his embrace and began to kiss her neck. Jaelynn felt like she was going to throw up. Germain was not the best looking of men. He was overweight, his belly protruding over his belt. He wasn't a tall man and almost looked square when you took in his height and his weight in perspective.

Jaelynn tried to pull away, but Germain gripped her upper arms more tightly, hurting her. She let out a whimper of pain.

"You had to know that we would sample your goods before offering you to our clients. Relax, baby. Just let yourself go along with Uncle Germain, and I promise I won't hurt you. Don't fight me."

Germain grabbed Jaelynn's face with one hand and pulled her body into him with his other hand. Suddenly, he released Jaelynn and said, "I think we could both use a drink. You go slip into some-thing sexy, and I'll fix us one."

Jaelynn escaped quickly into the bedroom and closed the door. Leaning against the door, she stifled a sob, swallowing it down hard. She knew what was about to happen and with whom, and she was dreading it.

Jaelynn went to her dresser and selected one of the new teddies Megan had insisted she buy and slipped into the master bathroom to change. Just then, she remembered what Megan had whispered to her just before she left the flat. Jaelynn picked up the tube; it was a lubricant with birth control. She had no idea what she was doing or even if she was doing it correctly. She put the teddy on and a short, silky robe over it and went back to the living room where Germain had made himself comfortable on her couch. His jacket and tie dis-carded lay over the back of the sofa.

Germain held out his hand, holding a drink for Jaelynn. She took the glass and took a slow sip of the amber liquid. She had no idea that Germain had put a small pill into her glass to help her relax and be more cooperative. The first sip of liquid burned her throat as it slid down. The second sip wasn't as bad. By the third and fourth sip, she began to relax. Before Jaelynn knew what had happened, they had moved into her bedroom, and Germain had his way with her. It was by far the worst night of her eighteen years.

Jaelynn waited until she heard Germain's soft, even breathing indicating he was asleep. She slipped quickly out of the bed and went to the shower. She let the scalding water run over her body, and she scrubbed every inch. She felt so dirty, so violated. No matter how much she scrubbed, she couldn't get the dirty feeling to wash away.

After the shower, she got into her sweats and fled to the living room sofa. She laid there for several hours, rocking herself and cry-ing. She hated her life. She should have listened to Kaelynn. There was something very, very wrong here.

Around 4:30 a.m., she drifted off to sleep. An hour later, she could here Germain fumbling around in the kitchen making cof-fee and toast. She hoped he would leave without bothering her any further.

Germain came to her just before he left the flat for work.

"Don't be late for work this morning. Just because you're our little dove doesn't mean you get any other special treatment. You still have to show up on time and work hard." He patted her bottom and said, "You were excellent last night." And with that, he left the flat.

Jaelynn stretched and got up. She headed for the shower again; she still felt dirty and ashamed. She hoped the scalding water would wash last night's violation away, but she knew it would not.

Jaelynn dressed and headed to work in her new car, which she now hated and wanted to get rid of. But the car was in the company's name as well as her own; she couldn't make any decisions regarding the car without their involvement. The entire situation was ironclad, and she knew it. She had backed herself into a hopeless corner. What was it her mother used to say? "You've made your bed. Now sleep in it."

The photo shoot today was for *High Fashion Magazine*, a Paris-based design house. It was on location at a beautiful mansion in a high-class neighborhood of London. The entryway was thirty-two feet from floor to ceiling with a beautiful crystal chandelier and opened up to a winding staircase to the second and third floors. Most of the photos were taken outside in the backyard around the crystal clear blue pool. Matthew Wilson was the photog today. Jaelynn liked working with him. He respected the models and treated them like people, not cattle.

"Tilt your head down and to the left just a little bit," Matt requested. Jaelynn complied.

"That's it. Yes, that's perfect. Now look at me please. Perfect, perfect. Got it. Thank you, ladies That's a wrap."

It was actually earlier than Jaelynn thought they would finish today; it was only 7:30 p.m., and she couldn't wait to get home and have another shower. All she wanted to do was put on her sweats and collapse on the sofa for the evening.

"Oh, Jaelynn," called Germain. "This is Mr. Housely from *High Fashion*. He would like to take you to dinner tonight." Germain saw that Jaelynn was going to decline, and he tightened his grip on her arm. Leaning into her ear, he whispered, "You go along and show him a real good time, just like you showed me last night!"

7

· ·

THE FOLLOWING DAY IN LE Havre, the surf was perfect. Jon-Pierre and Kae walked down to the beach, Jon-Pierre carrying his surfboard. Kae sat on a towel on the beach and watched Jon-Pierre surf for a while. After several nice wave rides, he came into shore and talked Kaelynn into giving it a try.

"No, no, no way. I wouldn't be able to stand up on that thing."

"Well, then lay on it and ride the wave into shore. I promise you, it is so much fun."

After some cajoling, Kae agreed to ride the board on her stomach. They both swam out to where the waves were forming. Jon-Pierre stayed with her until a nice-sized wave appeared. He helped guide her when to paddle and when to just ride. He body-surfed along as well, reaching the shore just seconds after she did.

The look on her face told Jon-Pierre everything; she was hooked.

"I want to do it again!" she exclaimed.

He grinned and said, "Let's go!"

They stayed out until early afternoon when they were famished and went to get some lunch. They stopped at the Fifties American Diner and ordered hamburgers, fries, and sodas. To Kaelynn, the food never tasted so good.

"There's nothing like surfing to stir up good appetite, right?"

"Yes!" exclaimed Kaelynn. "I can't remember when I've been so hungry, and I work out every day."

"Ah, the gym is nothing compared to surfing. Wait until tomorrow. Your abs are going to be so sore. Surfing uses muscles you don't often work in the gym."

51

He was so right. The next morning, Kaelynn went to get out of bed, and her entire core hurt. Jon-Pierre laughed lovingly at her. "You've got to come surfing with me as often as we can. You'll have incredible abs in no time."

Three months later, Jon-Pierre bought Kaelynn her own surfboard. Since Le Havre was only a two-hour drive from Paris, they continued to surf together whenever they could get over to the beach.

During the rainy months, they went to Espace Glisse de Paris indoor skateboard park. Kaelynn absolutely refused to try skateboarding. The possibility of getting seriously injured was far too great on wheels. The water was one thing, but wheels could easily render a broken bone, bruises, or worse, contusions. Kaelynn would not risk harming her body or looks, what she called her moneymaker.

* * * * *

Week after week, Germain or his brother, Georgio, had dates set up for Jaelynn with some big, important person. Over time Jaelynn slipped into depression. She knew how to do her job, both of them, and went along to get along.

One night when Germaine had not arranged any date for Jaelynn, she was allowed to go to dinner with Matt Wilson, one of the photographers. Jaelynn liked working with Matt and was looking forward to a nice dinner when suddenly she wondered if she was supposed to entertain him too. As it turned out, Matt wanted only to have dinner and a nice conversation, which they did. It was so refreshing not to be handled all evening with knowing expectations. Matt was a true gentleman, or at least tonight, he was.

Matt wondered how Jaelynn could make it through a day with how little she ate. She said she wasn't very hungry, but he had been watching her for several weeks now; she didn't eat during the day either. She had to be hungry. He had also noticed that she had bags under her eyes, a sure sign that she wasn't sleeping well either.

Matt wanted so much to talk to Jaelynn about what was going on behind the scenes, but he too knew what happened to girls who talked. Matt had seen the same photos of the plane crash that Jaelynn had been shown but was told a very different story. Somehow, he knew the whole crash had been carefully planned. He had seen both models chatting privately with Josh, his fellow photographer, and now all three were dead. No, he would never talk to Jaelynn or put her in any danger with the management or owners.

Over the next year, Jaelynn and Matt went to dinner together as often as they could. It was not a romance or even a hint of one. It was a growing friendship.

Matt knew Jaelynn was in deep depression. He had seen the pattern before. One model six years ago hung herself in her own shower, the only escape clause open in her mind. Then the two models and photog who died in the plane crash three years ago, and now, Jaelynn. How long could she last?

8

....

KAELYNN LANDED AT HEATHROW AIRPORT at 7:55 a.m. Monday morning. There was a full day of shooting planned for Sadie Williams, and four models from Johansen had been flown in. They quickly found out that they were joining six models from Farinis.

Kaelynn walked into the studio and immediately felt Jaelynn's presence. She looked around and saw her across the studio. Jaelynn was looking around for Kaelynn too. Jae was being dressed by one of the dressers for an opening shot.

Sadie Williams's designs were being featured in British *Vogue*. They had one week to get everything the publisher wanted for the layout.

Kae thought it would be a blast if she could stay with Jae for the week. It would be like old times when they shared a flat in Paris. But Jaelynn said that along with the free penthouse flat the Farinis paid for came the demand that Jaelynn host all kinds of dinner parties for the Farini's clientele. This week, she was called upon to host a high-class get-together for Sadie Williams and British *Vogue* executives. She told Kaelynn that her entire week was booked solid. Jaelynn didn't even know if she would be able to get away for dinner one night.

Kaelynn play punched Jae in the arm and said, "That's what you get for seventy thousand a year."

Jaelynn rubbed her arm and said, "You have no idea."

Kaelynn wondered more than once if she had missed out on a sweet deal. But then, she would never have met Jon-Pierre if she had signed with the Farinis. Matt Wilson was the Farini's photographer of choice. Kae knew why. Matt was a fantastic American photographer. He was a gentleman as well. Most of the other photographers were in the business to see how many models they could make out with by the time they were thirty. None of the models liked them.

All the models liked Matt. He was a dream to work with. He watched the models to make sure they didn't get too hot or sweaty, unless that's what the shoot called for. He also made sure they took regular breaks during the shoot. The other guys just wanted to get done as fast as they could so they could get into bed with one of the models. Kaelynn thought their work showed it too. But when Matt wasn't available, one of the other guys showed up.

Kaelynn was hoping that Jon-Pierre's reputation would grow to be like Matt Wilson's. Matt's work was truly something to aspire to.

Often on a first day of shooting, the designer is a mess and tries to micromanage everything, causing long, needless delays. Sometimes the designer hasn't even settled on the order of the outfits he or she wants to have used. At any rate, Sadie Williams had her stuff together. She didn't micromanage, and her lineup was rock solid. The shoot went well for the first day.

Kaelynn and Jaelynn were used for the majority of the outfits. Because they were identical twins, Sadie had them in almost every shot, together. Sadie commented that it was amazing to be able to mirror the models without have to plan everything for postediting. Normally, the photographer would have to take the same model in multiple outfits and then put them together in post by using photoshop and mirroring the model so that it looked like there were two. For this shoot, they actually had two. It was a win-win for everyone.

Matt worked the models and the outfit changes in a flow that moved smoothly throughout the week. By Thursday midafternoon, they were wrapped—all the shots and all the outfits captured. The models took a fifteen-minute break while Sadie, and the *Vogue* people looked over their planned layout and the shots. They were satisfied, and so the shoot was over by 4:30 p.m. Thursday.

Kaelynn beelined for Jaelynn to see if she was free for dinner.

"I'm sorry, I'm not. I have to host a party tonight for the *Vogue* clientele, and I'm hosting all day tomorrow out on the Farini's yacht for Sadie. I won't have any time for myself until noon on Sunday. Do you think you will still be in London then?"

"No," said Kaelynn. "I'm flying out Sunday afternoon for Australia for a shoot there."

And so their schedules crossed without any time to hang out together. This became the normal turn of events for the twins over the next two years. They found themselves on the same shoots many times, but Jaelynn's schedule would never open up for them to hang out.

Their conversations became late-night phone calls or quick snippets over changing room walls. It was not the life either of them had dreamed it would be when they started modeling together a year and a half ago. Kaelynn noticed that Jaelynn was looking more tired than usual. And no wonder, her schedule was so hectic, far more so than Kae's.

9

JAELYNN HAD NOT LOST COUNT of how many guests she had entertained. She kept a detailed calendar of appointments, with the company and the executives full name. She kept her book tucked away in her lingerie drawer. She hoped someday it would be useful against the Farinis. She felt so used and so old. She was only twenty, but she felt old. Shopping always helped lift the dark cloud she lived under. She had some time off coming; maybe she would call Kaelynn and catch up with her wherever she was working and just hang out.

Jaelynn logged into her bank account for the first time in a long time. She had never had to use her bank account. She had a company credit card, and everything else was paid for. She never even looked at her account. As the page loaded on her screen, her eyes grew wide in disbelief. She had twenty-four thousand euros—that was it. Where was her seventy thousand she had earned over the last year?

Jaelynn dialed Megan's number and waited for her to answer. *Crap, voicemail.* She left a brief message, "Megan, it's Jaelynn. Please call me. I have some questions about my paychecks." She hung up.

Twenty minutes later, her phone buzzed; it was Megan.

"Hello, sugar" Megan purred in sickening sweetness. "How are you?"

"Not too well," shot Jaelynn. "I just looked at my bank account. I seem to be missing about seventy thousand euros. Where is my pay for the past year?"

"Well, darling, some of the expenses on your account are not gratis, so they are subtracted from your salary."

"Seventy thousand worth? I couldn't spend that much if I tried."

"It is what it is, sugar," Megan said sharply. "Deal with it!" And she hung up.

Jaelynn was furious. How could they do this? After all she was doing for the company, how could they steal her pay as well. She dialed Georgio's number and waited. Georgio picked up on the second ring.

"Hello, Jaelynn," he answered. "How are you, darling?"

"Not too well, Mr. Farini. I just looked at my bank account. I seem to be missing about seventy thousand euro. Where is my pay for the past year?"

"You should talk to Megan about payroll matters, dear."

"I just got off the phone with her. She says it has all gone to cover spending that my expense account doesn't cover!"

"Jaelynn, if that's what Megan said, then that's what has happened. You know I don't deal with payroll and day-to-day details. I have people for that. Now run along and play nice with everyone, dear." And the line went dead; he had hung up too.

She sat her phone down, and it buzzed again. It was Kaelynn calling.

"Kaelynn! Oh gosh, it's so good to hear your voice."

"Jaelynn, it's good to hear yours too. How are you?"

"Okay, life as usual. How are you?" Jaelynn was very careful because she suspected that all her conversations were monitored by the company. She felt paranoid but was sure it was true.

"I have a week off next week, and I was wondering if we could finally have some time together?"

"It just so happens that I have a week coming as well. It would be great to hang out and catch up. Name the place and time, and I'll be there!"

"I was thinking St. Croix in the Virgin Islands. How about a week there?"

"Oh my gosh, that sounds so fantastic."

"Great, I'll make all the arrangements and send you a text by Friday."

"I'll watch for it, and make sure I am able to be gone for the week. Of course, I'll have to have a security detail with me."

"I'm so excited," said Kaelynn.

The girls chatted for another hour before hanging up. Their schedules had never matched before so they could get away together. Kaelynn texted Jaelynn that she would e-mail all the trip details because they were somewhat extensive. She had arranged to meet Jae in London, and then they would fly together from there. Jaelynn read the e-mail twice and logged all the travel arrangements into her appointment book. Attachments contained flight tickets and numbers as well as connection information and car rental reservations from the airport on St. Croix. They would drive to the resort and spend a week of nothing to do but enjoy themselves. They both worked hard and had earned a rest.

10

MATT LEFT FROM HIS FLAT in London and drove leisurely through the countryside as if simply enjoying a nice afternoon drive out of town. He arrived at the Wayfarer Inn exactly at 4:45 p.m. as instructed. He asked for the back corner booth and was escorted to his seat. The gentleman already seated spoke first.

"Good, you're on time. Were you followed?"

"No, I took all the back winding roads just as you instructed. I was the only car on the road the majority of the time."

"Good," replied the man. He was wearing a starched white shirt with a solid blue tie. His blue suit jacket lay across the back of the booth. He was crisp and professional.

"I've never done anything like this," said Matt. "I'm a little nervous. There is a lot at stake here. People have died trying to get out of this organization, and I don't want anything to go wrong."

"I understand," said the man.

"I don't even know your name," Matt said.

"Joe Richards, US witness security. This is what I do all the time, and if you do exactly what I tell you, when I tell you, everything should work like clockwork. But timing is critical to success. Do you understand?"

"I understand."

"So, give me the story."

"I work for a fashion model agency that tricks their models into signing contracts that actually lead them into sex slavery. The company pays for everything, and the girls have no way out. Six years ago, a model hung herself, and that's how she got out. Three years ago, two models and a photographer were killed in a suspicious plane crash, and that's how they got out. Now another model, a very sweet young woman barely twenty is caught in their lair, and I'm afraid we might see another suicide if I don't do something."

"We know all about the plane crash," began Joe, "and we also know exactly how they made it happen and look like an accident to the international aviation authorities. The Farini agency has been on our radar for a long time. We've just never been able to get inside. Do you think this girl will cooperate with us?"

"No, I don't think she will. That's why we are going to do this without her knowledge until the last minute."

"You've got to be kidding me! That will never work. We have to be able to have legitimate documents in place to get her safely out of the country without the agency ever knowing where she went. We cannot do this without her full cooperation."

"I believe we can, and it's the only way I'll agree to. You're not the only one who needs to be able to be anonymous. If this plan goes south, I want to be the only one that can be implicated. I will not put her life in jeopardy!"

"You are in love with her, aren't you!"

"That is not your concern. Do we have a deal?"

"If you can get us what we need as we progress, then yes, we'll do it your way. But if we hit any snags, you bring her into the process, or the deal is off. Agreed?"

"Agreed."

"I need her photo ID, her passport, her birth record and proof of residence to even get started."

"I can get those for you."

The man arched his brow. "I don't want to know how you get them, but they have to be originals. Copies will not do."

"I understand."

Joe continued to lay out the plan of when and where they would meet next to transfer the documents over to him.

11

···

In April, Kae asked Jon-Pierre if he could take a week off and get away too. They decided on St. Croix in the Virgin Islands. The prospect of getting away out of country just to relax was intoxicating.

Kae and Jon-Pierre were already set to fly out from Paris to London and then onto St. Croix. They made arrangements for Jae to join them from London on.

Jaelynn looked like death walking when she arrived at the airport. Never mind that she wasn't wearing make-up. Neither twin ever did when they were traveling; it cut down on being recognized. But Jae had dark circles under her eyes, and Kae could tell she was not only exhausted but also very depressed. She realized that Jaelynn needed this time of rest like her life depended on it, and it may very well.

The trio landed in St. Croix on a Sunday afternoon and wouldn't fly out until the following Sunday morning. The sun was shining, but a fine misty rain was in the air. It reminded them of Hawaii where it rains practically every day.

They drove to their hotel and started unpacking. It didn't take more than ten minutes because they were all so used to the travel routine.

They met in the lobby and ordered some early cocktails. Jae practically gulped hers down and ordered another. When her second drink arrived, Jaelynn noticed that Kae and Jon-Pierre had only taken a couple of sips of their drinks. Jae did her best to slow down, but all she wanted was to get to that buzzed place where she could begin to relax and not think about her life.

Kaelynn noticed what Jae was doing. She recognized the routine of drinking to forget. She had seen it in their father. He used to do the same thing after work. He would have several drinks and pass out in front of the TV.

She hoped Jae wasn't heading down the same path. Jaelynn had never been a party girl, but then, she had never had to host so many executives and throw so many parties either. Maybe the drinking was how she got through it all.

Once they were back in their hotel room, Kae talked with Jon-Pierre about Jae.

"Jon-Pierre, I don't like what I am seeing with Jaelynn. She is far more than just exhausted. There is no life in her eyes. She looks like death walking."

"I noticed, but I wasn't going to bring it up. She needs this week to be unplanned and chill."

"I agree. Let's ditch our planned agenda and just go with the flow of things from day to day. Jae may decide she wants to try surfing or go on some other touristy things, but unless she brings it up, let's chill as well."

"Agreed. I had a buddy commit suicide in secondary school, and she has that same look in her eyes. Like there's nothing left to live for. I don't want to scare you, but I am very concerned for her."

"Thanks for sharing that. I'm going to do my best to get her to talk. So how about this, you surf and leave us on the beach to talk."

"I can do that. It sounds like a good plan. I doubt she would open up with me around."

"She might not open up to me either. She's never wants to talk about work. It's like her new cardinal rule."

"Sounds to me like she's hiding something or trying to protect someone."

"Maybe."

Jaelynn slept almost the entire day Monday. She finally texted Kae around 5:30 p.m. to see where they were. They were down at the pool, and Kae invited Jae to join them. Twenty minutes later, she joined them at the pool with a drink already in hand. Kae suspected it was not her first.

Jon-Pierre suggested that they find a good spot for dinner before it got too late and they couldn't get a reservation. The settled on Savant near their hotel. They walked the few blocks in the cool evening breeze and enjoyed a relaxed evening. They talked about all kinds of places they had visited for their work and restaurants they had experienced in each. But the conversation never strayed from surface content. Jaelynn had four drinks during dinner. She was definitely buzzed when they walked back to the hotel. Jae called it an early night at 9:30 and went to her room.

Kaelynn didn't hear from Jae until 11:30 a.m. the following morning. Kae suggested they head down to the beach and enjoy some of the surf. Jae was up for that. They both wore conservative, one-piece suits, floppy hats to protect their faces from the sun, and sunglasses. It was getting harder to go out in public and not be recognized.

Jon-Pierre rented a surfboard and hit the waves. As soon as he was out of earshot, Kae turned to Jae and said, "Spill it!"

"Spill what?"

"What is going on with you?"

"What do you mean?"

"Jaelynn, let's not play games. You're way beyond exhausted, and you're drinking a lot. Talk to me. What is happening?" Kae pleaded.

"You know how hard a day of modeling is. After an already long day, I have to host a party for clients until wee hours of the morning. Then be up and ready to work again by 7:00 a.m. It's long days and nights with little sleep. It's exhausting. That all there is to tell." Jaelynn specifically left out the sexual details of her hosting job.

"Then why are you so depressed?"

"I'm not depressed. I'm tired," objected Jae. "Now if you could please stop interrogating me, I might be able to relax."

"I am not interrogating you. I care about you, and I don't like what I'm seeing."

"Well, whatever your motive is, please just let me be. I can only get away from work if you'll let me. I don't want to talk about work. Please!"

"Okay! I'll let it go."

"Thanks."

The girls walked the beach in silence for a long while. Jaelynn knew she was being watched. She kept seeing the same man and knew he was following them. He had all the markings of a Farini bodyguard or chaperon. They were keeping tabs on their big investment. Even on vacation, she wasn't truly free.

When Jon-Pierre came in from surfing to get some lunch, he could feel the tension; you could cut it with a knife. Later he asked Kaelynn, "What happened with you two? At lunch, I felt like I was sitting at the UN between two warring countries."

"Oh, Jae is obstinate and won't talk about what's depressing her. She won't even own that she's depressed to begin with. She says she is just exhausted and needs rest. She accused me of interrogating her?"

"Well, just let her rest then and avoid talk about work."

"It's almost like that's all we have in common anymore."

"Try, for her sanity and well-being, try. She needs you to be there for her the way she needs right now."

Kaelynn bit her lip, just like Jaelynn did when she was uncomfortable. "How did you get so wise?" she asked Jon-Pierre.

Jon-Pierre flicked Kae's nose with his index finger and said, "I've been hanging around you for a while."

"Ha ha, funny," she replied.

Wednesday morning, Jaelynn was up and ready to go to the beach by 9:00 a.m. She informed Kaelynn and Jon-Pierre that she wanted to learn to surf. Jae thought learning something new would take her mind off work and the horrible aspects of hosting clients. She knew she was nothing more than a paid prostitute who was trapped. She would try surfing just to focus on anything but the thoughts that consumed her days and the nightmares that haunted her nights.

The first thing Kaelynn taught Jae was how to ride the waves lying on the board. Jaelynn had a blast! They laughed and splashed all morning. It was great fun for them both, and now they were truly relaxing and having a good time.

After lunch, Jon-Pierre taught Jaelynn on the sand how to pop up on the board quickly. They practiced for almost an hour before paddling out. The first several waves Jae tried simply dumped her into the water. A couple of times, she got up for a few seconds and experienced the thrill of riding the wave. After three hours, she was exhausted and went back ashore to rest.

Kaelynn took the board and went out to surf with Jon-Pierre. They made surfing look effortless, and they could ride the same wave close to each other and never collide. It was like poetry in motion to watch them. Jaelynn sat back and enjoyed the show.

Around 5:00, Kae and Jon-Pierre came ashore from surfing for the day and prepared to go back to the hotel and clean up for dinner. As they were walking past the marina, Jae spotted a yacht that looked familiar; then, she saw them—their parents.

"Oh, Kae, look who it is! Mama and Papa just docking."

"Oh my goodness, you're right. We should go say hello?"

"God, no! Are you kidding me? We haven't gotten so much as a postcard in over a year. They don't care about us."

"Yah, I guess you're right. C'est la vie."

"C'est la vie."

They walked on as if there was nothing of interest to see.

Jon-Pierre was shocked. Kaelynn never talked about her parents. He knew they were sailing around the world, but he had no idea they hadn't contacted their daughters in over a year. He remembered that they left the girls when they were sixteen and thought that was appalling. What he just experienced was beyond his comprehension. Here the girls were on the same small island in the Caribbean, even in the same small town, Christiansted, but had no interest in even saying hello to their parents.

The trio went to the Bombay Club for dinner and had a wonderful time—good food, relaxing conversation that flowed much more smoothly. Jaelynn didn't order any alcohol tonight; instead, she drank local fruit drinks. They walked back to the hotel and could see their parents' yacht in the harbor. They were having some sort of party because there were a lot of people up on deck. They could hear the music from shore. But the girls turned the corner and kept right on walking to the hotel.

Jon-Pierre considered talking to the parents himself about their behavior toward their daughters but then thought better of it. The girls were adamant about not giving their parents the time of day. And they didn't the entire rest of the week.

On Thursday, the trio went on a guided horseback tour of the island. The horses were trained to simply follow the trail. It wasn't hard to just sit and let the horse do its job. They found the ride to be very fun, but they also identified muscles they didn't know they had.

Jon-Pierre said, "Wow, I found some muscles that surfing and skateboarding don't use. Whoa, I am soar." The girls agreed they were soar as well.

"Let's go to a hot dog stand for dinner. I don't think I can sit down tonight. I am so soar," said Jaelynn.

They opted to order room service and spend the evening watching old movies in the hotel room. It reminded Jae of Matt, and she told Kae about their day of rest and movie watching.

Kae could tell there was more than friendship between Jae and Matt, but she wasn't sure Jae was ready to admit it.

Friday and Saturday brought more surfing and soaking up the sun. Sunday morning came all too soon for the trio, and it was time to pack up for the flight back to London.

12

··

JAELYNN HAD NEVER INVITED MATT up to her flat, and he had never asked either. It was a boundary they had never approached. He spent the week working up ideas of exactly how he could get his hands on her documents.

Work continued and so did the hosting of parties and guests. Jaelynn was weary and ready for another vacation. It had only been a month since her week with her twin in St. Croix. *What a needed break*, she thought. Jaelynn didn't realize how worn out she was until she landed in St. Croix and had absolutely nothing to do or anywhere to be or anyone to host. She was able to relax and enjoy the pool, the sun, the beach, and the water. Everything was so colorful in St. Croix, the water was turquoise and clear, and she could see the tropical fish as they swam around her legs. She thought this must be what heaven is like.

Now back in the United Kingdom at her London flat, she realized that she could not do this hosting work for much longer. Something inside her was beginning to break, to crumble. She felt like she was disappearing and someone fake was taking her place. Modeling was hard work, long hours and grueling heat from the sun and lights—all things that are very bad for the skin. Hosting was hard on her body, and she never got much sleep on those nights. At twenty years old, she felt like she was forty, or at least what she imagined forty would feel like.

Matt was astounded at how beautiful Jaelynn looked when she got back from St. Croix. She looked radiant and rested. The bags under her eyes and the creases around them were gone. In three very long weeks working on location on three different continents, the old, weary look was back, and she was exhausted. They landed at Heathrow at 9:00 p.m. but didn't get through customs and back to her flat until after midnight.

Matt went with her all the way up to the penthouse with her luggage and saw her inside. She looked so done and broken. She turned to say thank you, stumbled, and passed out. Matt caught her before she hit her head on the coffee table. He picked her up and laid her on the couch. He stayed with her until she came to. Matt brought her some water and sat her upright. She sipped the water and asked what had happened. Jaelynn had a wary look on her face. Matt explained that she was so exhausted that she had passed out.

Jaelynn scratched her head and accepted his answer. She was still dressed, and they were in the living room, not the bedroom. Besides, Matt had never made a single move on her ever. She felt safe with him.

Matt insisted on walking her into her bedroom and making sure she was okay before closing her door and returning to the living room. He listened, wanting to be there quickly if she passed out again. When he saw the light go out under her door, he knocked softly, opened the door, and announced that he was going to sleep on the couch tonight just in case she needed him. He closed the door and started looking around the flat. It was large and spacious. The view from the balcony was breathtaking of the London skyline.

Matt continued exploring around the flat, ostensibly looking for a spare blanket and a pillow. He found what he was looking for in a closet of another bedroom. As he pulled the items from the shelf, he uncovered a metal document box. He pulled it out and took it to the bed where he sat down and opened it. Inside was Jaelynn DepProvoue's birth certificate. He pulled it out and put it in his jacket pocket. He would make a copy and find a way to return the copy to the box. Now all he needed was to get her passport and driver's license without her noticing him rummaging through her purse.

As Matt was returning to the living room, he saw Jaelynn's bag sitting on the kitchen island. He went to her bedroom door and opened it quietly to check on her. Her breathing was soft and rhythmic, ensuring him she was sound asleep. He returned to the kitchen and began looking through her bag. It had all the normal women's things, a make-up compact, mirror, lipsticks, and wallet. Aha, her driver's license. He slipped it out and dropped it into the pocket with the birth certificate. Now to find her passport.

The passport proved the easiest to find. It was in the side pocket of her travel bag with the top clearly showing. Matt dropped it in with the other documents. He thanked God for helping him obtain these documents so quickly. Matt threw his jacket over the back of a chair and headed for the couch. Truth was he too was quite tired.

Matt woke up the next morning with the sun streaming in the wall of windows. He could smell the amazing aroma of coffee brewing. He sat up and found Jaelynn in sweats sipping coffee at the kitchen island. He stretched and joined her. She slid a cup across the counter to him.

"Thank you," he said.

"No, thank you! Matt, I am so glad you stayed last night. I haven't slept that good since St. Croix. Thank you."

"My pleasure." Matt suddenly felt very awkward; his mouth was dry, and he didn't know what to say. He sipped his coffee instead.

Jaelynn asked, "What are your plans today?"

Matt choked on his sip of coffee and spilled it on the counter. "I'm so sorry," he sputtered and got up to get a paper towel. "Ah, ah, nothing today. I, ah, try to take at least one day a week to do absolutely nothing. I call it my day of rest. How about you?"

"Ah, well, I think I will take a 'day of rest' today as well."

They spent the day lounging on the couch and watching old black-and-white movies and eating whatever junk food they could come up with in the flat. It was the best day off Jaelynn had had in a very long time.

13

JAELYNN WENT ON WITH HER usual schedule for the next couple of months, working on and off with Matt as the photographer. She preferred working with him. The other photographers were all over the models whenever they got the chance. Jaelynn was used to being handled, but she didn't like the sleazy photographers doing it. Well, she didn't like anyone doing it but least of all the photogs. They would find a way to adjust the models and put their hands in inappropriate places.

Jaelynn suspected that the photographers had caught wind of the underside of the Farini business and were trying to get in on some of the action. She didn't even know how many models were involved in the dirty side of the business. What she did know was that she wasn't going to give any freebees to these guys. That's what made Matt so different. He'd had more than one opportunity to take advantage of her over the past few months, and yet he had treated her like a princess. It suddenly occurred to her that he might be gay. She didn't think so; she knew several gay men, and Matt just didn't fit the description in her opinion.

Photographers aside, Jaelynn was finding it harder to get through each week and particularly a week that had multiple parties for her to host. Since her vacation to St. Croix, it seemed that the number of parties had increased from one to three a week. It was getting to be too much. She wanted out badly but didn't know how to go about it. She didn't want anyone she knew and loved to get hurt in the process. She didn't want to die either. The *how* was extremely important, and she was at a loss.

In August, Kaelynn and Jon-Pierre went out to their favorite bistro in Paris to celebrate being together for a year. It was a beautiful evening in the city. They ordered their meals and shared in easy conversation. They were inseparable when Jon-Pierre was in town.

Jon-Pierre's reputation as a photographer had grown immensely in the past year. He had worked with many of the mega-models around the world and even on a couple of jobs alongside Matt Wilson. Matt and Jon-Pierre became fast friends. Matt was also very easygoing and willing to share all kinds of professional tips and knowledge with Jon-Pierre.

Kaelynn rarely ate dessert because of the calories, but Jon-Pierre ordered crème brûlée since it was such a special occasion. Just before the desserts arrived, Jon-Pierre knelt down on one knee and said, "Kaelynn, in you I have found the other half of myself. You are my soulmate. Would you do me the honor of marrying me?" He pulled a beautiful, simply cut diamond engagement ring from his pocket and held it up to her. Kaelynn's hands flew to her mouth, and tears welled up in her eyes.

Then she whispered, "Yes, it would be my honor."

That night when Kaelynn got home, Jon-Pierre suggested that they look for a flat together. He was working more and more in Australia and didn't use his flat more than one weekend a month. Kaelynn was gone just as much with her own work.

When Jon-Pierre had gone home, Kae called Jaelynn.

"Hey, Kae, how are you doing?" answered Jaelynn.

"Great actually! I'm engaged! Ah! Can you believe it?" she squealed.

"Oh my gosh," replied Jaelynn. "Congratulations!"

They talked for over an hour on the phone. At 12:30 p.m., they hung up. Kaelynn could not go to sleep; her head was spinning. They had not talked about the wedding or setting a date yet. She finally got up and started making a list of things that would need to be planned and carried out. Finally at 3:34 a.m., she went back to bed for a couple of hours of sleep.

Sunday afternoon, Jon-Pierre left for a two-week shoot on location in New Zealand. Kaelynn had a normal work week with

Johansen and decided to take some time to look for a new flat. Both she and Jon-Pierre had one-bedroom flats. Together they wanted to get two bedrooms so one could be an office for Jon-Pierre. Right now, his editing computer and printer and cameras were all in a small corner of his current flat—not an ideal setup for two people.

It didn't take long to find a nice two-bedroom flat in a good neighborhood, one they had agreed upon before Jon-Pierre left for New Zealand. The lease on the flat wouldn't start until November, still a month and a half away. But that would give Kae and Jon-Pierre ample time to give a thirty-day notice at their respective flats.

Jon-Pierre and Kaelynn moved in together at the end of October. They had barely finished unpacking when they jetted off together to the United States for a swimsuit photo shoot for *National Sport Magazine*. Jaelynn was also working on the same shoot along with Matt. All four were booked at the same hotel. But once again, Jaelynn was booked solid until Friday.

The shoot wrapped in the morning on Friday allowing all the crew to hang out at the beach. Kae and Jon-Pierre rented surfboards and showed off their surfing skills. Jaelynn was able to go to the beach and relax a bit also. So instead of surfing all afternoon, Kae decided to relax on the beach and bodysurf with Jae. They had so much fun together.

Back in London, Jaelynn left for work early Monday morning to keep an appointment with Mars Hillman, director of Fashion Design and Marketing for Mars-Hillman Fashion. Jaelynn liked Mars; he was an exuberant and flamboyant gay man who knew fashion. He lived fashion to the fullest, and he knew how to dress a model that was absolutely jaw-dropping.

Today Mars was working with several of the models one-on-one for an upcoming fashion show featuring many of his newest designs. The first model was his favorite, Jaelynn DepProvoue. She was tall, exquisitely beautiful, and graceful and carried herself so naturally that she attracted people easily. She was Mars's favorite because she wasn't a snobbish shrew like so many of the other models were.

When Jaelynn arrived, Mars's jaw dropped open, not because of her beauty, but because she looked like death walking upright today.

"My cherie! What is wrong? Are you feeling sick today? Have you had enough of the world? Is it your time of month? I can help you if you need! Tell me what I can do to make you better."

"Oh, Mars, thank you, my dear, dear friend. But you can't help me with my problem today. I just need a long vacation in an undisclosed location where I can disappear forever, or a week or two. Not likely to happen anytime soon though."

"Oh, cherie, I am so sorry. You look terrible. I insist that we sit and have some coffee first."

They sat in a luxurious glassed-in sitting area in the rear of his dressing studio. Everything was sleek and chic. The couches were modern yet comfortable. The coffee table was made from a single slab of marble with glass over the top. They sipped coffee in silence at first. Suddenly Mars pushed a button on the side of his chair and a set of soundproof doors closed in the existing walls. Jaelynn's eyes widened in surprise. She had no idea what was going to happen next. Mars leaned forward and said, "Cherie, we are now completely safe to have any conversation you would like. I am well aware of Farini's sex trafficking business. And I fear that you are caught in the very middle of it. Am I right?"

"Mars, I don't know what you're talking about. I am tired, and it's just an off week for me."

"Cherie, I have friends who can help get you out. You just have to say the word."

"You mean like the two models who tried to get out a few years back who ended up burnt to a crisp in a plane crash? No thanks."

"I had nothing to do with that. They didn't confide in me, cherie."

"Thank you, Mars, but I will be fine with a little rest."

"As you wish, my cherie, but if you ever change your mind, just stop by for Turkish Coffee." Mars winked at Jaelynn.

"How do I know that you're not trying to entrap me? Or record our conversation and turn it over to Farini?"

"My cherie, I am hurt. I thought our friendship was deeper than that!"

"I'm sorry, Mars, I just have to be so careful with whom I trust and talk openly with. This is such a fickle business."

"Yes, it is. Well, if you need my help, you now know that I am here for you."

And with a squeeze of the same button, the doors disappeared from where they had come.

They went about their business of fitting outfits and selecting accessories for the show. Two hours later, all of Jaelynn's outfits were tagged and bagged up for the show, and she was on her way to an open-air photo shoot. As she was driving across London, it began to pour rain.

When Jaelynn arrived at the shoot, Megan met her at her car.

"You're a half hour late, Jaelynn. What happened?"

"I was scheduled for fittings at Mars-Hillman. I came here directly after."

Megan looked suspiciously at Jaelynn, then declared the shoot was cancelled for the rest of the day due to rain. Jaelynn raised her window, relieved there would be no work today.

As soon as Megan got into her own car, she called Georgio's number; he picked up on the first ring.

"Where was she?" Georgio demanded.

"Mars-Hillman for the show fitting."

"Who was her chaperone?"

"None, she's trusted, remember? But I did have Hugo on her. He said she went into the back room where they sat and talked over coffee for several minutes."

"Keep an eye on her. She's looking tired and haggard. We may be reaching the end of her usefulness. Keep me apprised." He demanded and hung up.

Jaelynn was relieved she could go home and sleep all day if she wanted. And that is what she did. She didn't wake up until after 6:00 p.m. and ordered dinner to be delivered. She ate Chinese in front of the TV recalling fondly the day she and Matt had watched black-and-white movies all day. She had just taken another *day of rest* she so desperately needed. Maybe she could get through the next couple of weeks. They were scheduled to be in Los Angeles for numerous beach shoots. Jaelynn loved the beach. She hoped their hotel would have a beach view.

14

···

MATT HAD PAID DEARLY FOR a duplicate set of documents for Jaelynn. The duplicates looked as real as the originals. Getting them back inside Jaelynn's flat proved to be easier than he had expected. He waited until they came home late from a long shoot and offered to walk Jaelynn up to her door. She invited him in for coffee. As soon as the water was on to boil, Jae went to her room to change out of her travel clothes and into her comfortable sweats. Matt took the opportunity to replace all the documents.

Jaelynn passed right through all the checkpoints from London to Los Angeles without any problems or red flags.

Matt called Joe Richards, his US witness security contact, and let him know that he along with Jaelynn would be in Los Angeles and that he had the documents requested. They made arrangements to meet while he was on the West Coast.

The days were long and hot but being near the water was refreshing. The breeze picked up and blew a mist off the water over the shoot location cooling them off. All the models were in the pool at the hotel at the end of the day.

While in Los Angeles, Jaelynn was given a presidential suite at the Four Seasons Hotel at Westlake Village, only a few miles from the beach where they were shooting a swimsuit layout for Sports Fan. Of course, Jaelynn hosted the executives on Tuesday night, all four of them at the same time. It was exhausting.

On Thursday night, she hosted yet another executive. This one was a woman from a Malibu modeling and casting firm. Jaelynn had no idea what she was supposed to do with a woman, but she soon learned. The woman was insulant and demanding. She told Jaelynn what to do and how she wanted it done. Jaelynn did her best to please the woman and not throw up at the same time. She was nervous that Megan would not get a favorable report from the woman. That usually called for a discipline visit from Germain.

Friday morning, Megan showed up at Jaelynn's suite to see how everything went. She knew she had never sprung a female on her before and was a little nervous. Jaelynn looked like a mess. She had obviously been crying and hadn't slept much. Megan slapped her across the face and told her to pull herself together and be the professional they were certainly paying her to be.

Jaelynn took a quick shower and was ready to go in ten minutes. On the drive to the shoot, Megan told her that the executive had an exceptional time and had even thanked her for making sure she got a young girl with no experience with females. She said it made the whole experience that much more sensual.

Friday, they wrapped up in Los Angeles and would be flying out on Saturday back to London, and Matt still hadn't heard from Joe about getting together to drop off the documents. He was getting nervous when his phone buzzed. It was Joe.

"Hello."

"Hey, Matt. Meet me tonight, 8:55 p.m. at Top of Five. You know the place?"

"Yes, I know it."

"Come alone, and make sure you're not followed."

"I know the drill."

"Matt!" Jaelynn called out. "Come with us. We're going to dinner."

"Go on without me. My cousin is in town, and I've got dinner plans with him."

As soon as the girls' Uber pulled away, Matt called his own. He arrived at Top of Five at 8:50 p.m. Joe was already there. He made his way through the restaurant and joined Joe at the table where he was sitting.

The men greeted each other, and Matt slid a plane white envelope across the table. Joe slipped the envelope into his inner jacket pocket without opening it. They ordered dinner and talked about sports until 10:30 p.m. and then both left.

The next morning, the models and crew flew out of LAX back to London. Next week, they would be in New Zealand. It felt like the weeks were flying by to Matt. To Jaelynn, it felt like life was one week dragged into the next and the next and the next. She didn't know how much longer she could hold on. She planned to contact Mars the first chance she could justify a trip by his studios when they got back to London.

As they made their way to the baggage claim, they passed by a newsstand. The front page story on every London paper showed a large picture of Mars Hillman. Jaelynn grabbed one and read down the article. "Mars was killed in an explosion in his London studio just the day before," she exclaimed. The article went on to explain everything was a total loss and that there would be a memorial for Mars on Saturday next. Jaelynn felt like her heart was going to beat out of her chest. Somehow Farini had found out and had taken care of Mars. She felt sick to her stomach and dashed into the restroom.

When Jaelynn walked out of the restroom, Matt was waiting for her with her luggage. The other models joined them all in shock about Mars's death. No one wanted to say what they were sure was true, but they all knew, somehow Farini was involved.

The shoot in New Zealand went off without delay, and they wrapped on Thursday afternoon. Everyone was relieved they would be able to get back to London in time for Mars Hillman's memorial.

It rained the morning of the memorial. It was appropriate to the feelings of all who were in attendance. There was a large crowd; faces from all over the fashion world had flown in for the service. The graveside service that followed later in the day was by invitation only. There was mostly family but a few people Mars considered true friends. Matt and Jaelynn were among them, the Farinis were not. By evening, Jaelynn was exhausted, not unusual lately. Everything seemed to be taking a bigger toll on her, and she was in bed by 8:00 p.m. unless she was hosting.

15

∙∙∙

JAELYNN MISSED TWO DAYS OF work the following week due to sickness. She couldn't seem to get enough rest and had been throwing up with a slight fever.

On Wednesday, Megan insisted that she be seen by a doctor. Jaelynn assured her she would be better by Thursday, but Megan had her suspicions that Jaelynn might be planning some sort of escape. All the signs were present. She had seen them before enough times, the black circles under the eyes, too much weight loss, fatigue on the job, and now missing work because of "sickness." Megan knew something would happen soon by the pattern. The other times, the girls either attempted escape or suicide. Megan just wasn't sure which avenue Jaelynn might pick. She suspected the latter.

Wednesday afternoon, Megan had her answer. Jaelynn wasn't planning any escape; she was pregnant.

"You little fool!" spat Megan at Jaelynn. "Why didn't you use the preventions I gave you!"

"I did, I do, I don't know how this happened. Maybe it's the two and three guests per week you've been sticking me with. Even the best birth control has its limitations." Jaelynn shot back.

"Well, tomorrow we will take care of this little bump in the road. You'll need at least a week to recover. Why don't you call your sister and arrange a visit? I'll take care of the rest."

"What do you mean 'take care of it'? I don't want an abortion! That's going too far, and I won't do it!"

Megan slapped Jaelynn across the face. "You will do it, and I don't want to hear any whining about it before, during, or after! Do I make myself clear?"

"Crystal," said Jaelynn. She tasted blood in her mouth.

Thursday morning, Megan and a bodyguard picked Jaelynn up and took her to a small clinic in a seedy part of London. The place was untidy and dirty. The doctor looked like he had worn the same clothes for the past week; they were stained and dirty.

An hour and a half later, Megan tucked Jaelynn into her own bed back at her flat. She gave Jaelynn a prescription pill with a glass of water and told her to sleep as long as she was able. The pain was worse the first twenty-four hours.

Jaelynn felt awful, not only from the pain of the procedure but sick in her soul. They had killed her own unborn child. Abortion was a cardinal sin according to her Catholic upbringing. She was doomed to hell now. There really wasn't anything left to live for.

Megan made sure Jaelynn was asleep before she left the flat. She called Germain as she was in the elevator.

Germain picked up on the first ring. "Is it done?" he demanded.

"Yes, it's done. She's resting, asleep actually."

"I want her watched for the next few days. I don't want to lose this one to suicide. She is far too good. Everyone raves about her."

"She's going to visit her sister for a week. Nothing will happen while she's there."

"I'm going to have her watched anyway."

* * * * *

Back in Paris, things returned to the normal work pace. Kaelynn and Jon-Pierre had most weekends off and surfed as often as they could. When the weather was not conducive to surfing, Kaelynn watched Jon-Pierre at the indoor skate park. Jaelynn worked most weekends and only had Sunday to recuperate.

Three months after their vacation in St. Croix, Jae called Kae and asked if she could come spend a week at their home in Paris.

She had experienced an appendicitis and needed to recover from the surgery.

Jaelynn spent a week with Kaelynn recovering from her surgery. Jon-Pierre was working at the office in Australia for the week, so it was just the two girls.

Kaelynn asked, "Do you have any surgical bandage to change?"

"No," replied Jaelynn. "The surgery was laparoscopic. They went in through the belly button. That way, I wouldn't have any scars."

She lied to Kaelynn to maintain a plausible cover story and protect her and Jon-Pierre.

The week went easy because Kaelynn continued to work, and Jaelynn mainly rested and cried when Kaelynn wasn't home.

Friday afternoon, Jaelynn was asleep on the couch with a blanket pulled up over her nose. Jon-Pierre came home early from Australia and thought it was Kaelynn on the couch. He went over and snuggled his face down into the crook of her neck and started kissing her and calling her baby and telling her he had missed her all week. Jaelynn woke up and looked at him with shock and horror in her eyes.

Jon-Pierre pulled back and said, "What's wrong, baby?"

Jaelynn sat up and said, "I'm not Kae. I'm Jaelynn."

Jon-Pierre jumped back and immediately began to apologize. "I'm so sorry. Oh my gosh, I thought, oh dear god, I'm sorry, Jaelynn. What can I say, you look exactly like Kaelynn."

Just then, Kaelynn walked into the flat.

"What's going on?" she asked. She took one look at the situation and started laughing. And then Jaelynn cracked a smile. But Jon-Pierre was mortified.

Kaelynn said, "Baby, I forgot to tell you on the phone that Jae was here for a few days. You thought she was me, didn't you?"

Jaelynn said, "No harm no foul, Jon-Pierre. This happens to us all the time."

"Well, it doesn't happen to me. I am so embarrassed."

Jaelynn got up from the couch and walked toward Jon-Pierre and said, "It's okay. I missed you too, baby."

Jaelynn and Kaelynn were laughing so hard they both had tears in their eyes. Jon-Pierre looked like he'd just got caught with his hand in the cookie jar.

It felt good for both girls to laugh together over a classic twin mistake.

Over dinner that evening, the trio talked about possible wedding dates for Kae and Jon-Pierre. It was hard to settle on a date when Jon-Pierre didn't know when he would be in town. Jaelynn suggested that he present some possible wedding dates to his employer and ask if it would be possible to secure one of the dates off.

"I actually never thought about that. I think we could both do that and come up with a date to shoot for. What do you think?" he asked Kae.

"I think it's an excellent idea. Would you be able to do the same thing, Jae, because I'm not getting married without you there."

"Sure, I can ask. Why don't you guys select the date and get your companies to approve, and then I'll ask at Farini."

"That is a plan," said Kaelynn. "Thank you for the idea, Jae."

"My pleasure," replied Jaelynn.

On Saturday, Jaelynn returned to London.

16

Matt messaged Joe Richards via the secure app and phone he had been instructed to use from now on. He knew something awful had happened with Jaelynn. She hadn't been to work in a week. They were told only that she was sick. No more details than that. It was rare for a model to miss an entire week. Matt was worried.

It took over forty-eight hours for Joe to respond. It came as a phone call.

"I've got all the documents ready to go. When can we meet?" asked Joe.

"How about Saturday?" replied Matt.

"Great." And Joe proceeded to give a new location for Matt to meet him.

Matt overheard one of the models, Sophia, saying that Jaelynn was visiting her sister for the next week and would be back after that. The week seemed to drag by for Matt.

Saturday morning, Matt set out using Google maps to find the new location to meet Joe Richards. It was a quaint little inn about an hour outside London in the country. Joe had a plan, a bold plan that would have to be executed to the letter, down to the minute in order to pull it off.

Matt listened as Joe went over the plan step by step.

Step one: Matt and Jaelynn would plan to meet for dinner at a place they usually frequent. No other models or photographers would join them.

Matt would arrive before Jaelynn and secure a table near the rear of the restaurant. Matt would appear to be waiting for Jaelynn to arrive and order a beer.

Jaelynn would call an Uber and come to the restaurant's rear entrance in an alley.

Then Matt would get up to use the bathroom and leave out the back door and get into the Uber with Jaelynn. Matt would explain the next few steps quickly to Jaelynn emphasizing the urgency that the plan be followed to the letter to ensure success. He would give her all her new documents, a new driver's license, birth certificate, travel visa, and passport.

Step two: Together Matt and Jaelynn would ride to the magistrate's office arriving at 5:45 p.m., fifteen minutes before closing. There they would be married under Jaelynn's new witness security name, Grace. The marriage license was secured and all blood work completed. Joe even had Grace Wilson's green card ready for US entrance. Being married to Matt would allow Grace to enter the US with her new passport and green card as Mrs. Grace Wilson. It would also enable Grace to enter the US witness security program.

Step three: Immediately after being married, Matt and Grace would dash to Heathrow airport and catch the 7:15 Concord to New York City. They would each have a small carry-on, no checked luggage. The tickets were in the names of Matt Wilson and Grace Wilson. Their seats would be in business class so as not to attract attention. Via Joe, the US witness security program had made arrangements for all traces of Grace boarding and disembarking to be erased from surveillance footage.

Step four: Upon arrival in New York City, they would drive to Matt's NYC apartment for some rest. The following morning, Matt would take Grace to a yet-to-be disclosed airstrip.

Step five: Grace would be flown to an undisclosed location for three months. Once there, she would give depositions regarding the Farinis and their sex trafficking business. Grace would also work on losing her French accent and becoming Americanized.

Well, step one was all about getting Jaelynn to go along with the plan. This would be the most challenging feat by far, everything hinged on it. Timing everything would be so very critical. Should he tell Jaelynn about the plan and get her in now or spring the whole thing on her in the Uber when they met at the restaurant? The last thing Matt wanted was for Jaelynn to know the plan and get cornered by someone and blow the whole thing wide open. But not bringing her in could blow up in his face if she refused when he sprang the plan on her suddenly. This was going to require some serious thought and prayer.

To Jaelynn, Matt seemed like he had something serious on his mind during the next week. She could tell he was seriously distracted and awkward somehow. Something was going on because he wasn't his usual self. Jaelynn wanted to reach out to him, to offer a listening ear, if he would open up and share anything personal with her. He had always been so kind and good to her. She wanted to reciprocate. But how or where could she even approach him was a dilemma. She was being watched constantly, even at her own flat these days. She was sure she was being shadowed while in Paris with her sister the previous week.

Jaelynn was considering confiding in Matt. If he opened up to her about what was on his mind, then she just might.

* * * * *

One month later in April, Jon-Pierre and Kaelynn DepProvoue were married. Jaelynn was the maid of honor and Matt Wilson was the best man. It was a simple but elegant ceremony and outdoor reception on the beach. Jon-Pierre's family were all there and so happy to welcome Kaelynn to the family.

Jaelynn and the twins' paternal grandfather Jon-Luke DepProvoue were the only family present from the DepProvoue side. Kaelynn's grandfather walked her down the aisle and gave her away. Their parents were not even invited, primarily because nobody knew where in the world they were.

Kaelynn and Jon-Pierre planned to spend their honeymoon on the island of Maui in the Hawaiian Islands. They had done some exotic photo shoots there and loved the place. They spent two wonderful weeks relaxing and surfing and loving each other.

Upon returning from their honeymoon, life quickly returned to the familiar routine. Kaelynn had to make some changes to her legal name and her passport and travel documents. But work picked up like it hadn't even missed a beat.

Jon-Pierre was working more and more in Australia now, and it was hard for the couple to get quality time together. One weekend, Jon-Pierre broached the subject of them moving to Australia. Kaelynn still had three years left on her contract with Johansen. She wasn't sure she would be able to alter her term.

"I'll think about it though. I'm tired of being alone during the week. I really miss you."

"Me too," said Jon-Pierre.

17

···

FRIDAY WAS A SHOOT FOR *Playboy* Europe. It went quickly, and that afternoon, Matt slipped a note inside Jaelynn's bag as he was packing up his photography gear. Her bag, along with the other models' bags, and his gear were kept in a secure area and guarded by a Farini security person. Matt had to be very careful because if the security guard saw him, he and Jaelynn would be in serious trouble.

When Jaelynn arrived home, she tossed her keys and bag on the kitchen counter. Something in her bag caught her eye. She looked inside and saw the note. There wasn't any reason she should have noticed it; it was well inside her bag and out of casual sight. But she had noticed it and opened it.

The note read:

> *Meet me at Del Veccio's at 5:00 p.m. Take an Uber. Leave your car at home. Don't be late! I'll explain everything as soon as possible. Pull up in the alley behind the restaurant and wait for me there. I'll come out the back door. Please TRUST ME.—Matt*

Jaelynn bit her lip. Was this his way of opening up? He had never done anything like this before. Suddenly Jaelynn recalled several times Matt had looked out for her, cared for her even. She felt like she could trust him. He didn't say to bring a change of clothes or a suitcase or anything like that, so it wasn't a getaway. Jaelynn decided to do exactly what Matt asked her to do. It was 4:20. She would have to get moving in order to meet him on time. She called for an Uber instructing the driver to pick her up in the back alley instead of in front as usual.

Jaelynn changed clothes quickly, choosing a faded pair of jeans and a simple white T-shirt and a blue and white stripped long sleeve over shirt and her athletic shoes. She grabbed her bag then decided to leave it on the counter with her keys. She grabbed her appointment book on a whim and left her flat. She took the service elevator down to the basement level below the car park. She couldn't rationalize leaving her bag and keys at home; it just felt like she should. There was an air of mystery and excitement in the air that she couldn't explain.

Jaelynn stepped out the back door of the basement level and sprinted up the steps to the alley gate. The Uber was waiting right on time. She got in the car and gave the driver the address and instructions to pull up in the back alley.

The Uber pulled into the alley behind Del Veccio's at 4:58. They stopped at the back door and waited. At 5:01 the rear door opened, and Matt darted out and into the Uber slamming the door and giving the driver a new destination.

"Where's your bag?" Matt asked Jaelynn.

"I didn't bring it," Jaelynn replied.

He paused for a moment. "Good! That saves a step. Let's go, driver. Don't break any laws and don't draw any attention."

"What's going on, Matt?"

Matt turned to Jaelynn as the driver pulled out of the alley and headed for the byway.

"Do you trust me?" he asked.

"Yes. I'm here, aren't I?"

"Okay, this is huge, and it's gotta happen right now or it never can."

"What in the world are you talking about, Matt?"

Matt was careful to keep his face in the shadows, and his voice barely a whisper.

"We're escaping Jaelynn!"

"What! Are you crazy?"

"Sh. Sh." shushed Matt.

"They'll catch us and kill us!" whispered Jaelynn.

"Not if we follow my plan exactly. I've been working on this for six months, trust me? Please for God's sake, trust me."

"Okay, what's the plan?"

"Step one is that we're going to the civil register office right now to meet my US contact. He has all new identification papers for you including a green card for the US and..."

"And...?"

"And we're getting married."

"*What!*"

"Sh, calm down and listen to me please. We don't have much time. You will be given a new name, and we will get married. Immediately after that, we are catching the Concord to New York City, where I live. That's right now! Without delay, no time to consider...it's now or never, Jaelynn."

"Have you lost your mind? It will never work."

"Yes, it will. You aren't Jaelynn DepProvoue anymore. You are now Grace Janes and about to become Grace Wilson. When we get on the plane, no one will even know that Jaelynn DepProvoue is missing. I occasionally fly back to New York when I get a long weekend off like this one. We can get away. I have to come back to work like I don't know anything on Tuesday, but by then, you will be gone from New York and not even I will know where you are. It's the only way I could get you out safely."

"This is insane!" she sputtered. What about my sister?"

"Your sister can't know anything. That way, all her reactions will be authentic. It's the only way we can protect her."

"Why do we have to get married if I already have a new name and papers and everything?"

"It's the only way I can get you a green card to get you into the United States and into the witness security program."

"Witness security program? Are you telling me that I will have to testify in court about the Farinis?"

"Yes, eventually. But don't you want this to end for everyone? To never happen to any other young girls?"

"Yes, of course, I want to make this stop."

"We're here. Come on, we only have fifteen minutes to get this part done."

Matt whisked Jaelynn into the civil register office and went straight to the office of marriage. Joe was waiting. He approached them swiftly and thrust an overnight bag and a new purse into Jaelynn's hands. Inside the bag were all of Jaelynn's new documents: a driver's license, birth certificate, passport, and travel visa. He then quickly ushered them into the office where their papers were examined, approved, and a fast wedding ceremony took place.

"You may now kiss your bride," spoke the magistrate.

Matt turned awkwardly to Grace and saw equal shock in her eyes as he knew was in his own. He had considered everything except this part—the kiss, the actual "you are now husband and wife part." There they kissed for the very first time. It was brief but sweet and emotional. Jaelynn felt butterflies in her stomach.

As quickly as the service began, it was over, and the couple was rushing out of the office and into a Lyft on their way to the airport.

Grace leaned over to Matt and whispered jokingly, "If you wanted to marry me, you could've just asked."

For the first time in over an hour, the tension broke, and they both laughed. Matt put his arm around Grace's shoulder and hugged her.

18

. . . .

Matt and "Grace" got to the airport twelve minutes before their designated departure time. If they didn't make the plane, the whole plan was jeopardized. They jumped out of the car and ran through the airport as fast as they could. They had no luggage to check, so they headed straight to the gate. When they rounded the corner to their gate, the attendant was just beginning to close the door.

"Wait!" shouted Matt. "We have our tickets."

The attendant left the door open and quickly went through their bag and Grace's purse. Everything was fine, and they sprinted down the boarding gate and onto the plane. They found their seats in business class just as the plane's engine began to reverse and maneuver away from the gate. Ten minutes later, the plane was in the air. They were on their way to whatever new life lay ahead of them.

For Matt, it was going to be a very difficult period, acting in shock like everyone else, grieving Jaelynn's loss along with her friends and Kaelynn, her twin sister. Matt had to make himself believe that Jaelynn had actually disappeared. He prayed to God he would be able to pull it off. His life depended on it.

Matt looked over at Grace and smiled; she smiled back.

"I can't believe you would do this for me. You're putting your own life at risk by helping me. I will make sure you get a good return on your incredible investment, Matt."

"Not all men are all about sex, Jaelynn."

"Excuse me, sir. It's Grace to you now."

"Sh," Matt whispered. "We don't want anyone to overhear."

"Are you newlyweds?" asked the women to their right.

"Yes, we are," stated Matt. Grace blushed.

"Oh young love is so sweet and pure. God bless you both."

"Thank you," said Matt. He leaned into Grace and whispered, "It's a long flight. We can't talk here. You should get some sleep."

Grace leaned her head against Matt's shoulder and closed her eyes. "Thank you," she whispered.

They landed at JFK in New York at 3:09 Saturday morning. Matt got a cab and gave the driver directions to his apartment. Grace knew what was coming. They would get to Matt's apartment, and then they would have sex because that's what men expected. Then she might be able to get some actual sleep. She wondered how long she would belong to Matt before she would truly be free. Then again, things could be worse, much worse.

When they got to Matt's apartment, he showed her around. The apartment had a galley kitchen with a raised bar open to the main living area. The place looked like it had been built in the seventies or eighties. The bedroom was a fair size for having a king bed in it. There was one bathroom, and all Grace could do to describe it was that it was functional. There was another bedroom, much smaller, and it was set up as an office with large computer screens and photos strewn all around. It also had a comfortable-looking sofa. Matt told Grace to take the master bedroom. He would sleep on the pullout couch in his office. Grace was shocked.

"You mean we are not sleeping together?"

"No, not until the day you can look me in the eye and honestly say that you are in love with me," said Matt.

"Well, I could say that to you now."

"No, not like that. And you're only tied to my name for the next six months. Then you can get a divorce or whatever you want."

"You mean I'm actually going to be free? No contract or implied agreements or anything?"

"Nothing, you are free now. But I encourage you to follow-through with the plan so that you will also be safe," finished Matt. At any rate, it is late, and we are both exhausted. Let's get some sleep, and I will fill you in on all the rest of the details in the morning, or whenever you wake up. Okay?

"All right, but you are welcome to sleep in your own bed. I promise I won't take advantage of you." She winked at Matt.

"No, like I said…not without real honest to goodness love between us."

Grace woke up around 4:00 p.m. New York time with a headache like a hangover, only she hadn't had any pills or anything to drink. She stumbled to the bathroom and showered. When she got out, she wrapped a towel around herself and realized she didn't have any clean clothes. She slipped out to the living area and found Matt sitting at the kitchen bar sipping on coffee. He was showered, clean shaven, and dressed.

"Ehem," Grace cleared her throat. "I don't seem to have any clothes to wear. Was that part of your plan?" she teased.

"Already thought of that." He tossed her a bag from a local superstore. In it she found a new pair of sweatpants, size small, a V-neck T-shirt, some socks, and a pair of sneakers.

"Right, no underwear or bra."

"Oops, I forgot those. I wouldn't even begin to know what to choose in that department."

"Come on now, you've photographed me in lingerie many times."

Suddenly Matt felt awkward, and his face blushed with heat. "Yes, ah, well ah, that was not your own choosing. That was the marketer's choice. Ah yah, so, you'll have to pick out your own I guess."

"Okay, but you will have to go with me because I have no money and no credit cards, remember?" Grace called over her shoulder as she went back into the bedroom to put the clothes on.

When she came back out, Matt had poured her a cup of coffee and had it waiting at the bar next to him. He held out his hand in invitation to the open chair beside his. Grace moved forward and sat down next to him. Now she felt awkward, so she leaned over and kissed him on the cheek.

"Good morning, Mr. Wilson," she teased.

Matt blushed again and said, "Good morning, Mrs. Wilson," in return.

Joe called and delayed the next flight until tomorrow, so Grace and Matt went out shopping to get a few essentials. They stayed clear of high-fashion stores where Grace would be easily recognized. They found a Walmart, and Grace chose some more clothes and undergarments. She bought some comfortable oversized T-shirts because she found them easy to sleep in.

Grace stepped into the dressing room to try on the clothes she had chosen. They certainly weren't anything she had become accustomed to. They didn't fit well, and the quality was dearly lacking from the high-fashion clothing she usually wore. But they would work. After all, she was supposed to blend in, not stand out. They would do.

While Grace was in the dressing room, she could hear Matt talking to another man outside in the waiting area. It wasn't a voice she recognized, but then she didn't know anything about Matt's life in New York. She hadn't even known he lived here at all. She thought he lived permanently in London. She had a lot to learn if they were going to stay together even as friends.

When Grace came out of the dressing room, Matt was alone.

"Who were you talking to a minute ago?" she asked

"Oh, nobody really, an old buddy from school days. Hey, I was hoping to see some of those outfits on you."

"You will," she teased. "Do you have any more high-quality American stores you would like to show me?" She laughed.

Grace's laugh sounded so good to Matt. He hadn't heard her laugh in months. She looked better already too.

The next store they shopped at was Target, another American retailer. When they drove into the parking lot, Grace immediately pronounced the name Targét as if it were French. Matt busted out laughing.

"Are you making fun of my accent?"

"No, not at all. Targét is what people call this store to pretend it's a higher fashion shop. You said it exactly the same way, and it was funny, that's all."

"So this is really another Walmart with a different name then?"

"Not exactly, they do have some nicer things, and more things made in America."

"Is this important to buy things made in America?"

"Yah, sort of, as Americans, we want to support our local economies whenever possible."

"America and Europe are so very different. We are more like one big community, and America is so spread out. New York and Los Angeles are far from each other, and the culture is very different. Don't you think?"

"Yes, you're right. The east and west coasts have very different vibes."

They entered the store, and Grace immediately smelled popcorn.

"Oh, it's popcorn. Can we get some? It smells wonderful."

"Sure." Matt stepped to the counter and ordered a large popcorn and a Dr Pepper, something very difficult to find in Europe. He handed the popcorn to Grace, and they meandered down the main aisle into the women's clothing.

"Oh, I see what you mean about the fashion here. It is more chic than the Walmart store."

Grace tried on more clothes, and this time modeled them for Matt. He could tell the difference in fit and quality too but didn't say anything to Grace. He knew enough about women to know not to. She looked good. That's all that mattered. And he told her so. She grimaced at him but said, "Thanks anyway."

They finished shopping at Target and went to find some lunch. Matt took Grace to a place called Applebee's.

"Do they serve a lot of apple dishes here?" she asked innocently.

Matt chuckled. "No, actually, they don't. It's the name of the family who started the restaurant chain."

"Chain, like McDonald's?"

"As in a chain of restaurants, yes, but very different than McDonald's."

They were seated and given menus to peruse. Grace sat hers down after only a couple of minutes.

"There are so many dishes to choose from. You order for me. You know what I like."

Matt ordered a cheeseburger for himself, and the oriental chicken salad for Grace.

They talked about the next phase of Grace's freedom. Matt explained how witness security worked and how she would be taken to an undisclosed location for the next several months and that they wouldn't be able to see each other or even talk on the phone.

"So you won't know where I am or what I am doing? You won't know if I am well or happy or sad and lonely?" Grace asked.

"That's right. It's for the best, because then, I can honestly say that I have no idea what happened to you or where you are when the Farinis do their inevitable investigation. I will have gone home to New York like I was scheduled to. Unless they can find that old woman on the plane who asked if we were newlyweds, no one will ever know you were on that flight."

Matt continued, "It was genius that you left your purse and keys at your flat because now it looks like a kidnapping or something. That was a brilliant move on your part. Why did you do it?"

"Something in your note, you said, 'please trust me,' that made me think of leaving everything at home. I thought maybe we were going to the 'night at the zoo' event or something like that, and I didn't want to lug those things around."

Their food arrived, and Grace suddenly felt hungry for the first time in a long time. The salad looked so good. She picked up her fork and started to take a bite.

"Um, do you mind if we say a prayer of thanks before we eat?" asked Matt.

"Sure." Grace put her fork down.

"Heavenly Father, thank you for this food we are about to eat. Thank you for safe travels so far. We ask that you keep your hand of security on each of us the rest of the way. In the name of Jesus your precious Son, we pray, amen."

"Wow," said Grace. "That was beautiful. I was expecting the standard Catholic prayer."

Grace took a bite of her salad and was amazed at how good it was. She had expected an oriental flavor just by the name of the dish, but the crispy chicken and crunchy wonton noodles along with the greens was a marriage of flavors and textures all at once. It was delicious!

"Oh my goodness, this is delicious," she told Matt. "How is yours?"

"Very good, you wanna bite?"

"No, thank you. I've had a hamburger before."

They finished their meal. Matt paid the bill, and they left. They took the subway back to Matt's neighborhood and walked the few blocks to his apartment building. He lived on the 140th floor, and Grace was glad there was an elevator. She would not like to take that many stairs.

When they got in the elevator, Matt pushed the button for the 166th floor.

"I want to take you to the roof and show you the city at sunset," he told Grace.

"Why is there no floor 13 or 113?" Grace asked. Matt explained the superstition of the number 13 and why it is almost never used in a building or vessel.

"That's odd," said Grace. "Don't people know that the 14th floor is actually the 13th floor anyway? You can't just call it something else and change the truth. You might as well call it the 'the missing floor' for goodness' sakes."

Matt chuckled along with Grace. She was right. He loved how relaxed and fun she was now that they were away from London.

They reached the roof, and Matt opened the door. The sun was setting over the harbor just to the west of them. Matt showed her the view in all directions. There were some buildings that blocked the view of the Statue of Liberty.

"You know she was a gift from France, right?" said Grace.

"Yes, indeed she was. And she has stood in the harbor for over two hundred years. Amazing, isn't it? We Americans consider her one of our greatest national treasures. On behalf of the United States of America, I thank you, my dearest French friend." Matt bowed to Grace.

Grace playfully punched him in the arm and said, "You are most welcome, you goofball," a playful term she had learned from Matt. "Where is Ground Zero?"

Matt pointed in the direction where the twin towers used to stand.

"See those two spotlights shinning straight up into the night sky? That's where the towers stood."

"And now they are just…gone. Such a tragedy."

"Yes, it sure is. Now over there is Manhattan Island, and over there, all those lights that look like a carnival, that's Coney Island, an amusement park with lots of fun rides, hot dogs, ice cream, and cotton candy. So much fun!"

An hour later, they left the roof and descended to Matt's floor. It was eight o'clock, but Grace felt like it was three in the morning. She yawned and stretched and decided to go to bed early.

"What time do we leave in the morning. Do you know yet?"

"No, not yet. Don't set your alarm. I'll wake you up in time to get packed to go. I promise."

"Okay, then, thank you." She leaned in to hug him, kissed his cheek, and said, "Good night."

At 9:00 p.m. Matt's phone rang; it was Joe.

"Hey, Matt, how are things going? Have you noticed any eyes or tails on you?"

"None, everything is clear. What's the story in London?"

"No signs of awareness so far. For all they know, it's just another Saturday morning sleeping in. So no news is good news for now. How is Grace?"

"She's asleep. We got the supplies on the list you gave me. Everything is ready for the next step, including Grace. She is 100 percent on board."

"That's great. I will pick her up in the lobby of the building tomorrow morning at 10:00 sharp. Make sure she is packed and waiting in the lobby."

"Wait, I'm not going with you to the airport?"

"No, Matt, you're not. This is the end of connection for you."

"Oh, I see."

"Make sure you're seen by yourself or with your normal friends out and about this weekend in case you're being watched. Got it?"

"Ya, I got it."

Joe hung up, and Matt had a knot in his stomach. Suddenly he didn't want to let Grace out of his sight. But the plans were set, and it was out of his control. He poured himself a drink and took it out to the balcony. He sat for a long while sipping his drink and thinking about the tumultuous days ahead having to pretend he didn't know where Grace had gone or what had happened to her. The Grace he had enjoyed the past couple of days was the one he wanted to spend the rest of his life with. One thing was sure, he wouldn't have to pretend to miss her.

19

....

MEGAN GOT TO JAELYNN'S FLAT around 10:00 Sunday morning. Georgio wanted Megan to pop in on Jaelynn more often and unannounced. She rang the bell twice, then got out her own key and began to enter the flat. The door wasn't shut tightly and pushed open when she attempted to put her key into the lock.

Megan pushed the door open the rest of the way with a wary feeling in her stomach. It wasn't like Jaelynn to leave the door unlocked, let alone not shut and bolted. In fact, Megan expected the chain bolt to be on the door if Jaelynn was not up yet.

She entered the flat with caution. Megan saw Jaelynn's handbag on the bar and her travel bag on the floor by the couch. As she walked further into the kitchen area, she saw Jaelynn's keys on the table by her cell phone. She called out for Jaelynn; maybe she was in the shower. She went into the bedroom; the bed was made, and everything was neatly put away. The bathroom door was open, but Jaelynn was not there.

Megan dialed Georgio's number. "Did you have Jaelynn picked up for something last night or early this morning?"

"No, why?" Georgio asked tersely.

"I think we may have a runner. She's not here, but all her stuff is. Oh wait, I didn't look out on the balcony. It is a beautiful day. She may be out there."

"Well, look and be quick about it. If she is on the run, we need to find her fast."

"She's not on the balcony. It's all locked up."

"Call Matt right now and find out if she's with him. If she is, let me know."

Megan started to respond, but Georgio had already hung up. Megan dialed Matt's number, but it went straight to his voice mail which was normal for him on a weekend. This being a three-day weekend, Matt would probably be in New York, which meant if Jaelynn was with him, she may well be planning to run.

Megan called Germain and got him and the security team on a code red looking for Jaelynn. Meanwhile, Megan looked up Kaelynn's number and dialed it.

On a Sunday morning in January, Kaelynn got the worst phone call of her young life. Megan Stewart from the Farini Agency called Kae to see if Jaelynn had gone to Paris for the three-day weekend.

Megan asked, "Kaelynn, it's Megan Stewart, darling. I was wondering if Jaelynn had gone to Paris to spend the holiday with you this weekend?"

"No," replied Kae. "I haven't talked with Jaelynn since last Sunday a week ago. Why what's wrong?"

"Oh, nothing is wrong really. I just don't know where Jaelynn went for the weekend. She's not at her flat, but her handbag and car is."

"Well, something is wrong because Jaelynn would never leave her handbag at the flat if she were going somewhere. Have you called Matt? I know they are good friends."

"Matt went home to New York for the weekend, and Jaelynn did not go with him."

"This isn't good, Megan. Where are Jaelynn's bodyguards?"

"They had the weekend off."

"You need to find her because this doesn't sound good!"

"We are looking I assure you."

"When you find her, would you please ask her to call me and let me know she is okay?"

"I will, dear, 'bye now."

Kaelynn hung up the phone and turned to Jon-Pierre. She caught him up on the other side of the conversation. "Something is terribly wrong," she said. "Jae never leaves her handbag."

Jon-Pierre said, "Let's not jump to conclusions now. There may be a simple explanation."

"I sense some intense distress, Jon-Pierre. I'm calling Matt."

Kaelynn dialed Matt's private number, but it went straight to voice mail. She left a hurried message. "Matt, Megan just called me. They can't find Jae. Her bag and keys are at the flat, but there is no sign of her. Call me when you get this, please." Next she tried Jae's phone, but it just rang and rang then went to voice mail.

Monday there was no news. Kaelynn called Megan and Matt again. Megan said they were scouring footage of local transportation stations as well as checking with all Uber, Lyft, and taxi companies. They were coming up empty. Matt's phone went to voice mail again.

Kae was about to lose control. She wasn't sensing so much distress anymore but a sense of urgency to find Jae. She couldn't decipher her emotions. On one hand, she was frantic that something bad, like kidnapping, had happened, and on the other hand, an urgency to hear her voice and know she was all right.

Jon-Pierre did his best to try to keep Kaelynn calm, but the longer Jae was missing, the harder it was becoming. He was worrying too. Jon-Pierre called his boss to let him know they had a family emergency so he could take some time off. He updated his boss on what was happening and was told to take all the time he needed.

Megan left Jaelynn's flat, and everything just as she found it and headed for the office. When she arrived twenty-five minutes later, she went straight to Germain's office.

"What have you got?" she demanded.

"Watch your tone, Megan. You were supposed to be keeping close tabs on her."

"I have been! She hasn't given any indication she was planning something. I think we might have foul play."

"Did you talk to Matt?"

"Voice mail. It's a long weekend. I'm sure he went to New York. I talked with the twin sister. She doesn't know anything. She was very concerned, so she actually doesn't know where or what's going on with Jaelynn."

"I've sent an agent over to check out the flat and the garage. Is her car still there?"

"I didn't check the garage."

"You better call Georgio and update him."

"Let's wait until you hear back from your agent."

"Bingo! Matt was on a flight Friday night from Heathrow to New York. I'll pull up the boarding footage. Just a second…here it is…he boarded alone. Now for the footage from the New York end…here we go…disembarked alone. She's not with Matt."

"Well, then where in the world is she?"

"I'm sending a guy to check out the sister."

Germain's phone buzzed; it was Georgio. "What the bloody hell is going on, Germain? What is the status of Jaelynn?"

"We are looking for her now. We have been for the past hour. I don't know that she is missing perse, but she's not at the flat, she's not with Matt, he's in New York, I checked the flight footage, and Jaelynn was not on the flight."

"Check the sister."

"I've already contacted Kaelynn, and she sounded legitimately surprised that we were looking for Jaelynn. She says she's not there—"

"Send someone to check personally. You can't trust the sister."

"I've already sent an agent to check."

"Check all the outgoing flights from Friday night to this morning—"

"Georgio! I know how to do my job. I'm already in process of checking outgoing everything, including Ubers and Lyfts."

"Keep me informed! We've got a lot invested in this girl."

"I will," said Germain," but the line was already dead.

Reports began to pour in form the security staff. Jaelynn was not on any outgoing plane, train, car rental, Uber, Lyft, or bus.

She wasn't at her flat, and her sister came up clean. Now Germain was scouring shopping footage and street cameras all over the city to see if any camera caught a glimpse of her somewhere, anywhere.

By Monday, the entire Farini underworld was in full panic mode. It was as if Jaelynn had simply disappeared into thin air. Georgio and Germain decided to file a missing person's report to enlist the help of Scotland Yard. Germain made the call with Georgio breathing literally down his neck.

"Hello, I'd like to report a missing person."

Germain proceeded to give them a detailed description of Jaelynn, her occupation, and last known whereabouts. Once the report was filed, a detective would be assigned and contact them for a meeting.

Within the hour, Detective Whitmore rang at the agency front door. He was immediately ushered into Germain's office. Whitmore had worked on the case of the two models and photographer two years ago.

"Lost another model, have we?" he stated somewhat condescendingly.

Germain shook Whitmore's hand and said, "We've been looking everywhere. We think she might have gone on holiday, but her handbag, identification, passport, car, and keys are all in her flat. Mrs. Stewart found the door unlocked and slightly ajar Sunday morning."

"Why didn't you call us Sunday then?"

"We wanted to check her known holiday locations and other possibilities before bothering Scotland Yard."

"Oh yes, well, I see. Let's begin at the flat, shall we? I hope you haven't disturbed everything and gotten fingerprints all over the place."

They left the agency office for the penthouse. When they arrived, everything was just as Megan had found on it Sunday. After taking a quick look around, Whitmore called a forensic team to get fingerprints and any other evidence they might find for clues to Jaelynn's disappearance.

There were no fingerprints other than Jaelynn's, Megan's, and Matt's. There was no sign of a struggle or anything out of place that would raise suspicion. Jaelynn's disappearance was a mystery.

20

Tuesday morning, Matt returned Kaelynn's call.

"I just heard myself. Something is definitely not right. Jae wouldn't just up and disappear like this," said Matt.

"Matt, tell me what's been going on, please? I know Jae has been stressed and depressed, but she wouldn't talk to me about it."

"I know, I saw the same thing. Believe me, I'm all over this here, and I will keep you updated."

"Thanks, Matt. I know you love her as much as I do."

"She's my best friend." Matt choked up a little, and when he did, Kae lost it and began to cry.

"I can't lose her too."

"I know, honey. I'll keep you up to date. I promise. Put Jon-Pierre on."

Matt talked for a few minutes to Jon-Pierre then hung up.

By Tuesday, evening the story hit the news. The report suggested foul play with no confirmation yet. They mentioned her handbag, a car, and keys at the flat and ended the story with the fact that no ransom information had been received.

Matt called Jon-Pierre and Kae right after the story. He assured them he was staying very close to the investigation, but that he too was beginning to suspect something foul. Kae couldn't even talk. She could only sob and try to listen.

Jon-Pierre came on the line and asked, "Matt, could there have been a ransom call, and the Farinis aren't telling anyone?"

"I wouldn't put it past them. I've been pestering Scotland Yard and the Farinis nonstop for information. If there has been a call, they are being extremely quiet about it."

"I don't trust those Farinis. Something has always been shady about them. I'm going to hire our own private investigator to look into this. Maybe we will get some real answers."

"I wouldn't waist your money just yet, Jon-Pierre. Scotland Yard is very thorough on cases like this."

"I have to, Matt, for Kae's sake."

"I understand. Well, let's keep each other up to date, all right, my friend?"

"Absolutely."

* * * * *

Joe arrived at Matt's building in New York City at exactly 10:00 a.m. Grace was waiting as requested in the lobby. She was wearing a pair of blue jeans and a white T-shirt with a pair a sneakers, some of the new clothes purchased the day before. Joe was pleased. She blended in well. She had a small travel bag. They got into Joe's unmarked car and headed east to Republic Airport in Farmingdale.

The flight plan was logged, the plane fueled, loaded and ready to go when Joe pulled the car directly adjacent the steps. Grace stepped out of the car and boarded the small jet. She turned halfway up the stairs to find Joe pulling away in his car. A flight attendant at the top of the stairs motioned Grace to hurry onto the plane.

It was a beautiful Gulf Stream 5, spacious with the finest amenities. Grace settled into a leather seat and buckled in as the attendant stowed her bags in the luggage compartment. Grace asked the attendant, "Where are we going?"

"I'm sorry I can't answer any of your questions until we are in the air," she said politely. Then she went to the front of the plane and buckled in herself. Within minutes, the jet thrust forward and took off. The last time Grace had felt this alone, she was standing on a dock with Kaelynn waving good-bye to their parents as they set sail around the world.

They hadn't been in the air long when an official-looking man stepped out of the cockpit area and took the seat opposite of Grace.

"Good morning. I'm agent Keith Hartman, and I will be handling all communications with you form here on out. I'm sure you have a lot of questions. Let me see if I can fill you in on the most important details, and then we can address any other questions you have."

"First of all, you are now in the US witness security program. That means that the US government has granted you asylum to protect you from harm while awaiting a trial where you will testify against the Farini crime organization. We have been tracking the Farinis for a very long time. We've tried to get an agent inside the organization, but the last one was killed in a suspicious plane crash. The Farinis paid off an inside man with the aviation investigators and got them to rule the plane had a bizarre bird strike.

"We were ecstatic when your friend approached us about helping get you out of the organization. We could never have hoped for a better opportunity. It took about six months to get through all the processes here in the US to get your request approved. The rest you know all about because here you are.

"Now for the next part of the process, we have given you a whole new identity. In fact, according to your new background check, you were born here in the United States in Casper, Wyoming. This file contains all your new history. You will need to read and memorize it. You have to know it forward and backward because everything you used to be is gone, and this is who you are now."

Keith handed the file to Grace. "Now I'm sure you want to know about your sister and your parents? Until the trial is over, you may not contact them for any reason whatsoever. If there is some sort of emergency, I will be your communication source. I will keep you informed on important issues with your family, but your family will always believe that you are still missing."

"No, Mr. Hartman. It will break my sister's heart!"

"Which would you rather have, a sister with a broken heart or a dead sister? Because the Farinis will kill her if they even think she knows where you are!"

"I get your point."

"Your new profile indicates that your parents were killed in a car accident when you were fifteen. So you won't have new parents to try to get to know."

"That's fine."

"We know where Kaelynn is, but we haven't been successful in locating your parents. Can you shed some light on their whereabouts?"

"No, we haven't seen or heard from them in over three years."

"Okay, then let's leave well enough alone on that front. We're heading to Worland, Wyoming, where you will live with an agent couple who will work with you on acquiring an American accent and understanding American culture. They will also help you memorize and recite facts from your new background and develop plausible back stories.

"The US government has agreed to fast-track citizenship for you should you wish to become a US citizen. It is not a requirement, but it is highly recommended. Your status shows that you were born here, but if someone savvy tried to dig deeper within the dark web, they might be able to uncover results that US citizenship would give us the ability to expunge."

"What do I have to do to become a US citizen?"

"Marty and Mitch will help you with what you need to know to pass the citizenship test. Then it's a private swearing in by a judge, and your part is done. Legally then we can expunge everything from your real past and lock in your new profile so long as we don't uncover any illegal activity."

"What kind of illegal activity?"

"Only what you've been arrested for. And since you have never been arrested, you're in the clear."

"Okay, that's fine. Where is this Warland place?"

"It's *Worland*. It's in the middle of nowhere. It is largely farm and ranch territory. Trust me, no one will find you there."

"What about Matt?"

"Not even Matt will know where you are. Is there something going on between you two that I should know about?"

"You mean besides the fact that we're married?"

"Besides that."

"Isn't that significant? I mean we are married, and I'm not with my husband, and he doesn't know where I am. Don't you think that's a bit of a plot hole?"

"Oh I see. No, not really. The marriage is only on paper right now. We can handle future plausibilities as they arise."

"Oh, so my past is erased, and a new past written in its place, but my future is up to plausibility? That's comforting."

"It's not like that exactly. It's just that we have the next three months mapped out. You're tucked away in Wyoming giving depositional testimony, and Matt is staying the course in London as if you are really missing. We can't pull this off without Matt convincing the Farinis that you truly are missing. Meanwhile with your help here, we are building a solid case to bring them down."

"Okay, I get it now. What about after the trial?"

"After the trial, it would be best if you remain Grace Wilson, with or without being married to Matt. Wilson is a pretty common name here in the States, so it's plausible that you just happen to have the same last name."

"And we're back to plausibility again."

"Sorry, there are a lot of unknowns in your future."

"*Hmm*, just like real life."

The captain announced they were on approach to Casper, Wyoming, airport and for everyone to buckle up. They landed smoothly and taxied to the terminal. It was a small airport, so they disembarked onto the tarmac and walked the remaining distance to the terminal. Grace had only one bag, so there was no need to go to luggage claim. A Lincoln Town Car was waiting for them. They got in a settled down for a two-hour drive to Worland.

"You're gonna like Marty and Mitch. They have a real nice spread of land with a river that runs through it and a lake. You can fish, hike, and really get back to nature."

"Keith, I've never been to nature, so I don't possibly think I can get back to it."

Keith chuckled. "I think once you get used to it, you'll really like this place. It will be a bit of a culture shock at first. It's miles from any town or stores, but it's quite peaceful too."

Suddenly Grace wasn't looking forward to the next three months. She was going to be all alone with two strangers in a foreign land far away from civilization as she knew it—no one to talk to, can't contact Kaelynn or Matt. What in the world would she do with her time? She had always filled her days with work. Now there was no work. On the brighter side, there wouldn't be anymore entertaining either. She was beyond grateful for that.

21

MATT WAS WORKING DAY AND night trying to stay as busy as possible so as not to think too much about Jaelynn being gone. He took as much freelance work as he could handle. When he wasn't working, he was trying to find out what was happening with the search for Jaelynn.

Most of his news, he got from other models; some he got by directly asking Megan what the news was. The answers were always the same—nobody had seen her and nobody knows what happened to her.

After a week of searching, Matt felt the Farinis eyes swing back to him. Germain was asking old questions again like, "When was the last time you saw her? Where were you the Friday and Saturday night when Jaelynn disappeared?"

When Matt had enough of the probing in his direction, he proceeded to blow up at Megan and Germain, asking, "Where were you guys? Where was Jaelynn's security detail? Why weren't they protecting her? It looks to me like someone kidnapped her, and you guys have nothing!"

"Calm down, Matt," Germain soothed. "We aren't trying to say you had anything to do with Jaelynn's disappearance. It's just that we keep hitting brick walls. So we're going back over everything we know to make sure we haven't missed anything. We know you're clean. We're just hoping there's something you forgot or remember now that you didn't when we first went over it."

"Well, I can see you didn't waste any time replacing her. You already have a new model, and she's living in Jaelynn's flat, so maybe you guys are just trying to cover your own asses."

"Matt, please, we're trying our best here."

"Well, what does Scotland Yard say?"

"They are hitting dead ends too. It's like she simply vanished into thin air. There is no trace of her anywhere. Look, Matt, we know you and Jaelynn were close friends. We gave you two a lot of leeway because we trusted you both. We were hoping maybe she had contacted you or reached out or something that could help us find her."

Matt drug his hand through his already tossed hair. "No, I haven't heard a word. I've even talked with her sister, and she hasn't heard anything either. If there's one thing I know about Jaelynn, it's that she would never leave her sister in the dark. If she could let us know she was safe, she would talk to Kaelynn. I'm sure of it."

"Okay, Matt, now that we're all on the same page, we'll keep you up to date as new developments come around."

"Thank you, guys, I appreciate that."

Matt left the office and headed for the employee entrance.

Megan asked, "Are you really gonna let him know everything we know?"

"Bloody no. I won't tell him squat. But I am keeping him under surveillance."

Kaelynn and Jon-Pierre decided to hire a private detective to find out what happened to Jaelynn. Kae was sick with worry. It was not like Jae to do something like this. There had to be some sort of foul play.

Certainly Scotland Yard had the good sense to consider that a kidnapper would use gloves so as not to leave any fingerprints. It's the only scenario that made any sense at all. Jaelynn wouldn't leave her bag and her keys when she left her flat for any reason. She never left the door unlocked, and she usually had it bolted. Nothing she was being told made sense.

Jaelynn never said anything untoward about the Farinis, but Kaelynn knew Jae too well to think everything was "just fine" as she always answered. Kae could see that Jae was unhappy, losing weight, and not sleeping well. She also knew that she was depressed. But Jae wouldn't talk about any of it. She always said, "I don't want to talk about work. How are you doing?" And so the subject of work was always avoided.

Kaelynn never trusted the Farinis or Megan Stewart. There was something shady going on, and it was dangerous, or Jae would talk to her about it. Everyone knew about the two models and a photographer who had lost their lives in the plane crash. They all had suspicions too, but there was no proof of a coverup, so subject closed.

Jon-Pierre located a reputable private detective named Lucas Page. Kaelynn and Jon-Pierre met with him over coffee at a local café. After going over everything they knew, reports they had been given, and what they suspected, Lucas had another suspicion. He wanted to check things out before tipping his hand to the couple.

Lucas could see the genuine distress in Kaelynn over her twin sister's disappearance and wanted to help shed some light on the subject for her.

After the meeting, Lucas called a close personal friend he had made years ago at Scotland Yard to dig up any additional information. What he found out confirmed his suspicion, but they couldn't talk about it over the phone. They would have to meet in person. They made arrangements to meet at a pub in London as they had done many times while Lucas was there on business.

Before he left for London, he met with Kaelynn and Jon-Pierre again.

He began with, "I have found some additional information that I can't talk about until I confirm it for myself. But I strongly suggest that you make peace with Jaelynn's disappearance. I don't think she's coming back even though we haven't found a body. I encourage you to plan a memorial service and begin to work through your grief. Even if we find a body, you're probably not going to see her again."

Kaelynn was devastated. "When can you tell us all the details?"

"Maybe never. It may just have to be that way."

"I can't accept that! I have to know what happened to her!"

Kaelynn was on the verge of hysteria. Lucas looked at Jon-Pierre pleadingly. Jon-Pierre tried to console Kaelynn, but she would have none of it.

"I deserve to know what has happened to Jaelynn. We're twins! If she were dead, I would know it in my soul. She is not dead! She's alive. I can feel her. You have to find her before it's too late!"

Kaelynn collapsed into Jon-Pierre's arms sobbing uncontrollably. Lucas apologized and excused himself while Jon-Pierre comforted Kaelynn.

The following week, Lucas met with his Scotland Yard friend, James Smythe. They shared a beer together and caught up on each other's lives before diving into the DepProvoue case.

"I can't tell you everything, but I can tell you enough that you can piece together the rest. I can tell you that the United States government is involved at the highest level. I can tell you that Jaelynn was not kidnapped or in any way harmed."

"So she is alive?"

"Ya, if she were dead, I think that would constitute being harmed, don't you, ole chap?"

"Okay, Smart ass, what else?"

"I can tell you that Jaelynn DepProvoue is not anywhere in Europe."

Lucas leaned in, and so did James.

"So witness security?" whispered Lucas.

"I can neither confirm nor deny such speculation," replied James with a wink.

Thursday, Lucas called Jon-Pierre and told him he had some leads he was working on but that it didn't look good. He thought it would be in everyone's best interest to go ahead with a memorial service for Jaelynn and begin to move on with their lives.

Jon-Pierre was stunned. "What do your leads say?"

"My information is not complete yet. The authorities are searching the rivers and canals first. They have to rule out suicide before they can move on to possible foul play. But if what I think has happened, you'll never see Jaelynn again."

"Tell me what you know, please," begged Jon-Pierre.

"That's all I can tell you right now. Urge Kaelynn to have the memorial as soon as possible."

Kaelynn was devastated by the turn of events. "Someone knows something they aren't telling us, Jon-Pierre. I want to know what is happening with my sister. If she's dead, where is her body? I don't want to have a funeral for her without knowing for sure she is dead! My gut says she's alive! Damn it! How can I bury her?"

"I know, baby, this is the hardest situation. I do understand. As long as they haven't found her body, we should assume she is still alive."

"I can *feel* her, Jon-Pierre. She is alive."

"Okay, let's have the memorial so everyone else can move on. What if Jaelynn ran, you know, like those models that were in that plane crash? But what if Jae is still on the run. I know that sounds crazy, but what if the memorial would actually help her?"

"You're talking nonsense, Jon-Pierre. But fine, we will have a memorial. Call the church."

22

ONE WEEK LATER, ON A gloomy Saturday morning, a memorial service was held for Jaelynn DepProvoue in France at the Cathedral Saint Alexandre Nevsky where the family attended while the girls were growing up. The service started at 10:00 a.m. It was a fine service with many of Jaelynn's modeling coworkers in attendance plus her friends from her school days. Even some of Jae and Kae's teachers came.

There was no casket because there was no body found. So the service focused on Jaelynn and her life, as it should—how happy she was as a child, how she loved to sing and write little songs that Kaelynn performed dances to for their parents. The priest spoke of her modeling career, naming all the high-end fashion houses she modeled for.

Finally the priest talked about life and the hereafter. He talked about heaven and our blessed savior Jesus Christ and his Holy Mother, Mary. The rosary was recited, and the service ended with the Holy Eucharist.

There was a reception that followed with lots of food and beverages. Everyone wanted to talk to Kaelynn about what had happened, and they were all so sorry for her loss. It was a hard day for Kaelynn. In her heart, she didn't believe Jae was dead, but in reality, it certainly appeared that way.

Lucas attended the service but did not talk to the family. He slipped in just after the service started and left directly after it ended, avoiding the reception altogether. What he had to say could wait for another day.

Matt also attended the service for Jaelynn. Kaelynn, whom he had met several times with Jaelynn, insisted that Matt sit with her and Jon-Pierre in the family section.

"But I am not family," Matt protested.

"You are as close to family as Jaelynn ever had. She talked about you all the time. If I didn't know better, I would say you two were in a serious relationship."

Matt blushed at this revelation and sat down. Jon-Pierre shook his hand. Kaelynn started to ask Matt what he knew about Jae's disappearance. Jon-Pierre tightened his grip on her hand and whispered, "Not here, honey," and she stopped.

Matt leaned close and whispered to Kaelynn, "At this point, no news is good news, but I think this memorial service is a very good idea. It will help us process what we have experienced over the past few weeks."

"You don't think she is dead, do you, Matt?" Kaelynn asked pointedly.

"I can't say if she is or isn't. They haven't found her or her body, so who's to say. But if it were a kidnapping, it would seem to me that someone would have gotten a ransom note or call by now."

"How do we know the Farinis haven't gotten one and just aren't saying anything?"

"I suppose that's still a possibility."

Just then, the service started, halting their conversation for the present.

There was no doubt that Jaelynn was a loved person judging by the sniffles and sobs that Matt could hear throughout the cathedral. Kaelynn sat quietly between Matt and Jon-Pierre. There was an occasional tear that ran down her cheek but no hysterics or exuberant displays of emotion. She wasn't emotionless, but she was handling the service remarkably well.

Following the service at the reception, Jon-Pierre did not leave Kaelynn's side. He was a rock solid pillar for her. Matt could tell how much they loved each other. It was on pure, unfiltered display today.

Kaelynn turned from an old childhood friend to the next people in line waiting to give their condolences, and it was the Farinis and

Mrs. Stewart. Kaelynn almost lunged at them, but Jon-Pierre was able to subdue her in time. She hissed at them, "You were responsible for her. You were supposed to protect her and keep her safe. How dare you show up here like you actually cared about her. She was just a big payday to you. Get out. You're not welcome here. *Get out!*"

The Farinis and Megan quickly left the reception not wanting to draw any more attention to themselves.

After the reception had been going on for about an hour, Matt got a table and filled three plates with foods offered at the reception. He coaxed Kaelynn and Jon-Pierre over to the table to sit and rest for a bit. He announced to the guests that since all had been greeted through the reception line that Kaelynn was going to sit a while and get something to eat. Most of the guests respected this request and did not interrupt them.

Matt asked, "How are you holding up, Kaelynn?"

"I'm doing okay, but I am ready for this day to be over. It just feels so wrong putting her to rest when we don't even know what happened."

"This is the hardest kind of memorial, and I can understand your feelings. But if not for us, then for her hundreds of friends who loved and cared about her, this is very appropriate. Try to think of it that way."

"Well put," said Jon-Pierre. "That's a good way for us to think about it, Kae."

Kaelynn agreed and began to relax a little. She didn't feel like eating, but she did take a few bites of food.

When it was clear that the reception was winding down and people began to leave, Jon-Pierre called for their car to be brought to the main door. He invited Matt to come to their home for a bit of rest before he began the six-hour drive back to London.

Only when they arrived at Kaelynn and Jon-Pierre's flat did Matt truly begin to relax. He realized that he had been tense trying to be strong and brave for Kaelynn. As his body began to relax, the reality of what happened today began to sink in. He reminded himself that he had to believe Jaelynn was gone so that he would appear to be in true mourning. In a way he was, because Jaelynn *was* gone, but Grace was very much alive.

Jon-Pierre insisted that Kae lay down and get some rest. He poured her some water and gave her a couple aspirin and something to help her sleep. She took the pills without hesitation and went to lay down.

Their flat was a nice size with two bedrooms and two bathrooms. The view from the balcony wasn't spectacular, but it wasn't hideous either. It reminded Matt of the view from his apartment balcony in New York. The flat was furnished with a white leather sofa and love seat. There was a beautiful white rug on the floor under a stunning cut glass coffee table. The hardwood flooring was traditional and well cared for. To replace it in today's market would cost thousands of dollars.

The kitchen was open to the dining and living area. The cabinets were all white as was the granite countertops and backsplash. The bottom of the island was painted a dark ocean blue, the only splash of color in the open area. It was quite stunning. Matt could see Kaelynn had done all the decorating. It was very similar to Jaelynn's tastes.

Jon-Pierre came back into the room from getting Kaelynn settled for some rest and moved to the kitchen.

"Café?" he asked

"Yes, please," responded Matt. "How is the photog business treating you?"

"Treating me? I don't understand."

"How is work going?" Matt clarified.

Jon-Pierre chuckled. "Oh, it is good. I am as busy as I want to be. These last few weeks though have been very hard as I am sure they have been for you as well."

"Yes, they have been. But I have taken on as much work as I can to keep busy and try to not go around busting peoples' heads open who should have been watching Jae and keeping her safe. And to boot, I can't get a straight answer out of anyone. They just say, 'we're still looking for her, there's no trace.' I am so sick of hearing that. No one can disappear without a single trace. Someone knows something, but they're not saying anything."

"For me, I have had to cut back on my work for Kae's sake. She needs me more than ever now. She has been an emotional wreck like you. She screams at people sometimes when they try to placate her with a simple answer like 'we're looking,' same as you."

"I'm sorry this is happening to you guys."

"It's happening to you too and to everyone who loves Jae. Can you tell me what was really going on with her work? Kae is sure that something not good was happening, but Jae wouldn't talk about any of it."

"It is the same with me. Whenever we weren't working, she didn't want to talk about work at all. Anything but work was okay, but work was a taboo subject. I could tell she was depressed, exhausted, and fragile emotionally. I tried to get her to open up, but she wouldn't."

"Kae tried on our holiday to St. Croix too, but she was, how you say, tight-lipped?"

"Ya, that sounds right. I think honestly she didn't want to talk about it because whatever was eating at her was quite distasteful. I would only be speculating if I tried to imagine what was bothering her. I think she felt like not opening up was somehow protecting all of us. It's the only reasonable answer I can come up with."

"But you were with her more than we have been the past two years. Surely you have some idea of what might have happened to her."

"Like I said, it would be pure speculation, and I have no proof of anything really."

"Hmph, that is what is making this whole thing so difficult to swallow."

"I agree." Matt had a knot in his stomach from lying to Jon-Pierre and Kae. He agreed to spend that night on the couch at Kaelynn and Jon-Pierre's flat. He would leave after breakfast in the morning.

The next morning, Matt awoke to the aroma of rich coffee. He pulled himself up from the couch to see Kaelynn in the kitchen just pouring a cup for herself.

Just as she set the pot back on counter, Matt asked, "May I have a cup?"

Kaelynn nearly jumped out of her skin. She turned around shocked to see Matt. "Oh my goodness, I didn't even see you there. I thought you left last night, but…I'm so glad you stayed. It was too late and too exhausting of a day to try to drive back to London."

"I'm sorry, I didn't mean to frighten you. I thought Jon-Pierre would have told you I stayed over."

"No, I was out for the night. Jon-Pierre couldn't have woke me if he blew an air horn next to my ear." She poured Matt a cup of coffee. "Do you take cream or sugar?"

"No, just black, thank you."

"I can see why Jae loves you so much. I'm glad you stayed. I'd like to talk with you about Jae and her disappearance."

"Okay, what's on your mind?"

"In my heart, I am confident she is alive, somewhere. As a twin we have this, connection, you know? We just know stuff about each other."

"Well, to be completely honest with you in my gut, I feel like she's alive too."

"I knew it! I knew you were too calm at the service yesterday! Nobody can love someone and not shed at least a few tears at a memorial."

"Why do you insist that Jaelynn and I are in love? It's not like that with us."

"I think thou dost protest too much, Mr. Wilson. If you could hear the way Jaelynn talked about you in St. Croix and every other time we talked on the phone, you would know she is head over heels in love with you."

"Or maybe I was a safe topic for discussion something other than her work. She wouldn't talk about work, ever, even if we were on the same shoot. 'No work talk,' she would say."

"She did the same with me, but a sister knows when her twin is in love, and that girl is in love with you."

"Well, she never showed any signs of that with me."

"And what about you? I can tell you are in love with her too."

"I don't know. That's a bridge we never crossed. I mean I care about her a great deal, and yes, I love her, but it's more like best friends love each other."

"Well, every good relationship starts with friendship, no? You'll know when the time is right."

"That is if we ever find her."

23

GRACE AND KEITH'S CAR TURNED onto a dirt road that at one time had been covered with gravel. It was lined with fences on both sides. There was no house in sight. After driving for five minutes, Grace began to wonder how far each house was away from another.

She asked Keith, "How much space is there between houses out here?"

"Well, these folks have three hundred acres, so about half a mile to the next property. I don't know how many acres they own, somewhere in the neighborhood of six hundred, so probably a mile to a mile and a half."

"How much is that in kilometers?"

He opened his phone and ran the calculation. "Just under one kilometer from one property line to the next."

"My goodness, that's far. I have never seen so much land with nothing on it. It boggles the mind. Wait, they have cows?"

"Yes, they have cows and sheep on this ranch as well as chickens, so you will have fresh eggs every day. I think you're going to like it here. All this wide open space, clean, clear air to breath and blue sky to die for."

They drove several more minutes then went up over a small hill. A large house came into view. It looked like some of the mansions Grace had been in on photo shoots.

"What a beautiful home!" said Grace. "How many people live here?"

"Just Marty and Mitch. Their children are all grown and on their own."

"Teenagers, are they?" said Grace dryly.

"What? Teenagers? No, they're in their late twenties and early thirties. Why would they be teenagers?"

"Oh, it's nothing. It's just that my sister and I were living on our own at sixteen."

"You've got to be kidding me?"

"No, it's true. Our parents sold everything we owned, leased a flat for my sister and me, then bought a yacht to sail around the world. It was a deal my father made with my mother when we were born."

"That is terrible. Do they check in from time to time?"

"No, we have received three postcards in four years, one at Christmas and one on our birthday. Great parents, huh?"

"They wouldn't get 'parents of the year' in the US, that's for sure."

The car pulled to a stop on a huge cement driveway. As they were getting out of the car, the front door opened, and a couple, mid to late fifties, came out to greet them. Introductions were made.

"Grace, this is Marty and Mitch Garrison. Marty and Mitch, this is Grace Wilson." Keith got Grace's bag from the trunk of the car.

They walked up some steps to a large front porch complete with two rocking chairs, a cocktail table, and a bench swing. Grace could envision herself sitting alone out here in the evening taking in the beauty of the pure blue sky and the massive mountain range in the distance.

They entered the house into a large foyer that went from the ground floor all the way to the top of the second floor. There was a beautiful grand chandelier hanging in the open space. It was stunning.

The entryway opened up into a large living area, which opened up to a small dinning space adjacent to a grand open kitchen. It reminded Grace of Kaelynn's flat but on a much grander scale. Nothing was white except the kitchen cabinets. Everything was done in rustic browns, tans with splashes of colors utilizing burgundies, greens, and rust.

The rooms were warm and inviting. The furniture looked very comfortable. The eat-in dining area had a high table that required stools to sit at. Grace had never seen anything like it before.

"Come on in," said Marty. "Mitch and I don't stand on much ceremony here, but with all the dirt and dust, we always take our shoes off at the door."

Grace quietly slipped her Tom's shoes off and left them on the shoe mat at the door. She walked into the living room, and they all sat down on the couches. They were comfortable. Grace thought she could easily curl up and fall asleep on them. Her body was still on London time.

"Would you guys like some lemonade while we go over the rules?"

"There's rules?" asked Grace.

Keith jumped in, "Yes, there has to be rules, and we would love some lemonade."

Mitch picked up a manila envelope from the large wood coffee table and opened it up. Keith pulled a similar file from his briefcase and handed it to Grace.

Marty came back to the living room with a tray of glasses with ice and a pitcher of lemonade with real cut lemons inside. She poured four glasses and distributed them.

Just as Grace took her glass of lemonade, a large yellow lab came bounding into the living room and jumped right onto Grace causing her to spill her drink all over her top and pants.

"Tiny," scolded Mitch, "down, boy."

Immediately Tiny sat down by his owner, tongue hanging out panting. Marty jumped up. "I am so sorry, Grace. Come with me. I'll show you to your room so you can change. We'll just have to do things a little out of order this time," she called over her shoulder to the men.

They went up a large staircase to the second floor. They rounded a corner at the top that led to a long, wide corridor with several doors. Marty showed her each room. One was an office with a cozy-looking fireplace, a nice mahogany desk and matching chair, and another comfortable-looking couch.

The second room, across the hall, was to be Grace's room. It was large with two big windows that let in a lot of light, which Grace loved. The bed had four grand posts and sat high up off the floor.

There was actually a small step stool at the side to get up onto the bed. Another thing Grace had never seen before. There was a fireplace in her room as well and an attached bathroom with a large soaker tub and a huge walk-in shower. Everything was huge in this house.

Grace asked, "Does it get very cold here? I noticed there are fireplaces in each room."

"It gets very cold in the winter, and the fireplaces do help keep the warmth in, but we have central heat throughout the house, so we don't actually depend solely on the fireplace. It's really more for ambiance."

Marty continued to show her where the towels were and the laundry shoot.

"What is a laundry shoot?" Grace asked.

So Marty showed her how to open the shoot door and drop an item down to the laundry room on the first floor. Grace thought that was very clever.

Marty showed Grace the dresser and told her to go ahead and put her clothes right in the drawers because she was going to be here for a few months. Then she slipped out of the room.

Grace went into the bathroom and took all her wet clothes off and dropped them into the corner on the floor for now. She wasn't sure about using a laundry shoot for her undergarments. It felt strange that someone else might be handling her underwear and bras. She washed the sticky residue off her arms and legs then dressed in a pair of jeans and a white button-up shirt.

When Grace came down the stairs, the conversation in the living room came to a stop. The men were struck by Grace's beauty. Grace wondered if they were talking in confidence, so she asked, "Am I interrupting?"

Keith replied, "No, not at all. Come on down, and we'll get back into the file review. Mitch and I go back a long way, and we were just reminiscing about some old cases we worked together."

Grace sat down again but did not reach for her drink. Tiny was lying on the floor at his master's feet. He looked so sad, like he had just gotten in very big trouble.

Grace said, "Your home is quite beautiful. Have you lived here long?"

"About thirty years," replied Mitch. "We just had a full remodel two years ago, so it looks all fancy and new now."

Grace liked the easy way Mitch carried himself. He was relaxed and comfortable just like his home.

Keith interjected, "Let's get down to business now."

Grace picked up the file Keith had given her and opened it up to the first page. It was her new dossier. "Grace, you will need to memorize this dossier from top to bottom as we discussed on the plane. It is the new you. Do not deviate from it!"

"Okay," Grace replied.

"Moving onto the next section, these are the rules we referred to earlier. One, you are not to make any phone calls to anyone for any reason. Two, you are not to leave the property without Marty or Mitch with you. Three, when you do go out in public, let Marty and Mitch do most of the talking. Let them answer questions for you and don't feel like you need to make any friends."

"So basically you want me to be a snobbish, self-absorbed super-model? I can do that," said Jaelynn tongue-in-cheek.

Keith laughed. "Something like that. It's just easier if you say very little. Your accent alone will draw attention to you. We don't want that."

"I get it," Grace replied. "I am very used to being seen and not heard. It goes with the job."

"Okay, next section. You will be working on your testimony and depositions over the next few months. There are a couple of examples in here to give you an idea of what to expect. US offi-cials will be facilitating the interviews for the depositions. I've made arrangements for them to come here so you will not be required to travel at all. The more you lay low and out of sight, the better chance we have of keeping you safe."

Grace thumbed through the testimony section. It was a bit overwhelming.

"Don't worry, Grace. You have several months to work through this part."

"Okay," she responded.

"The last section is for citizenship. If you decide you want to become a US citizen, this section will walk you through the process. It's important to know that the path to citizenship can take up to five years, but like I said on the plane, the government has agreed to fast-track yours under the circumstances in six months."

"Wow," said Grace. "That's impressive. What are the benefits of becoming a citizen again?"

"Becoming a citizen allows us to literally erase more of your past. We can even arrange for a body to be used in recovery purposes to put all those questions back in London to rest. Being a citizen will allow you to be Grace Wilson for the rest of your life. Not becoming a citizen could result in you going back to being Jaelynn DepProvoue after the trial."

"Why would that be a concern?" asked Grace.

"Right now, there is a 1.5 million dollar contract on you." Grace felt like she had been punched in the stomach. "We might not get everyone in the Farini organization once we go to trial, which could leave you wide open for them to find you when the trial is over. None of us want that. But witness security only protects you until the trial is over and you have witnessed for the prosecution."

"So becoming a citizen is almost my only option if I want to stay safe? If I testify at trial, everyone is going to see me, and they will know who I am, so how will witness protection help me anyway?"

"That is a very good question. You will witness as Jaelynn DepProvoue not Grace Wilson. Grace Wilson will never become known during the trial. Once the trial is over, we will relocate you again, hide you for several months, and then relocate you to a permanent place of your choosing. Los Angeles, San Francisco, Chicago, New York City, any large city is a great place, but then small, charming towns work too. So you will have options, but only as a citizen of the US. As a noncitizen, once the trial is over, you're on your own. We're not asking you to make that decision today. Again you have several months to consider your options."

"What about my sister?"

"You can't see or talk to your sister!"

"What about after the trial?"

"That will depend on how many of the Farini organization we are able to take down."

"What about Matt?"

"No contact with anyone anywhere but in these walls."

Grace bit her lip. "You know, the Farinis stole my life two years ago. Matt pulled me out of it in a flash. I hardly knew what was happening three days ago. And now, I can't see or talk to anyone from my past. It feels like my life is being stolen by the US government."

"I understand how it feels."

"Do you? Have you ever been plucked out of your life and erased from everyone you have ever known and loved?"

"No, I haven't. But I've walked through the process with many people, and I can understand it from the point that everyone feels the same way you do now. And I'm sorry for that. It's all for your protection and the protection of the ones you love. If we are able to get the whole organization, you will be able to resume all your previous relationships if you so choose."

"I'm sorry, Keith, I am just really tired. My body is still on London time."

"I understand, Grace. If you want, you can get some rest before dinner, and we can talk more this evening. I am not leaving until later tomorrow afternoon. And I'm sure you're going to have more questions after you've had some time to mull over our conversation."

"Yes, I would like to get some rest if you don't mind."

Marty and Keith both stood up along with Grace as she headed for the stairs to her room.

Once in her room, she crawled up on the bed and began to cry. Her entire life as she had known it up to this day was gone. Matt was the only person in her world who knew she was alive. Everyone else thought she had disappeared and presumed dead. How awful that must be for Kaelynn.

Grace hoped that Matt would somehow let her know that she was alive and safe. But according to the witness security rules, he probably couldn't. Besides if anyone knew she was alive, they might not act appropriately and draw suspicion to themselves. The Farinis did not take kindly to people who withheld information.

Grace hoped and prayed that Matt would be able to keep his head about him and act like she was truly gone.

24

MATT TOOK HIS TIME ON the long drive from Paris to London. With average traffic, it usually took five hours and forty-five minutes. Today, Sunday, traffic was very lite. But he took his time and tried to enjoy the countryside. He arrived at his flat in London just after 8:00 p.m. He was stiff from sitting so long, so he decided to take a hot shower before beginning some photo editing he needed to get finished.

The shower worked on relieving the stiffness in his muscles. He made himself a sandwich with some chips and cola, then headed for his office where he did all his post-photographic work. Opening Adobe Photoshop, he started working through thousands of shots to edit. He remembered the day they were taken. It was at the McClain mansion over in Scotland.

It was a beautiful day, and the models were all glowing in the natural light by the pool. They were shooting for two clients at the same location—something the Farinis seemed to excel at, packing two days of work into one long one. Today they were shooting for a make-up company and a swimsuit line.

The models were all dressed in their different outfits and made up with the company product by the make-up artists. The daytime and indoor shots were taken first. When that was finished, they all switched to swimsuits and outdoor poolside shots. When the girls started getting hot from the lighting and sunlight combination, they simply slipped into the pool to cool off. They could dip down to their neck but not get their face or hair wet. It made the long, hot day more bearable.

As Matt was shuffling through the shots, he ran across Jaelynn's photos. Oh she was beautiful. There was a simple purity in her face and smile. Her poses showed her unassuming ease. She had no idea how beautiful or photogenic she was. It was the one thing that made her so good at what she did and so valuable.

The irony of it was that the other girls tried their hardest to look and act like Jaelynn, but because it was not their true nature, it didn't come across to the camera. The camera didn't lie. It captured the truth. It was postediting that covered up any visible flaws. Like a pimple, covered with make-up was still a pimple. But once it was worked just right in postediting, it was like it was never there.

Yeah, postediting worked great on skin, hair, and nails, but there's nothing you can do about the overall look from the person's eyes. They say the eyes are the window to the soul, and Matt would add that the camera captures the essence of the soul absolutely.

Matt worked into the wee hours of the morning on the editing. He was about halfway finished when his eyes stopped focusing, and he gave in to fatigue and went to bed. He laid there tossing and turning for a couple of hours but couldn't sleep. He finally gave up and turned on some old movies. It reminded him of the day of rest he and Jaelynn had taken together only a few months ago.

It seemed everywhere he turned or whatever he had to work on brought him full circle back to Jaelynn. *Oh God, keep her safe, please. This nightmare has to come to an end for these young girls.*

Matt wasn't naive. He knew what Jaelynn had to do for the Farinis. He knew other girls had to do the same thing, but they didn't get the car, the wardrobe, or the penthouse like Jaelynn did. Jaelynn was special, and the Farinis knew it.

Matt was watching *An Affair to Remember* for the umpteenth time. It was one of his favorites. His college roommates had teased him for being a softy, a hopeless romantic, and some even called him a fool because of his natural sensitivity. But he never had a problem getting a date if he wanted one.

He remembered showing this movie to Jaelynn; she had never seen it probably because it's an American classic. She cried several times during the story as did he at the end. She had hugged him and thanked him for showing her such a special movie.

Now it made him cry for a different reason. He missed Jaelynn. He didn't know if he would ever see her again. He hoped so. He himself was planning to be available to testify against the Farinis, but he didn't know how much his testimony would be of help. What he knew and what he could testify to didn't match. He knew what was going on, but he didn't have any hard, factual evidence to contribute to the prosecution.

The entire prosecution's case depended on Jaelynn linking what they had evidence of to the actual commission of the crime, forcing young girls into sex trafficking for the profit of the agency. It wouldn't be easy for Jaelynn. Matt knew she was ashamed of what she had to do. That's why she would never talk about work. He understood.

* * * * *

Georgio asked Megan to bring him Jaelynn's appointment book. Megan's mouth dropped open.

"I don't have Jaelynn's appointment book. I thought you had it."

"I do not have it. You better have gotten it from Jaelynn's flat before the police took over the investigation."

"I didn't see it at her flat before the police arrived."

"Get your bloody ass over there and get me that book. If the police have it, we are royally screwed."

Megan left directly and raced over to the flat. The police line "do not cross" tape was still up. Megan opened the front door and ducked under the tape. She searched the flat thoroughly but could not find the appointment book. She began to panic and started looking under the mattress, unzipping the sofa cushions and searching inside. She looked in boxes, through dresser drawers and closets all to no avail. The book was nowhere to be found.

* * * * *

The next few weeks were a blur for Kaelynn. All the news was the same—there was no new news. Kae started to decline into depression herself. *Damn it! Jaelynn, where are you and what are you doing to us? Are you safe? Please let me know you are safe.*

25

GRACE BEGAN EACH DAY WITH breakfast with the Garrison's. Marty and Mitch worked side by side in the kitchen. Grace initially sat at the large island bar and sipped weak American coffee while Mitch or Marty tried to make small talk. At first, it was quite awkward. Grace had learned the value of being seen and not heard. But these people seemed to genuinely want to draw her out and get to know her.

On the third morning, Marty finally said, "Grace, we know you've been through a lot, and we know that it's not easy to talk about. So you don't have to talk about anything you're not comfortable with. But here's the thing, in our experience, healing begins when you are able to start opening up everything you have bottled up inside you. As humans, we naturally tend to stuff painful emotions and memories as far down inside us as we can to protect us and to hold on to the real person we are."

"You have been forced to do things that would make any normal human being blush, cringe, hide, and retreat into oneself. You're not the first victim of sexual abuse we've worked with. We want to help you heal, not just put your testimony together for the prosecution, but to really begin to heal. You are the victim. This was done to you. You didn't choose this."

Grace whispered, "But I did. I signed the contract."

Marty's heart broke. She went to Grace and took her hands in her own. "No, honey, you signed a *contract*, one that didn't say anything about allowing your body to be used by any man the agency sent your way."

"But I accepted all the perks, the wardrobe, the car, the amazing penthouse."

"You may have, but that did not give the agency the right to expect sexual favors or demand sexual activity from you. Don't you see how they have manipulated the circumstances and threatened you with your life and your families' lives to get what they want? *You* are the victim here. You have been emotionally and physically abused, and Mitch and I want to help you heal. And yes, we want to help you bring these scumbags to justice and to put them in prison for the rest of their lives."

"It wasn't just men. There were women too."

"*Oh*, Grace, we are so very sorry, honey. Please, let us help you."

"How? How can you help me? Can you make the nightmares stop? Can you undo what they have done to me? You know I was a virgin when I started working for the Farinis? I was a virgin the first time Germain made me have sex with him. Nothing can change any of that!"

"No, you're right. We can't make any of that go away. And pretending it didn't happen won't help either. What will help is talking through the pain, the way it made you feel and looking at what a healthy relationship looks like. I imagine you would like to have children, wouldn't you?"

"I don't know if I will ever be any good for anyone. I don't know how to behave with a man other than what I have learned, which turns my stomach, so no, I don't see myself ever having a good relationship with a man or having children. I don't even know if I can have children."

"Well, part of the rehab process is that you will be able to see a doctor who will examine you physically and work with you on your physical health."

"The only doctor I've ever seen ripped a human life from inside me, stuffed me with gauze, and told me to sleep it off. You don't just sleep that kind of thing off."

"No, you don't."

Grace took her plate to the sink and rinsed it off. She placed it into the dishwasher and began cleaning up the kitchen, anything to get out of this uncomfortable conversation. Marty, having a doctorate in marriage and family therapy, recognized the maneuver and joined in the cleanup. When the dishes and kitchen were almost clean, she said, "I am going for a horseback ride this afternoon. Care to join me? I could show you around the property and what we do here from day to day."

"I've never ridden a horse before."

"I'll teach you."

"Okay, sure." Grace liked being with Marty. She felt like she could trust her and Mitch.

Grace was wiping down the last of the countertops when Marty opened a drawer in a little desk area adjacent to the kitchen. She pulled out a leather-bound journal full of blank lined pages. She handed it to Grace.

"Here, I find it helps to write things down. Memories, moments that were fun, or bad. Just write…it's therapeutic."

"My goodness, this is lovely. Thank you!"

Grace went up to her room and sat at the little desk. She laid the journal down and opened it to the first page. She picked up a pen and wrote her name on the line that said," This Journal Belongs To."

She entered, *Jaelynn DepProvoue.*

26

GRACE TRIED TO WRITE SOMETHING in the journal every day. If it was supposed to be therapeutic, then she would try it.

The first few days were short little sentences like,

> *I really like it here. I thought I would be so lonely, but there is a lot to do, and I have a lot of time to think.*
>
> *I like Marty and Mitch. They are very kind and seem to know just how much to push me and when I need them to stop. I feel respected, like a real person with them. Kind of like what I feel when I am with Matt.*

But as the days turned into a week, Grace felt something inside that had cracked before and pulled her inside herself begin to allow some light to shine through. Yes, she was still broken, but there was a light that hinted at a promise of restoration and healing.

The depositions started the beginning of the second week of being with the Garrisons. At first, they were simple questions about the recruiting and the first contract while the girls were still in school. The interviewers, as they called themselves, brought a stenographer with them. They said her job was to record everything we said, and she did, every word.

The following day, they got into the second contract and the pay increase and why Kaelynn didn't sign with the Farinis again. She had to tell them as much as she could remember about conversations with Megan while shopping for clothes and cars and flats. It was exhausting. She would give anything to be seen and photographed again instead of going through this grueling process. And they hadn't even gotten to the sex yet. How awful would that be, telling these men all about her activities with other men. Ugh, that she was dreading.

In the meantime, Grace was journaling more and more. It seemed the deposition questions drudged up all kinds of memories, and Grace had no shortage of things to write about each day.

Marty had taught Grace how to ride, and they went out a couple of times each week. It was fun, and the fresh air was rejuvenating. The ranch, as she learned it was called, sprawled on and on. Grace found out she had muscles she had never known existed after the first day of riding. Marty just laughed and told her she would get used to it soon enough. Grace loved the feel of the wind in her hair as she bounced along with the horse. She could endure a few sore muscles for a few weeks.

* * * * *

Matt was struggling to get through the days. He had no idea how much he had looked forward to working with Jaelynn. He missed her so much. He thought about how Kae had accused him of being in love with Jaelynn and how he had scoffed at her. But now, he wondered if she was right. He had never been in love as an adult. He knew he liked Jaelynn a lot, probably loved her like a best friend even, but love as *in love*, maybe Kaelynn and Jon-Pierre were right.

Matt contacted Joe Richards and asked if they could meet again.

"What for?" Joe asked with caution in his tone.

"Ah, I want to talk to you about Kaelynn," Matt lied. He suddenly felt like a schoolboy getting caught with a crush on a classmate.

"What about Kaelynn?"

"Well, I was wondering if it wouldn't be advantageous to get her testimony."

"No, you're not. You want to know how Grace is doing. Now listen, you calling me is putting everyone in jeopardy. You can't call me again! You understand!"

"Yes, but listen, I'm at a pay phone, an honest to goodness old school pay phone. Can't you tell me a little about how she's doing?"

"She's fine. You promised me you could handle this."

"I know, but I didn't know I was in love with her." There, he had finally said it out loud. He was in love with Jaelynn, Grace as she was now.

"I told you that weeks ago, remember? As long as you keep your head down and mouth shut, she will be safe and fine. You could singlehandedly bring this whole operation down. We don't know who is on the agency payroll or an inside informant. So do not call me again!"

"I won't. Thanks for the update."

"Hey, kid, I'm sorry I came down on you so hard, but we think we might have a snitch on the inside here. So please, don't blow this now."

"Okay, I'll do my part. I promise."

So a snitch on the inside? That didn't sound good at all. Joe was either very paranoid, which he may well be, or he had a sixth sense about each case that kept him and his clients safe. Matt chose to believe the latter.

* * * * *

After the second week of interviews, the next part of the story would be the sexual part, and Grace was feeling very agitated at the probability of having to talk about the sex with these men. But she was in this for the sake of all the other girls, not just herself. She would endure what she had to endure.

Before the interviewers put the last of their notepads away, she asked shyly.

"Is there any way that the next part of the interviews could be handled by Marty? I would feel so much more comfortable with a woman, no offense to you, gentlemen."

"No offense taken. We anticipated the discomfort of the coming testimony and have arranged for a woman interviewer. Her name is Cassy, and she will be here on Monday. If you would feel more comfortable, you can ask Marty to sit in with you. That would be perfectly acceptable."

"Oh, thank you. That is a relief. Thank you. I really appreciate that."

That afternoon while Grace was writing in her journal, she stopped and thought of Matt. She missed him so much. She didn't realize how close they had become. They were best friends. Truth be told, Matt was her only friend aside from her sister and Jon-Pierre who lived six hours away.

In her journal, she wrote:

> I'm so glad Matt is in my life. If it weren't for him, I know I would've found a way to end everything, maybe by overdose or some other means, but I know I couldn't take much more. I'm sorry, I know that suicide is a sin, and I would probably end up in purgatory, or worse, maybe even hell, but I just couldn't take any more. Matt saved my life, and I will always be grateful to him for that.

There was so much more she wanted to write tonight, but she was exhausted from the day's interviews and nearly fell asleep on her journal. She put everything away, donned an oversized white T-shirt, and slipped into bed. She was asleep in less than five minutes.

Saturday after breakfast, Marty invited Grace to sit on the front porch in the rockers with her while they enjoyed more of Marty's weak American coffee. It paled in comparison to her customary French coffee.

Once they were settled on the porch, Marty asked how the interviews were going.

"Fine, I guess," was Grace's answer. "They are asking questions, and I am answering them and filling in the details for them. It's actually quite exhausting."

"I can tell," replied Marty. "If you ever want to flesh some of the details out, I am a very good listener."

"I know that you are. And you were right about the journal. Writing things down is therapeutic. I think it is really helping me process some of this. In fact, I was bold enough to ask for a woman interviewer from here on out. I started to keep my mouth shut, but then, I realized that's what got me into this whole mess to begin with. I'm actually kinda proud of myself."

"You should be," said Marty. "Listen, I haven't told you this before now because it can be intimidating at first with coming to a new home with people you don't even know and all, but I have a PhD in marriage and family therapy."

"I don't know what that means. I'm sorry."

"No need to apologize. You're in a new country with new customs and terminology. It means I have a doctorate in psychology where I help people work through all kinds of problems and situations. I help people save their marriage, learn how to communicate between parents and children, help children deal with divorce or being abused, anything involving family dynamics. I've worked with young ladies, such as yourself, who have been raped or sexually molested growing up. Granted I've never worked with someone trapped in sex-trafficking before, but I am here for you in any way I can be."

"Thank you. That means a lot. I was wondering if you would be willing to sit with me through the next section of interviews? It's going to get pretty crazy and detailed, and well, it would be nice to have a friendly face with me on my side of the room."

"I absolutely will, Grace. It would be my honor. Have you given any more thought to becoming a US citizen?"

"Yes, I've been thinking about that quite a bit. I have some questions though. I know France doesn't allow dual citizenship. So if I become a US citizen, I lose everything I've worked for in France. Does the US allow dual citizenship?"

"Yes, it's not stated anywhere in our Constitution, but it is not prohibited either. So it's allowed. However, if France does not allow it, then of course it's a moot point. How much do you figure you will lose financially?"

"About fifty thousand euros, that's about forty-four thousand US dollars."

"How many years were you employed by the Farinis?"

"Three and a half years. And that is if they handled their books legally. They skimmed a lot out of my pay accounts, so I'm not certain."

"At forty-four thousand dollars in retirement, how much were they paying you a year if you don't mind me asking?"

"The last two years seventy thousand euro each, the first year was twenty thousand. The second year, I got the seventy thousand plus a new wardrobe, a new car, and a new penthouse flat. But as you know, it came at a very high price, and they skimmed most of the money. They paid for everything, or so I was told. But it's my fault for not staying on top of my own finances."

"Are you thinking that you deserved their illegal activities just because you were young and believed what they told you. I assume the contract you signed clearly stated that they would skim your earnings to pay for things they told you were included?"

"No."

"The contract clearly stated that you would be required to provide sexual services as demanded by management?"

"No."

"Then why would you be surprised if they didn't handle payroll and retirement taxes correctly? And better still, why do you think you deserve it?"

"I shouldn't, I guess."

"If I were you, I would start thinking that you're not going to see a dime of 'your money.'"

"Ya, I'm sure you're right."

"How are the language lessons coming?"

"You tell me, how is my American accent sounding?"

"Very French," Marty chuckled.

"Ugh, I know. It's been two weeks, and no progress at all."

"Wow you really do have high standards for yourself. What would you tell someone who was trying to learn French with a proper French accent?"

"I would say that it's too soon to expect so much progress."

"Well, tell yourself that!"

They both laughed.

"Let's go for a ride," Marty suggested. "You've been working so hard you deserve a break."

They saddled up and took a three-hour ride that extended into the early afternoon. When they got back and cleaned up, they had some lunch. Then Grace went to her room to try to think things through. Marty had dispensed a great deal of truth today. She lay back on her bed and within minutes was asleep.

Grace slept through dinner that night. She awoke at 11:30 p.m. with a nasty kink in her neck. She had obviously slept for hours without moving at all, a sure sign that she was physically and emotionally exhausted. She got up and took a hot shower, towel dried her hair, put on her T-shirt, and went back to bed.

Sunday was a lazy and relaxing day. Marty asked Grace if she wanted to go into the nearest town and do a little shopping. Grace declined by saying, "No, thank you. I think I'm going to take a day of rest."

27

....

MONDAY MORNING CAME AND THE most dreaded part of the interviews with it. Grace didn't want to get too specific, but she had no idea what direction the interviewer's questions would take her.

The interviewer, Cassy Freeman, turned out to also be a professional psychologist. That seemed a bit odd to Grace. She didn't know if she was going to be interviewed or analyzed. Perhaps a little of both.

Grace informed Cassy that Marty would be sitting in as moral support. Cassy was fine with that.

"You might be wondering why the government would send a professional psychologist to conduct seeming routine questions? But due to the nature of what you've been through, we all agreed that you would be best suited with an interview that took certain sensitivities into consideration," started Cassy.

"Let's get started. How did you become aware that certain sexual favors would be required as part of your contract?"

"Well, I was still seventeen when the second contract was offered. The first contract was very specific and included none of the sex stuff. The second contract was for fifty thousand euros more than the first, and it was a term of five years."

Grace went on to try to explain why she signed the contract without asking more questions. She felt like she needed to defend her actions.

Cassy interrupted, "Grace, I am not judging you or your decisions, so please don't be nervous about that. We have a lot to talk about today that will be unpleasant enough, for which I wish to apologize for in advance. But this is such an important part of the deposition that we have to get into unfortunate details, things that I'm sure you don't want to say out loud but are critical to the case."

"Okay, I'm sorry. What was the question again?"

Cassy repeated the question, and Grace pulled out her appointment book. She opened it and flipped through a few pages then gave the exact date to Cassy. "Will you require the name of the client?" she asked.

"If you have it, that would be fantastic. Is that your appointment book?"

"Yes."

"May I look at that for a moment?"

"Grace handed the book over to Cassy. She began to flip through the pages and was astounded at the detailed schedule of appointments for hosting and whom Jaelynn was hosting. This was an absolute jackpot!

"Grace, who knows you have this?"

"I grabbed it out of habit when I left the flat. I didn't know I wouldn't be going back."

"So do the Farinis know you have it now?"

"I don't know what the Farinis know."

"Good point. But, Grace, this book is going to make this week of questions so much easier for both of us. I would like you to go through this book and stop on the dates where you were required to host a client and give me some of the details of the evening."

Grace bit her lip. This was the part she was so dreading. "Okay," she answered hesitantly.

"I want to know who was there for the party portion, or how the client came to be with you for the evening. Whether he wanted to take you to dinner or the company had a party at your flat, things like that."

"Okay."

And so the interview began to take shape. Cassy wanted specific details that she explained would constitute coercion on the company's part toward Grace. After each hosting date was discussed, Cassy would ask Grace if she needed a brake or would like to pause a few moments.

At 4:00 p.m., they called it a day for the interview. Then Cassy asked Grace, "Do you have any questions, Grace? Any at all?"

Grace did, "Why do you need to know the details of what I did with the client?"

"Oh, Grace, it's not what you did with the client. It's what the company allowed their clients to do to you. You were not a willing party to these expectations. You were a victim. For all intents and purposes, you have been raped repeatedly over the last three years, and that's not okay. Tomorrow I want to talk with you about some of the other girls. Because we know you are not the only one trapped in this horrible sex trafficking agency."

Before dinner, Cassy went outside to make a private phone call. She dialed her boss's number at the state department who was over-seeing Grace's witness security and working with the authorities try-ing to build an ironclad case against the Farinis.

"Guess what?" she asked. "I have Jaelynn's appointment book for the past three years! It has everything in it. All the appointments, who the client was, everything!"

"This is unbelievable! Good work, Cassy."

"I didn't do anything. Jaelynn is the one who brought it with her. Get this, she left her handbag and keys, but brought the appoint-ment book. We've got the Farinis by the kahunas!"

"Good job, Cassy! Now work your magic on our fragile witness."

"Yes, well that's going to be another matter altogether. She is so broken. She feels responsible for her actions. Get this, she thinks because she signed the contract without asking more questions that she got what she deserved. Can you believe that? These people are pure scum."

"Oh, and one more thing," added Cassy, "not all the clients were men."

"You're joking."

"I would not joke about something like that."

"Well, if anyone can help our girl, you can."

The rest of the week went by rather quickly and wasn't as bad as Grace thought it would be. She began to treat each appointment with a detached indifference. When it came to describing the sexual activity that took place, Grace recited facts simply and clearly. The interviews were not as painful, mainly because of her appointment book. Why she grabbed it but left her bag, she had no idea. But she had, and it was ironclad proof of coercion according to Cassy.

They talked about as many of the other girls as Grace could with any certainty that they were being made to have sex also. She told Cassy about plan A and plan B and how she was sure many of them were plan B girls.

On Saturday morning, Cassy needed time to put her report together and spent a good portion of the day in her room. Marty and Grace went for another long horseback ride. This time, they went to a part of the ranch Grace hadn't been to yet. They came up over a hill to a beautiful valley that lead to a river. They rode down, dismounted, and sat along the river's edge while enjoying some sandwiches Marty had thought to pack.

Marty broke the silence. "Grace, I want you to know how much I admire you, your strength, and your courage. You are wise beyond your years, and you are handling all these interviews with great, well, grace. Whomever chose your new name picked a fitting one for you."

"Thank you," said Grace softly. "I'm just now starting to get used to it. It still feels awkward."

"It probably will for some time. Have you been able to journal much?"

"Oh yes, I can't seem to stop writing. Most of it is coming out in poetry and songs."

"Good! I'm glad it's working for you."

"When I was younger, I used to play the guitar. Do you think I might be able to get my hands on one sometime when we go into the city?"

"I can do you one better than that. Our son, Zach, used to play guitar. It's still in his room in a case. You're welcome to play it."

* * * * *

Back in London, Interpol, with the assistance of the US Justice Department, were fitting all the pieces together for their case against the Farini agency. With Jaelynn's appointment book and testimony, they were confident that other models would become case witnesses as soon as they took the Farinis and those who worked with them in the sex trafficking ring into custody on formal charges.

But before the raid, they wanted to ensure Jaelynn's future would be safe. Grace had decided to become a US citizen. The United States provided an unidentified cadaver that fit Jaelynn's general description. The report was that the British authorities had pulled a car and a body from the Thames River. The body had been trapped under debris and missing for about four weeks, matching the time frame of Jaelynn's disappearance. The official autopsy report identified the cadaver by dental records to be the body of Jaelynn DepProvoue of London.

Matt saw the report on the nightly news as did Kaelynn and Jon-Pierre. Matt called Kae as soon as he saw the news. Kae was hysterical, and so Jon-Pierre handled the call.

"I am so sorry," Matt consoled. "I was absolutely sure in my gut that Jae was still alive. How is Kaelynn taking the news?"

"It's one thing to have a memorial with someone missing and presumed dead and quite another to have an actual body to bury."

"I know," soothed Matt. "I am so sorry," he said again. He could hear Kaelynn in the background and could envision her rocking herself back and forth as she kept repeating, "No, no, no, it can't be true."

Matt called Scotland Yard to see if they needed any other identification, but they assured him they had made identification in the only manner possible.

The Farinis issued a brief statement acknowledging that Jaelynn was indeed found and how profoundly sorry the entire Farini family was for her loss. The whole agency was like a family, they stated, and Jaelynn's loss was like losing part of that family.

The next day, Scotland Yard agents raided the Farini's organization and arrested Georgio, Germain, and Megan along with twenty-eight other people in their employ who aided and abetted the sex trafficking.

With the agency torn apart, Matt decided to close up his London shop and move back to New York. He would never work in Europe again.

* * * * *

Kae confirmed that she could still feel the special connection she had with Jae and that she couldn't believe she was dead.

"There was not enough of a body to bury," said the London coroner. He said there was no sign of a struggle, meaning possibly Jaelynn had been drugged before the car went into the river. He also said Jaelynn's body was in the passenger seat, and the car had slammed into a tree and exploded. There was no evidence of anyone else in the car.

Kaelynn decided to have whatever ashes were available of Jaelynn's packed into a crematorium container and given to her. She needed something concrete to hold onto, something to prove that they had found Jaelynn at last.

This was quite different from the memorial service. That was surreal, almost like a dream. It felt like little snippets of an event pasted together to form a service. At least that's how Kaelynn remembered it. The reception was somewhat of a blur as well. Except for the Farinis, she remembered that quite well. And she remembered the following morning when Matt had decided to accept their offer to spend the night. Kae laughed at the memory. He nearly scared her out of her skin.

But now, she had concrete proof that Jaelynn was gone. It didn't feel right. Was she just in a huge state of denial and shock? Maybe. But why could she still feel Jae? She could feel emotion that felt like shame, regret, and great loss. But why would she be feeling these things if Jae was dead? The twin connection should have been severed the moment Jae died in that car. It was strange.

28

GRACE HEARD THE NEWS ON the US national news. She was shocked to find out that she had been found, decomposed beyond recognition in a river. After the initial shock, she began to laugh. She laughed uncontrollably for several minutes as she felt a colossal weight lift off her. Marty and Mitch were familiar with this type of emotional release. They had seen it many times before.

Marty and Grace hugged.

"You're officially free, Grace. You are no longer being looked for."

"I guess I'm officially Grace Wilson forever now."

"Yes, dear, and now the true healing can begin."

Over the course of the next three months, the news covered the Farini agency and the underbelly of its organized crime business. Things that Grace didn't even know were uncovered and added to the charges against them. Along with sex trafficking was murder for hire, grand theft, and money laundering, a large illegal gambling ring and a mafia-type organization to keep people quiet about the other illegal activities.

The Farinis would never see the light of day again. But Megan and some of the others decided to turn state's evidence in hopes for a lighter sentence. With Jaelynn's appointment book and testimony in hand, Megan was in as deep as the Farinis.

* * * * *

Four months later, Kaelynn decided to fly to Australia to surprise Jon-Pierre. She landed at Kingsford airport at 4:00 p.m. Friday afternoon. She texted Jon-Pierre asking him to pick her up at the airport, and they would stay in Sydney for the weekend together.

Jon-Pierre was ecstatic that Kae was there. What a wonderful surprise. He wanted to show her around some cool places they never got to see when they were working. He picked Kae up and took her out to a nice Aussie steak dinner. After dinner and before dessert, Jon-Pierre asked Kae, "What made you decide to fly down under this weekend?"

"I wanted to give you a gift." She pulled a small box out of her handbag and slid it across the table to Jon-Pierre. He grinned and looked sheepishly at her.

"Whatever we are celebrating, I didn't get you anything."

"Just open the box. You've given me plenty."

Jon-Pierre opened the box and took out a tiny, little pair of baby booties. He looked from the booties up to Kae with a questioning look. Kaelynn had a gleam in her eyes.

"Congratulations! You're going to be a father. See, baby, you've already given me a wonderful gift."

Jon-Pierre teared up and choked down some water. "I'm gonna be a father?" he asked. "How long have you known?"

"A couple of weeks, but I wanted to see a doctor first and confirm everything was okay."

"Is everything okay?"

"Yes, silly. I'm fine, the baby is fine. We are due in June."

"Are you feeling okay? We shouldn't have had wine tonight."

"You didn't even notice the last two weeks I haven't had any alcohol."

"Ugh, I'm so dumb not to have noticed."

"Baby, don't be so hard on yourself. We've been living on different continents the past year. It's okay. But listen, I talked to Mr. Johansen, and he reminded me of the pregnancy clause in my contract. If I became pregnant, then Johansen has the right to withdraw the remainder of the contract. I never paid much attention to the clause because back then I never intended to have children.

"But now I am so happy. I want to have our children. I can hardly wait. And Johansen will let me out of the remaining two years of my contract. So if you want, I can move to Australia to be with you. There is nothing holding me to Paris anymore."

Just then, their cheesecake dessert arrived. They shared it together with hot coffee.

Jon-Pierre was beaming and grinning from ear to ear. He looked like the Cheshire cat from *Alice in Wonderland*.

At Jon-Pierre's apartment that night, they celebrated their love and their new little baby growing inside Kaelynn. The next morning, Kae got up and packed their lunch and got ready to go surfing. Jon-Pierre objected, telling Kae she wouldn't be surfing anymore while she was pregnant. Kaelynn assured him the doctor had told her to keep doing the things she normally does as long as it is comfortable to do so.

They went out surfing to one of Jon-Pierre's favorite local beaches. It wasn't as crowded as the tourist beaches. They had a wonderful day catching some perfect waves. By 3:00 in the afternoon, Kaelynn was exhausted and ready to go back to the apartment. Jon-Pierre was all worried that Kae had overdone it.

When they arrived back at the apartment, Kae took a shower, braided her hair, and laid down on the bed while Jon-Pierre took a shower. When Jon-Pierre got out of the shower, Kae was asleep.

Kaelynn worked as usual for the next two months. She remembered when they were little that Jae always played with the little dolls and treated them like babies. She recalled Jaelynn talking about being a mother and how much different she would be from their mum. Kaelynn assumed the sadness was because she also wanted to be a mom but didn't have any prospects on the immediate horizon. Kaelynn thought Matt and Jaelynn would have made wonderful babies if they would both had gotten on the same page and realized they loved each other.

29

FOUR MONTHS AFTER ENTERING THE witness security program in the USA, Grace Wilson was sworn in as a US citizen, in a private ceremony, at the Garrison ranch. Matt flew in for the occasion.

When Matt got out of his car at the Garrison ranch, Grace ran and jumped into his arms. It was so good to see him.

"You saved my life." She said, "Thank you," over and over.

Matt hugged her while spinning in a circle. It was so good to hold her finally.

"You did it, Matty. You kept your head together and helped pull a huge organization down. I am so proud of what you did."

"Well, I am now officially in the witness security program too, but I don't have to change my name like you did. I just get to hide out at this beautiful ranch with this beautiful woman until the court hearings are over."

Later that evening, the Garrisons put Matt's luggage in Grace's room. The dossier indicated they had gotten married, and they assumed that it was a true marriage. Marty and Mitch endured Grace's continuous talk about Matt. They knew what Jon-Pierre and Kaelynn knew. And judging by the reunion in the driveway this morning, it appeared that they had a couple who was deeply in love in their home. They had no idea that the couple were the only ones who didn't know how they felt about each other.

Once inside Grace's room, Matt recognized his luggage. He began to apologize to Grace.

"Oh, I'm sorry. I should've specified a separate room and that we weren't actually married that way," said Matt

"Well, I've been thinking about that a lot, actually. I have missed you so much. I have come to realize that I am in love with you. But if you're not okay with this arrangement, I can sleep on the sofa, and you can have the bed. It's very comfortable. And I'm used to sleeping on the sofa."

"I wouldn't hear of it," said Matt. "We can share the bed because I am head over heels in love with you."

They shared a deep and passionate kiss that erased any doubt from either of their minds about how the other felt.

* * * * *

Within three months, Kaelynn had closed up their flat in Paris and moved all their things to the apartment in Sydney. As it turned out, the apartment in Sydney was too small for three Laurents. Jon-Pierre had one bedroom set up for his office, and there wasn't much room in their bedroom for a baby. So they began to look for a new place to live.

They found a three-bedroom house in Dover Heights, Sydney, for sale. The husband's work had transferred him and the family to Los Angeles, California. They needed to move quickly, and so they were motivated to negotiate the price on the house. Three weeks later, Jon-Pierre and Kaelynn moved into their new house.

Kaelynn was able to surf up until her seventh month of pregnancy. After that, she couldn't adjust her balance with her growing "bubble," as Jon-Pierre called it. They wanted to find out if the baby was a boy or a girl, but the baby wouldn't cooperate. It kept crossing its legs whenever the ultrasound devise came near. Jon-Pierre was positive the baby was a sweet little girl who was being modest. He told Kaelynn that a boy would want to show off his package. So it was definitely a girl. Kaelynn wasn't so sure, but she kind of hoped it was a girl for Jon-Pierre's sake. He clearly wanted a little girl.

Two months later, Addison May Laurent was born. Jon-Pierre was so proud. He held both of his girls while mommy nursed little Addie. The renowned photographer now had a new focus for his work. Jon-Pierre couldn't help himself.

Every stage of Addie's life was fully documented by her papa. Jon-Pierre contemplated opening a local photography studio where he would specialize in child and family portraits. Kaelynn loved the idea because it meant Jon-Pierre would not be traveling any longer.

Kaelynn started to pick up her phone to call Jae, then put it down remembering she was gone. And her heart broke again. She had been following the story on the news about the Farini's organization being raided and all the organized crime being uncovered. She was horrified to learn about the sex trafficking. She cried for several days at the understanding that this is what Jaelynn was hiding. She knew now that the Farinis would have threatened to kill Kae to keep Jae cooperative.

Even though all this new information was coming to light, Kaelynn could still feel a connection with Jae. She tried to talk to Jon-Pierre about it, but all he would say was, "Stop living in a fantasy land. Jaelynn is gone, they found her body, Kae! She's dead, and you're just torturing yourself by not moving on!"

Kaelynn would retort back, "You'll never understand the connection we have."

It was a touchy topic between them. Jon-Pierre wanted Kae to accept the facts that Jae was dead. But for some reason, she just wouldn't.

30

....

Jon-Pierre called Matt on a Saturday morning and ran the idea of the portrait studio by him. The studio would give common people the royal treatment that a supermodel gets with hairstylist and make-up artists and professional photography. Matt was impressed.

"I can't believe no one has thought of this before," said Matt. "This is a fantastic idea. I can see it really taking off. And when it does, I want to be your first franchised owner and open a studio in London. What do you say, buddy?"

"You're on. I am so glad you think it's a good idea."

"What does Kaelynn think of it?"

"I think she's behind it because I want to do it. I'm not sure how much she believes in the idea."

"To be honest, if she goes along with it just for you, that's an amazing show of support and love. But I bet she thinks it will be a success as well."

"She wants to have another baby real bad. This venture is going to hit our savings big, so a baby is gonna have to wait."

"And she is willing to do that? Put another baby on hold?"

"Yes."

"Go for it, buddy. Do it!"

"Thanks, my friend."

"In fact, I want to invest fifty thousand euros in it. Can I be a background partner?"

"Yes, sure that would be fantastic!"

"Done. I'll send you a check this afternoon."

"Thanks, man."

"My pleasure, bro. I always wanted a brother. Being an only child always sucked."

Jon-Pierre and Kaelynn signed a one-year lease on the soon-to-be studio on Oxford Street. They spent two months setting it up—lighting, backgrounds, dressing rooms, hair, and make-up stations. Things began to fall into place in rapid succession.

Jon-Pierre started contacting people in the industry to see if they were interested in settling down and not having to travel so much. He found more people interested than he needed. So he devised a plan where they could all work in a job sharing type of environment. Make-up artists could work out of Sydney and have a home base. But they could also take off on location whenever they wanted and work for whomever they wanted. Their income would no longer be based on how much they traveled and how many different agencies they were working for.

Several of the hairstylists got together and worked out a rotation where one of them was always available for the studio while the others were away on location. It worked especially well for those who had spouses and children at home.

Jon-Pierre decided to call the business Laurent Fashion Studios. Jon-Pierre was still not entirely convinced that Kae was fully behind him like she insisted she was.

Their sex life had declined since their conversation about putting another baby on hold. He took it to mean she wasn't happy with the decision. He brought the subject up one night after Addie was put to bed.

"You're mad at me, aren't you?"

"Mad? No, baby, I'm not mad at you."

"I think you are mad because we have put having another baby on hold. We haven't had sex in six days."

"We've both been working on the new studio, and I've been taking care of the baby pretty much by myself. It's been a lot of work and quite exhausting to be honest."

"But sex always exhilarates us."

"Well, it used to. I'm so sorry, Jon-Pierre. I'm glad you brought this up tonight instead of just suppressing it."

"We promised we would talk things out, that we would never go to sleep angry at each other."

"I might fall asleep, but if you want to have sex tonight, I am willing."

"How about tomorrow morning when we wake up."

"Which time, 2:00 a.m. or 6:00 a.m.?"

"Touché. Let's try for 8:00 a.m."

The studio opened in September just as students were heading back to school. In the first week of being open, they booked twenty-seven senior photo shoots. They were officially in business.

Since Paddington attracted a lot of tourist, they decided to keep a couple of slots open each day for walk-ins. The first day, they had four walk-ins. The results were stunning, and the clients were astounded. They kept saying they never knew they could look so good. Jon-Pierre would tell them that everyone had a beautiful model within them; they just needed the right team to bring it out.

Jon-Pierre had several binders of models he had photographed over the years of his career. They were meant to showcase his abilities as a photographer. Occasionally someone would come in and want the studio to make them look like one of the models in the book. Often a brunette would want to look like a blonde. Jon-Pierre would sit down with them and begin to show them the features they possessed that he would bring out in the photography process. That usually got them to stop wanting to look like someone else.

Jon-Pierre found out very quickly that he could easily handle another photographer. He called Matt to see if he was ready to jump in. But he was booked for the next four months.

31

....

JAKE VANCE, THE DISTRICT ATTORNEY that would be prosecuting the Farinis, came to the Garrison ranch to help prepare Grace for her live testimony. They practiced cross-examining her for hours, deliberately tripping her up so that she could handle anything the defense attorneys tried to throw at her.

After five days of this grueling practice, the attorneys felt Grace was ready. She would be their star witness, sprung on the defense at the last possible minute to testify. By the time they called Jaelynn DepProvoue, the case would be so far along that Judge Hainley would be reticent to allow any delaying tactics from the defense.

Because the case had crossed borders into several foreign countries including Italy, Portugal, Spain, Prague, the United Kingdom, Australia, New Zealand, the United States, and Canada, it was decided that the trial would be held in Los Angeles, California.

Jury selection took two weeks. When a competent jury was deemed to have been seated, the trial began.

The judge pounded his gavel and called the court to order. He ordered the prosecutor, Jake Vance, to begin with his opening statement.

"Thank you, Your Honor. Ladies and gentlemen, the case before you is clear and solid. The defendants, Mr. Georgio Farini, Mr. Germain Farini, and Mrs. Megan Stewart have been charged with illegal gambling, prostitution, sex trafficking, and contracting for murder. For each of these charges, the prosecution will present witnesses and proof that the defendant did in fact engage in these criminal activities.

"You will hear testimony from young women who were offered contracts to model for the Farini modeling agency and were then forced to perform unspeakable sexual acts as part of those contracts. They will testify that the Farinis threatened to kill their families if they talked about their activities with anyone.

"You will hear testimony from those involved in the illegal gambling. And finally, you will hear testimony from a person who was hired to plan and execute murder of two models and a photographer who were trying to escape the Farini organization.

"Presenting you with the facts and testimony of those involved is my job. Your job is to hear that testimony and weigh the facts of the case against the Farinis and render a verdict of guilty or not guilty. You will be asked to render that verdict on each of the illegal counts they have been charged with.

"If I do my job well, your job shouldn't be difficult. As I said, the case is solid, and the facts are clear. I want to apologize for some of the testimony you will have to hear in this case. Some of it might make you sick to your stomach. For that, I am sorry, but you have to hear from the victims themselves what they were forced to do.

"Now the defense, they are going to try to prove that the models have fabricated their stories. They may even try to make you believe that the models got together and concocted the whole story about being forced into sex trafficking and their families being threatened. Your job will be to look at all the factual evidence and come back with a verdict that represents the facts and only the facts.

"Thank you all for honoring our great system of government where the accused can be judged by a jury of their peers. Your service is invaluable in this matter. Without you, our justice system would be incomplete.

Thank you."

The Farini's defense attorney, Joe Crawford, stood up and began with his opening statement.

"Ladies and gentlemen, I too want to thank you for your service in this matter. In this case, you are going to hear terminology from the prosecution like statutory rape and sex slavery. These terms are designed to make you feel something for the witnesses that simply isn't true. The prosecution's case is built on disgruntled employees who got together and concocted their story to prey upon your good sensibilities. The prosecution has no evidence that proves the employees were coerced by threat of life or bodily harm to perform sexual acts with clients. The truth is that each and every model who chose to participate in the optional sexual activity was paid a higher rate than those who chose not to.

"You might be asking yourself, 'Isn't that prostitution?' And the answer is *no*. It is not. Not according to the laws of the countries the girls were employed in. Both France and the United Kingdom allow for such activity so long as the participating parties are doing so willingly. So don't let the prosecutions fancy or demeaning terminology trick you. They do not have one piece of concrete evidence that proves the models were ever coerced. Thank you."

By the time the opening statements were competed, it was 3:30 in the afternoon, and the judge adjourned for the day. Since it was a Friday afternoon, court would not convene until 8:30 Monday morning.

The defense attorneys spent the remainder of the afternoon assuring their clients that the prosecution didn't have enough to convict on the sex trafficking. The one possible witness who had any records was dead, and her appointment book had never been found. If the prosecution did have her appointment book, they would have to declare it in pretrial evidence, and they had not. If they had it and didn't divulge it, then the defense would call for a mistrial and get one.

Joe Crawford, found his clients quite distasteful. They were clearly guilty, but that didn't matter. It was their job to defend their client to the best of their ability. That meant tearing apart any and all witnesses the prosecution put on the stand. It was that simple. But Joe hated like hell having to treat these girls that way. They had already endured some terrible situations, and now it was his job to persecute them for their willing actions.

It was times like these that he hated being a defense attorney. With six children to put through college, he had chosen defense work because it paid more. Normally he could stomach his clients, but the Farinis were by far the worst clients he had ever defended.

After reviewing the prosecution's evidence, Joe asked Judge Hainley to allow him to recuse himself. But His Honor, Douglas Hainely, would not allow it. He told Joe that he might believe his client to be guilty, but that did not recuse him form fulfilling the law of providing them with a proper defense. So Joe was stuck with the Farinis.

32

MONDAY MORNING CAME QUICKLY FOR Joe Crawford and his defense team. The first part of the trial would consist of the prosecution presenting their case against the Farinis. The defense's job was to discredit as much of the testimony of each witness as possible.

Joe had a team of six attorneys working with him on the case. Four of these attorneys did nothing but concentrate on little innuendos in the witnesses' testimonies and quickly jot down cross-examination points. Then they would pass their notes up to the other two attorneys at the table with Joe. These two attorneys would sort through the key cross-exam points and give the best ones to Joe ASAP so that he could review at a glance and be ready for cross.

The first witness was Chloe Standly, an eighteen-year-old model who had been working for the Farinis for two years, since she was sixteen. After she was sworn in, the prosecutor began his questioning. He guided Chloe through an obviously very rehearsed testimony. After getting through all the preliminary testimony about how Chloe came to work for the Farinis and her basic modeling requirements, the prosecution got down to the illegal part of the job.

"Ms. Standly, how did you come to know that you would be required to perform sexual favors and acts with Farini clients?"

"After the first year working for the Farinis, I was offered a five-year contract of fifty thousand euros each year. That was a thirty thousand increase form the first year. About a month after signing the new contract, Germain Farini told me that I was required to entertain clients after hours. I thought he meant to wine and dine them, but he said that and anything else they wanted."

"What did he mean by 'anything else they wanted'?"

"I asked that same question. He slapped me on my backside and said, 'Anything, honey,' and winked at me. I said, 'You mean sex?' And Germain pinched my cheek and said, 'See, you're pretty and smart.'"

"What did you do then?"

"I told him that I wasn't hired to do that, and he said, 'You better reread your contract, sweetie. Your contract says modeling and any other activities deemed necessary by the Farini agency or their clientele.' I told him I didn't care what was in the contract and that sex was absolutely off the table."

"What did he say to that?"

"He said… he said he didn't care if I did it on or off the table, but that I would do it or my family would be killed. Then he showed me some photographs of two models and a photographer who tried to leave the agency a couple of years ago. They were trapped in the wreckage of an airplane and obviously dead. Then he said, 'See how that worked out for them?'"

"So Germain Farini threatened you with bodily harm?"

"He threatened to kill me and my family."

"Objection, Your Honor," shouted Joe Crawford for the defense, "showing the witness some pictures doesn't mean that's what's going to happen to her!"

The judge replied, "Objection overruled."

"I have no further questions, Your Honor."

"Cross-examine."

"Yes, Your Honor. Ms. Standly, your employee record shows that you have been reprimanded on more than one occasion. Isn't that true?"

"If by reprimanded, you mean raped by Germain, then yes."

"Your Honor, can you instruct the witness to answer with a simple yes or no please?"

"Ms. Standly, isn't it true that you have a reputation of being defiant?"

"Would you please define 'defiant'?"

"Your Honor, please instruct the witness to answer my questions."

"She asks a valid question. Define your question for her. Then I'll instruct her to answer. I'd like to hear what your definition is as well."

"Very well. Defiant means not doing what you are told to do."

"No, never as a model."

"No? Did you refuse to drive all night to a new location and insist on driving the following morning instead?"

"It was 3:00 a.m."

"Yes or no!"

"Objection, Your Honor. The witness is trying to answer the prosecutor's questions."

"Sustained."

"I have no further questions."

Jake Vance quickly rose. "Ms. Standly, please continue the answer you were interrupted on."

"It was 3:00 in the morning when we finished that shoot. We had started at 7:30 the previous morning, and the next location was a five-and-half-hour drive. All of us models were exhausted. It was too dangerous for us to try to drive. We waited until we got some sleep."

"Nothing further," said Jake.

"The witness may step down. Court will recess for lunch and will reconvene at 1:30 p.m."

By the middle of the second week of the trial, the prosecution had called fourteen models to testify to the sex trafficking of the Farini agency. But none of them had any hard proof, just their testimony under oath.

On Wednesday of the second week, Judge Hainley asked Jake Vance if they intended on calling all forty-eight of the models employed at the time of the raid to testify. Jake replied no that they had only two more and then would be able to hand the case over to the defense.

The next witness called was Angela Hansen. Her testimony was primarily the same, and after an hour, she was handed over for cross-examination.

Joe Crawford began, "Isn't it true that you were fired from the Farini agency?"

Angela responded, "No."

"No? I have an employee termination form that says otherwise."

"Objection, Your Honor! Facts not in evidence."

"Sustained. Let's see that form." The judge looked the form over and called both attorneys to the bench for a sidebar. He handed the form to Jake. Jake noted that the form was dated the day of the raid and the time notated was thirty minutes after the raid took place. Jake informed Judge Hainley that the witness couldn't have possibly been given this form or fired because the agency had already been raided by the time notated.

The judge sustained the objection and told Joe to move on to another line of questioning.

Joe said, "I have no further questions of the witness," and sat down. He leaned over and whispered something to his client that made Georgio angry, and his face turned bright red.

33

THE TRIAL FOR THE FARINIS was in full swing by October. Jon-Pierre and Kae followed the progress on the nightly news and the Internet. They even found a YouTube channel that played snippets of the trial proceedings. It was obviously bootlegged footage, but it was straight from the courtroom.

So far, it looked like the prosecution had a good case against Georgio and Germain Farini and Megan Stewart. Kaelynn never did feel comfortable around any of them. She thought Megan was the biggest fake. She was always so sweet when you did exactly what she wanted. But if you stepped out of line, she became a horrible shrew.

Kae could only imagine what those people had put Jae through. She was hoping they would get the death penalty. She followed the trial as close as she could because she was hoping they had uncovered evidence that the Farinis had arranged for Jae's death. So far, that had not come up. In fact, Jaelynn's name had not come up at all.

One day, the person who was putting the bootleg videos up online decided to livestream the trial that day, and Kaelynn just happened to be watching. Addie was down for a nap.

Jake asked for a sidebar with Judge Hainley. He presented a witness who had prior to today not been on the witness list but was extremely pertinent to the case before the court.

The judge adjourned court for fifteen minutes as the attorneys went into Judge Hainley's chamber to discuss the witness.

Jake presented the judge with the witness security documents. The judge took several minutes looking over the documents and ensuring their legality. When His Honor was sure everything was above board, he stated that the prosecution would be calling Jaelynn to testify.

The defense attorney looked as though he had been sucker punched. He pleaded with Judge Hainley for a continuance in order to prepare for the witness. But Judge Hainley denied the motion and told both sides that testimony would resume in five minutes. The defense again asked for time, just a day, he pleaded.

Judge Hainley again denied the motion and reminded them that witness security was designed to protect an important witness and therefore did not have to comply with the customary rules of evidence and witness testimony.

They returned to the courtroom and waited for Judge Hainley to call, "Be seated." Joe whispered the news to his clients. Jake Vance stood and loudly called Jaelynn DepProvoue to the stand. The court-room erupted in confusion. Everyone realizing this was the model found in the Thames River in London.

The judge pounded his gavel and called, "Order! Order!"

The back doors opened, and Jaelynn DepProvoue entered the courtroom looking like the model she was. Grace was dressed classy in matching cream-colored pants and blouse with a navy waist-length blazer. She walked with great poise to the witness stand. The court official swore her in, and she promised to tell nothing but the truth so help her God.

Kaelynn was glued to the computer screen watching the lives-tream. When the camera came back on, Kaelynn could see her twin sister, Jaelynn, walking down the center aisle to be sworn in as a witness.

Kaelynn was crying when she saw Jae walk into that courtroom. She was alive! Kae kept saying, "You're alive!" over and over. She couldn't believe her eyes, yet she could because she had always felt Jaelynn. She knew she was alive. Every fiber of her being would not allow her to accept that she was dead because she could still feel her presence. Now she knew why.

Kae watched, glued to the screen, as Jaelynn took the stand and testified. She recounted numerous encounters where she was forced to have sex with company executives and clients of the organization.

She told how the Farinis would threaten to kill her twin sister if she breathed a word of what was going on. They showed her photographs of two models and a photographer who were killed in a plane crash and insinuated that would happen to anyone she told. Or to herself if she wasn't fully her best at all times with clients.

Jaelynn answered questions for the entire morning and into the afternoon as the prosecution went over her statements, testimony, and appointment book with a fine-tooth comb. Jaelynn had gone into detail of sexually explicit activity with named clients of the Farini agency and Germain Farini as a frequent participant. She referred to her appointment book at every question to ensure that her answers were correct to the best of her recollection.

"What happened on January 30th according to your appointment book?"

Grace hung her head as tears welled in her eyes; her voice was barely above a whisper as she answered, "I was forcibly taken to have an abortion."

"What do you mean by forcibly?"

"Megan had a security guard come along with her. He held my arm tightly in the car on the way to the clinic."

"What happened next?"

"The guard forced me into the clinic and onto the procedure table where he and Megan held me down."

"Then what happened?"

"The doctor pulled my unborn child limb by limb from my body and tossed them into a bucket."

"Objection!" shouted the defense. "I think we all know what an abortion is."

Jake responded, "The testimony shows the nature of force used and the emotional as well as physical trauma it caused the witness."

"Overruled," said Judge Hainley. "Would you like a short recess to compose yourself?" the judge asked Jaelynn.

"Yes, please," she replied.

Kaelynn cried through the majority of the testimony. At the same time, she was so proud of her sister. She held her own emotions in check. She was poised and in complete control.

The defense attorney got up and tried his best to discredit Jae's testimony by attacking her appointment book as being completely fabricated over the eight months she was in witness protection. But the judge and the prosecutor were able to shut that down right away and effectively the defense as well.

Kaelynn kept trying to contact Jon-Pierre, but his cell phone was off when he was working. Finally she called the studio line and ask to speak to him ASAP, saying that it was an emergency.

Jon-Pierre finally called Kae back thinking something was wrong with the baby.

"No, no, the baby is fine. It's Jaelynn. she's alive! I knew it. I told you I could feel her. She is alive!"

"Okay, okay, Kaelynn, calm down. You're not making any sense. You and I both know that they found Jaelynn's body. She is not alive."

"Turn on your phone. I just texted you a link. It's a video from today's trial, and Jaelynn is the witness!"

Jon-Pierre turned on his phone and pulled up the text from Kae. But the video wouldn't play because it had been a live feed and was over now.

"Nothing is coming up, Kaelynn. Listen, I've got one more client to photograph, and then I'll come right home. I won't stay and do any editing tonight."

All the way home Jon-Pierre prayed that he could talk some sense into Kaelynn. If not, he was afraid he might be dealing with a wife who was losing her mental faculties. He didn't want to think about what that might mean for them.

When he arrived home, Kae was nursing the baby and was very calm. He thought maybe Kae had come to her senses on her own. She finished feeding the baby and got up to burp her. She walked into Jon-Pierre's office and went straight to his computer. She typed in the address of the YouTube channel they had been watching for days. Right at the top was the video from today's live stream.

Jon-Pierre sat down and began to watch the video. Within a few minutes, the prosecution indeed called Jaelynn DepProvoue to testify. And into the courtroom walked Jaelynn herself. She really was alive. Jon-Pierre was speechless.

"Well, I'll be damned," he exclaimed. I am so sorry I doubted your twin connection, baby." They watched the entire testimony together. Jon-Pierre was flabbergasted at what was actually going on at the Farini agency. It made him feel dirty that he had ever worked for them.

Kaelynn called Matt, but his phone went straight to voice mail. She wondered if he had seen any of today's testimony or if he knew about Jaelynn being alive.

She tried to find the prosecution law firm and call them in an attempt to get ahold of Jaelynn. Clearly Jaelynn had walked out of her life and into witness protection leaving everyone and everything behind. Literally her life depended on it. Well, come to think of it, so did Kae's, Jon-Pierre, and now Addie's too.

Kaelynn mentioned this to Jon-Pierre. He said, "What courage, what poise and grace. She was amazing. She is amazing."

"I'm glad I didn't know anything when Megan called me to see if she was visiting that day," said Kaelynn.

"That's probably why she handled it the way she did, baby. To protect you, and us."

At 3:30 p.m. on the second day, the prosecution rested their case and handed everything over to the defense.

Even after two days of Jaelynn's testimony, the defense was still reeling at the fact that the model whom everyone thought dead had in fact been hidden in witness protection for nearly eight months now.

The defense chose to attack Jaelynn's appointment book as being made-up. They attacked it saying that she had been working on fabricating it for six months while waiting for trial. Of course there was no foundation for this accusation, so Jake objected with the fact that the book had been evaluated and documented six months prior to trial and entered into evidence as such two days ago.

Next, the defense went after Jaelynn as a willing participant. He asked her if she had enjoyed any of the sexual activity. She responded that it was abhorrent. Then he asked, "Surely then you must have gotten some pleasure from the women clients?"

At this, the entire courtroom burst out in angry objections. Jake was on his feet the instant the words were out with an objection.

The judge pounded his gavel for order and stated, "The witness will answer the question."

Jaelynn responded, "I found it to be some of the worst nights of my life."

Matt was not in the courtroom for any of Jaelynn's testimony. He waited patiently with Mitch and Marty at the ranch and prayed for her the entire time she was testifying.

The defense rested their case, and the attorneys prepared to present closing arguments. By Friday, the case was handed to the jury for deliberation. The jury took three hours to return with a verdict of guilty on each charge against Georgio and Germain Farini as well as Megan Stewart.

The Farinis and Megan Stewart would be sentenced in three months from the end of the trial and would most likely be given life sentences without the possibility of parole, exactly what the jury recommended.

34

GRACE REJOINED MATT AT THE Garrison ranch for another three months. They would be hidden there until final sentencing took place and all the guilty agency personnel put in their final prison destinations.

The three months allowed Grace to get some very much-needed psychological therapy. There were years of abandonment and sexual abuse to deal with.

Three months gave Grace and Matt time to get to know each other as husband and wife. Grace had a lot to work through. She had no idea how to be a wife. Her mother hadn't served as a good role model. Grace's only experience with sex was filled with horrible memories. So the first few months with Matt were a huge period of learning to enjoy each other and learning what should be left behind.

Matt was extremely patient and gentle with Grace, knowing there was a great deal of damage to be repaired and healed. He knew that only God could truly heal the damage done to her. He prayed that Grace would come to know Jesus the way he did. He also understood why she had no desire to get to know a God who allowed such hideous things to happen to her.

Two weeks later, Matt Wilson called Jon-Pierre and Kaelynn. He was making arrangements to fly them out to the secret location where Jaelynn had been hidden. They would have to follow his instructions to the letter, or they wouldn't be allowed to see her. After all, she was in even more danger now than when they thought she was dead.

Jon-Pierre and Kaelynn said they would agree to anything in order to see Jae.

A key arrived in the mail with instructions of what PO box it would open. The instructions said to go to the PO box, and there would be detailed instructions inside. The key was from Matt Wilson.

Jon-Pierre went to the post office and opened the PO box. Sure enough inside was a letter addressed to the PO box. The letter itself read:

> *Go to Camden Airport on Monday afternoon at exactly 2:45 p.m. Drive directly onto the tarmac up to a blue Gulf Stream V airplane. The stairs will be lowered and the engine running. Leave your car, and board the airplane. A man named Keith Hartman will meet you on the stairs. As soon as you are boarded and seated, the plane will take off. It has special clearance. That is why you must be on time. It's critical. The plane and pilots have authority to file their flight plan only after exiting Aussie airspace.*
>
> *Once you've left Aussie airspace, Keith Hartman will fill you in on important details regarding the flight and Jaelynn.*
>
> *Thank you for trusting me.*
>
> *Matt*

Jon-Pierre showed Kae the letter. She was overjoyed that they may get to see Jaelynn soon. It had been almost a year since they had even talked to each other. Jaelynn didn't even know about Addie.

Jon-Pierre said that if they went according to the letter that he would have to shut the studio down and postpone a week's worth of appointments. The studio had been doing tremendously well, and he wasn't sure how shutting down for a week would affect business.

He called a fellow photographer to see if she would be willing to fill in for a week. She was willing and had only a one-day shoot where she was unavailable. Rescheduling one day of appointments wouldn't be a huge problem.

Jon-Pierre apprised his staff of what would be happening the following week and put them all to work rescheduling the appointments that couldn't be covered. They closed the studio that day and posted a sign that it was closed due to a family emergency.

With that settled, Jon-Pierre, Kaelynn, and Addie set out for the Camden Airport. It was about an hour drive by taxi. They arrived ten minutes ahead of schedule, but the plane was right where Matt said it would be. They boarded and got seated. It took a few minutes to get Addie's car seat buckled in properly. By the time they were all buckled and ready, the plane was taxiing to the runway. Jon-Pierre asked Keith where they were headed and got the usual answer, "I'll fill you in once we are in the air and out of Australian airspace."

Once they cleared Australian airspace, the seatbelt sign went off, and they were able to fully relax. Even Addie had gone to sleep, which was a blessing for Kaelynn.

Keith began, "As you know by now, Grace, formerly Jaelynn, is in the witness protection program in the United States."

"We didn't know Jaelynn was in the United States, but now that you say that, it makes sense," said Kaelynn. "Why do you refer to her as Grace?"

"I'm getting to that now. Jaelynn and Matt Wilson were married in London before they left the UK for the US. It made it much easier to get Jaelynn into the witness protection program if she were married to a US citizen, which Matt is. Jaelynn's new name is Grace Wilson. You need to get used to calling her Grace because Jaelynn DepProvoue is gone forever now. I'm sorry about that, but it has to be that way. If you were to slip up and call her Jaelynn in public, it could cost her her life. I don't mean to sound dramatic. It is that serious. We have already thwarted at least six known attempts on her life by intercepting professional assassins hired to find and eliminate her."

"You mean she can never go back to our given name?"

"No, not if she wants to stay alive."

"You said she and Matt got married?"

"Yes, they didn't have to, but it made the whole process much easier on the US end. Now there are some rules we need to go over before we land. One, no phone calls to or from each other, ever. There are more contracts on Grace now than there were before the trial. Two, call her Grace, get used to her name being Grace as fast as possible. Her life depends on it. Three, never mention Wyoming after your visit. Your home could be bugged when you get back. These people will stop at nothing to find Grace now that she has testified in open court. Four, absolutely no contact with each other unless you are face-to-face. No mail, no letters, no texts, no postcards nothing. Five, Grace and Matt will be moving away from the witness protection house they have been in for the past year almost. You will not know where either of them are at any time. If you do cross paths by chance in public, *do not* under any circumstances acknowledge each other. Are these rules clear and understandable as I have explained them to you?"

"Yes," they both replied. "I'm a little overwhelmed by this," stated Kaelynn. "I thought Jae, I mean Grace, would be safe after her testimony. Why is she still in so much danger? Will she ever not be in this kind of danger?"

"The Farini's criminal organization is far reaching. An international task force has been working to take them down for over ten years. They have associates in every major city in the world. When Jaelynn first disappeared, they put out a hit contract on her worldwide. That contract still stands. Should anyone find her and take her out, the reward for the hit is 1.5 million US dollars."

"Wow," said Jon-Pierre. "It's going to take some time getting used to calling her Grace. But we definitely will do our best."

They landed at John Wayne Airport in Southern California to refuel. A new flight plan would be announced when they left the Long Beach area. They were headed for Casper, Wyoming. They were taking every precaution to protect their witness.

Two and a half hours later, the plane landed in Casper, Wyoming. The passengers disembarked and walked directly to a Lincoln parked on the tarmac adjacent the plane. When all four passengers were properly secured, they left the airport heading southeast toward Worland. It would be another two-and-a-half-hour ride.

Addie was getting very restless. She wanted to get out of her seat in a bad way. Kaelynn finally gave her a bottle to help calm her. She drank the bottle, then needed a diaper change. After the diaper change, she did not want to get back into her car seat. Kae rocked her for a while, and she finally went to sleep again. She secured her back into the car seat. There was still another hour until they reached the small community of Worland, Wyoming.

They finally turned off of the main highway onto a dirt road. They stayed on that road for at least twenty minutes. There were some cattle and some sheep. Finally they came up over a small hill, and a large home loomed on an adjacent hilltop.

The car pulled to a stop on a huge cement driveway. As they were getting out of the car, the front door opened, and an older couple, probably mid to late fifties, came out to greet them followed by Matt. Introductions were made.

"Kaelynn and Jon-Pierre, this is Mitch and Marty Garrison, our witness protection hosts."

"Well, my goodness if you don't look exactly like Grace!" exclaimed Mitch.

"Yes, you do. I guess you two are identical twins?" said Marty.

"Yes we are. Where is Jae, I mean Grace?" asked Kaelynn.

Grace awoke to hear voices outside her window at the Garrison's ranch. She yawned and stretched to find that Matt was already up and gone from their room. That wasn't like him. He had been so protective of her since the trial, well since he had come to Wyoming actually.

The voices outside sounded excited and happy. Grace moved to the window to look down at the driveway. It was Kaelynn and Jon-Pierre. She couldn't believe her eyes. She grabbed her jeans and tried to put them as she ran toward the door. She got her foot caught in the waistband and toppled over onto the floor. She didn't miss a beat. She rolled onto her back and kicked into the pants. She had them buttoned and zipped by the time she got to the bedroom door.

Grace bounded down the steps as fast as she could and out the front door. She was yelling Kaelynn's name all the while she was running. They met in the middle of the driveway in a huge, happy hug. Both girls were crying, tears rolling down their cheeks. They were so happy to be together after almost a year of being completely out of contact.

Grace kept apologizing for having to keep Kaelynn in the dark and allowing her to believe she was dead. She told her it was the only way to ensure Kaelynn's safety.

"I know," said Kae. "Matt told us everything when he called to arrange our trip out here. He wanted it to be a surprise. So, surprise!"

They walked arm in arm into the house. Grace didn't even notice that Jon-Pierre was holding a baby. Matt and Jon-Pierre were completely forgotten. They both looked at each other and shrugged. The two inseparable girls were together again. They had so much to catch up on.

For the next two hours, the girls talked nonstop. Marty was holding Addison when Grace finally noticed the baby.

"Where did that baby come from?" Suddenly, Grace realized a lot had happened in the past year. "Oh my God, you have a baby?"

"Yes, Auntie Grace meet your niece, Addison. We call her Addie for short."

Kaelynn handed Addie to Grace to hold.

"Oh my goodness! Addie, aren't you so sweet?" Grace marveled at how Addie was a perfect small, little person. Addie kept looking from Grace to Kae and back in bewilderment.

"My goodness, she is beautiful. And I love her name, Addison."

Finally Matt invited Jon-Pierre outside to shoot some hoops on the basketball court.

"Congratulations, Jon-Pierre," said Matt. "What a joy it must be to have a baby in the house."

"Thank you, Matt. It's actually a whole lot more work than I thought it would be. But Kaelynn was ready. She wanted to stop working and move to Australia. You know about the new studio and all that."

"About that, how is it going?"

"Wow, it took off like a rocket. We are booked for the next six months. I purposely keep two spots open each day for walk-ins since we're located in a tourist area. It has been great. I love working for myself. Like this week for instance, I was able to get Lacy Langford to come and fill in for four of the five days we'll be gone."

"Lacy Langford, ya, she's got a great eye for portraits. Good call."

"I'm ready to add another photographer whenever you guys want to move to Sydney."

"Oh, man, we could never do that. We can never be close to you guys. It would be too easy to find Grace."

"Ya, I forgot about all of that for a moment. Sorry, man."

"No worries. Grace and I may want to open a studio in the US somewhere. It can't be like yours though, again with too close to find Grace and all. I will do whatever it takes to keep her safe!"

"I understand."

Back inside the house, Grace held little Addie and played with her on her lap. Kaelynn filled Grace in on the past year in her life— finding out she was pregnant, how she told Jon-Pierre, moving to Sydney, and opening up the new studio.

Grace was in awe of her sister. She was a mother.

"I remember growing up you never wanted to have children. You were absolutely sure that you would never change your mind, remember?"

"Yes," Kae chuckled. "I do remember. But everything changed when I found out I was pregnant. I mean everything. I knew Jon-Pierre would be so happy, I was happy. It was all so different than I thought it would be. And besides, I don't have to be a mother like mum was. I can and will be a great mum to Addie."

"I know you will be. I think you already are. And it's clear that Jon-Pierre adores her."

"Yes, he does. He plays with her every chance he gets. Now that we have the studio, he's been doing more of his postediting there instead of at his home office. He says it's nicer that way because when he's home, he can focus on us and not have work hanging over his head."

"That's good. Good organizing on his part. You are a very lucky girl, Kae. I sort of envy you."

"Envy me? Why?"

"Because you are living the dream now. Handsome husband…"

"You have a handsome husband too."

"Cute, beautiful little baby…"

"You'll have one soon enough, you'll see."

"Somehow, I don't think that's going to happen real soon. Besides, Matt and I have a long way to go before either of us will be ready for children, if ever. I have a whole lot of therapy I need to work through. I have so much to unlearn. So much emotional baggage to take care of. I don't even know if Matt will want to stick around much longer. We only got married to help get me into the US and the witness protection program. When all the dust settles, he may want to move on."

"Oh, I don't see that happening!" said Kae. "That man adores you! Don't you see that?"

"I don't know. I have spent so much time and effort numbing myself to men that I seriously wonder if I'll ever be any good for a husband."

"Jaelynn! I mean Grace! You stop that nonsense right now. I see the way you two look at each other. You know you're in love with him. The whole world can see it. And he's head over heels in love with you. You two are perfect for each other. Jon-Pierre and I have known it for a couple of years now. It's always best to have your spouse also be your best friend."

"I guess you're right. I just feel so broken and used. It's hard to let my guard down."

"Well, you can trust Matt. Did you know he made all the arrangements for us to visit? He said it took over two months to convince whoever the powers-to-be are to allow it."

"I didn't know that. I didn't know you were coming. I'll be sure to thank him later," she said with a glint in her eye.

The girls were inseparable for the rest of the week. They took walks, they went for a ride one day, and they were so happy just being together. Marty loved helping take care of little Addie while the girls were out. Mitch even enjoyed her, playing patty-cake with her and marveling at her laughter.

Jon-Pierre and Matt talked a lot about the new studio business and what kind of work Matt wanted to do next. Matt showed Jon-Pierre the photos he had been taking on the ranch with Grace. Jon-Pierre thought Matt just might be the best photographer in the world right now. The photos were stunning; the lighting was just right in every one of them. It was one thing to master lighting within a studio where you had absolute control over the lights. But to master the natural light of outdoors was something else altogether. And Jon-Pierre told Matt as much.

All too soon, the week was over, and it was time for the Laurents to head back home to Australia. Grace was all in a funk over it. She had no idea when or if she would ever get to see Kae again. She would give anything to be able to move to Sydney to be near them, but she knew that was not possible. A car arrived Friday morning to take them back to Casper to board another unmarked government plane back to Sydney.

Matt knew that Grace was sad because of their departure, so he planned a picnic down by the river for Monday afternoon. They went for a long leisurely ride and stopped at the river for lunch. Matt spread a blanket on the ground and pulled the picnic basket from the back of his horse.

There was cold fried chicken, potato salad, and barbeque beans for lunch. Matt had even remembered to bring plates, cups, and utensils. He had thought of everything. He even brought some cheesecake for them to share for desert.

"What made you decide to do all these today?" Grace asked.

"Well," he began, "I knew with Jon-Pierre and Kae and little Addie leaving this morning that you would be sad, and I wanted to plan something to help cheer you up."

Grace chuckled and said, "Kae was right, you are the perfect man for me."

"Yes, and you are the perfect woman for me. You do know that, don't you?"

"I don't know if I'm the perfect match for you. But I can tell you that I feel very lucky to have you in my life."

"For now and forever, for as long as we both shall live," said Matt.

Grace blushed at the memory of the night they were married in London and said those vows.

Matt said, "I meant those words then, and I mean them now."

Grace felt so awkward; she didn't know exactly what to say, so she said, "Me too."

That night as they lay in bed, Grace thanked Matt for bringing Kae and Jon-Pierre to Wyoming. She told him how much she loved him, and then she showed him.

Grace was thankful that Matty, as she affectionately called him now, was patient and loving with her. She had a lot to learn and even more to unlearn. But one thing she knew without a doubt was that Matt loved her, and she loved him.

35

JON-PIERRE, KAELYNN, AND ADDISON LANDED at Camden Airport outside of Sydney, Australia, on Sunday evening. With a seventeen-hour time difference and a fourteen-hour flight, they were all exhausted. Addison was absolutely cranky, and they still had a long drive home.

It was eleven-thirty by the time Kae got Addie calmed down and into her own bed. She fell into bed beside Jon-Pierre wiped out. Jon-Pierre was already snoring softly, assuring her he was asleep. She was careful not to wake him because he had a full schedule of work tomorrow at the studio.

Two hours later, Addie was awake and crying. Kae went to her, changed her nappy, and nursed her. She went back to sleep but not soundly. She was awake again two hours later, and they went through the whole routine again.

At 6:30 a.m., Addie woke up again. Kae rolled out of bed to go get her and found Jon-Pierre changing her diaper. He finished the job and handed Addie to Kae who took her and crawled back into her own bed with her. She laid on her side and nursed Addie until she fell back to sleep. And so did Kaelynn. Jon-Pierre finished getting ready for work. He leaned down and kissed both of his girls good-bye and left the house.

The studio fared so well with Lacy Langford filling in for Jon-Pierre that he decided to talk to Kae about offering her a full-time position. They could easily double the amount of portraiture business if they had another good photographer. Jon-Pierre decided to talk with Kae about it tonight over dinner.

"What would you think if I offered Lacy Langford a full-time position as photographer at the studio? She did a fantastic job while we were gone, and the staff seemed to like her. We could double our business with another photographer."

"It sounds like a good idea if you think the work is there to support it."

"Oh, it is. We've been turning down appointments."

"It sounds like an easy decision to me. Are you sure Lacy is the one?"

"Not 100 percent. She may not want to quit the freelance work she's doing now. I'll have to ask her and give her time to think it over. Eventually I would like to open another location, and Lacy could learn all the business end for about a year with me. Then, she could run the new studio. What do you think?"

"Like I said, it sounds like very good business sense, if Lacy is interested."

"I think I will call her tomorrow and thank her for filling in for the week and see what she thought of it. Any objection to inviting her and her husband for dinner on Friday night to discuss the plan?"

"No. That's fine with me."

All three of the Laurents were in bed sound asleep by 8:30 p.m. that night. The jet lag had really hit them hard coming back from the United States and loosing seventeen hours of time.

Tuesday afternoon, Jon-Pierre called Lacy Langford to thank her for filling in for him the previous week and to see how things went from her perspective. She told Jon-Pierre that he had really started something special. She told him that she heard the receptionist turn away at least two groups of tourists that had walked in after seeing just the window photos and dressings.

Jon-Pierre said, "That's another reason why I am calling. Kaelynn and I would like to invite you and Jim over for dinner Friday night. I want to talk to you about a possible partnership."

Lacy accepted the invitation and said she would see them on Friday night.

Friday evening came, and the Langfords arrived for a delicious dinner of steak frites with a light and airy chocolate mousse for dessert. After dinner, Kaelynn served classic French-pressed coffee, and they sat in the living room to talk about the possible partnership.

Jon-Pierre asked Lacy first if she was interested in working locally and not traveling as much to which she replied, "Jim and I have actually just been talking about that. We really want to start a family, but there is just no way with my work schedule. And once we do have a baby, I don't want to be traveling all over the world anymore. You guys have made the transition. How is it working for you?"

"It's great. No more traveling week after week and barely having time to do laundry before you fly out again. Plus, we were both working with schedules like that. Being in one place and working a more traditional type of job has been so refreshing for us. And having Addie now, I can't imagine trying to work my previous schedule. Neither can Kae, right?"

"Absolutely. I would rather die than try to work my old schedule and be a mother."

Jon-Pierre laid out the plan of working for one year together in the same studio and then looking at the possibility of opening another studio that would be Lacy's to run. They covered the financial aspect and the potential for growth along with the business. If everything worked well utilizing this model, they could each then look for other photographers of their own caliber to repeat the process.

Lacy mentioned Matt Wilson right away as a possible studio owner, but Jon-Pierre assured her that Matt was not in a position to do so.

Lacy and Jim wanted to take some time to talk it over and get back to Jon-Pierre and Kaelynn.

36

Matt and Grace were scheduled to be released form witness security the following week. Now that all the personnel from the agency that was involved in the illegal activity was in jail and not likely to see the outside for the rest of their lives, Matt and Grace could breathe a little easier. There was one small but potent possible detail that remained. The French police, London's Scotland Yard, Interpol, and the US government weren't sure that they had identified all the enforcement personnel the Farinis used. There were many private contractors available to continue searching for Jaelynn DepProvoue and Matt Wilson, especially with 1.5 million US dollars at stake.

The Farinis had far-reaching connections they could utilize on the outside of prison. So it was decided that Grace would never return to her former life as Jaelynn DepProvoue, a model. She would continue as Grace Wilson and remain in the United States.

Matt could continue his photography career and travel as he liked, but he chose to stay inside the US and close to Grace. Now imperative restoration was in full force. It was time to get Grace the help she needed to heal.

Marty had become instrumental in the beginning stages of Grace's healing. Grace met with Marty once a week in a formal therapy session. Grace was finding her way through issues of being abandoned by her parents at age sixteen, being forced to have sex with total strangers, both men and women, and her own feelings of getting just what she deserved. Her mother used to tell her and her twin, "You've made your bed. Now you have to sleep in it."

Matt was patient and kind. His heart broke for all that Grace had gone through in her twenty short years. He prayed for her healing daily. Matt knew there was no way to erase all the negative things Grace had been through, no more than anyone else. But he knew that God could restore health and beauty where destruction and ashes had been sewn.

Grace drank in this new life where she felt loved and safe. The wide open spaces of the Wyoming ranch gave her a sense of security. The property was so beautiful—the rolling hills, the valley where the river ran through the property, and the small lake that lay on the other side of the ranch.

Marty and Grace rode together several times a week just for the beauty and therapeutic value of the land. Grace got Matt into riding as well. Together they had explored the four corners of the ranch. They learned how to stay away from the cattle because they liked to chase riders on horseback, effectively scaring Grace away.

Matt took advantage of the scenery to photograph ever-beautiful space on the ranch and Grace at every opportunity he could. He even took some stunning new photographs of Marty and Mitch Garrison on horseback. He and Grace had a giant portrait of them on glass made to hang in their home. When they presented the gift to Mitch and Marty, they were amazed at the quality of Matt's work. It was something they would treasure as a family heirloom all their lives.

It was time for Matt and Grace to move on with their lives and step away from the Garrison's ranch and establish themselves somewhere in this country. Matt didn't want to go back to New York because that would be an easy place for the Farinis to search for them. They didn't know Grace's new name, but they knew Matt's.

Matt contacted their witness protection agent, Keith Hartman, and asked if they could meet one last time. Keith agreed. They met three days later at the Garrison ranch.

"How are you doing, Keith?" asked Matt as the two men shook hands.

"Just great, Matt. How are you guys doing?"

"Well, we're doing real good here."

The two men sat down in the living room as Matt got right down to the point of the visit.

"As you know, Grace and I are nearing the end of our time here at the Garrison's. It's been an honor to be here with these folks. But it's time for us to be on our own, and I have some concerns and some questions."

"Okay, Matt, that's what I'm here for. How can I help?"

"My concern is that the Farinis have a lot of contacts in the mafia world and could have a hit out on me. Wherever I go as Matt Wilson, I am a target because I helped get Jaelynn out of the organization and into protection."

"Do you know how many Matt Wilsons there are in the US?"

"A lot?"

"More than four thousand. Do you know how long it would take to check out that many Matt Wilsons? A very long time. I don't think that's going to be a problem."

"I disagree. I want to continue my photography. It's all I know. And wherever I go, Grace will be with me. You'll never convince me that they aren't looking for her. I just think we need a new last name. Something they won't be looking for."

"Well, that's not a bad idea. It would make finding you a great deal harder. What did you have in mind?"

"Nothing specific. I just want Grace to be safe."

"Agreed. How about Adams? It's simple, very common, and I'm sure there are thousands of them as well."

"Adams sounds fine. Do you think the decision makers above you will go for it?"

"Oh, I'm pretty sure they will. It's a relatively easy request, and it won't take more than a week to make it happen."

"Great, man, thank you."

"What else is on your mind?"

"We are weighing the options of where to live, big city, medium-sized, or small town. Eh, what do you think?"

"Well, a medium to big city is fairly easy to hide in, probably a whole lot of Adams living there. Easier to avoid close friends, etc., but a small town has its value too. A small community allows you to have a life with friends. You won't stand out as not fitting in after a while. You're not likely to be found there because it's far more costly to look there. Both options have pros and cons. I think it boils down to the kind of life you want to live.

"You said you wanted to continue your photography. How likely is that in a small town? On the other hand, you could be asked to have a gallery showing in a larger city and that could draw attention to you because of your signature style. See what I mean?"

"Yes, that's what we've been weighing as well. I take it we should keep a low profile wherever we end up?"

"It's not a bad idea, but it's not mandatory either."

"Come on, man, we're talking life and death here."

"Yes, we are. That's why you're getting new names."

"What would you do if you were in my shoes?"

"The first thing I would do is have Grace dye her hair blonde and keep it professionally done, eyebrows everything. The next thing I would do is decide to have a baby as soon as possible. That will change her figure a bit and make her not look so much like a supermodel, if you know what I mean. You should dye your hair too, make it look more like a beach guy, shave off the mustache and beard. You could keep some stubble if you like, but lose the facial hair."

"Okay, maybe we should have plastic surgery and get a whole new look altogether!" retorted Matt."

"You asked me what I would do. That's what I would do."

"Fair enough," said Matt. "I'm sorry I'm really nervous about this decision."

"It's okay. This is always a stressful part of transition. I'm here to help you. You just need to decide one thing at a time. Start with the physical appearance. Give it a few weeks to get used to."

"I'll talk to Grace about it."

Grace was coming down the main staircase when she heard Matt.

"Talk to Grace about what?" she asked.

Matt filled her in on their conversation.

"Keith, will I ever be able to model again?"

"No, that's definitely off the table if you want to stay alive."

"Okay, I was just asking." Grace raised her hands as if a gun were pointed at her. "Then it doesn't make much difference to me if we're in a city or a town. I have loved living here on the outskirts of a small town."

"What about the hair and the baby?" asked Matt

"I'm okay with the hair. The baby is subject for another day."

Keith felt the sudden change in the conversation and knew it was time to go. He asked Matt if he had any other questions. Matt didn't at the moment. Keith rose to leave. At the door, he said, "Listen, I only live about forty minutes from here. I've never told anyone that. I can be here, and we can talk anytime you like. Unless I'm out on another case nearby."

"Thanks, bro, I appreciate that," said Matt.

They shook hands again, and Keith got into his car and drove away. Matt and Grace were standing on the porch as the sun was beginning to set. Matt said, "Now, about the baby?"

Grace gave him a little punch in the ribs and said, "It's a bit too soon to talk about babies if you ask me."

"Why is that?"

"Because you and I are still getting to know each other, and I'm not ready to add a baby to the mix."

"Nonsense, we've known each other for four years now."

"I still have so much to work through. I feel like my plate is very full right now."

"Fair enough," said Matt.

Grace hadn't told Matt about the forced abortion the Farinis had made her have a year and a half ago. It was one of her most painful memories both physically and emotionally. There wasn't a day that went by that she didn't think of her baby.

Matt on the other hand had read everything printed about the trial, which included the graphic testimony about the forced abortion. He respected Grace's privacy and had recognized the pain that clouded her eyes on several occasion when a baby was mentioned or the subject was brought up. He vowed he would never press her on the subject but allow her to tell him in her own time, if ever.

To Grace, it didn't matter that she didn't know who the father was. The baby was part of her. It was hers. She had guessed about the probable due date. She grieved the awful pain the abortion would have caused her unborn child. Oh, how she hated the Farinis, pushing her around like she was nothing but a pawn in their financial game, someone that could be used, abused, and cast aside when they eventually were done with her. If Matt hadn't rescued her when he did, she was fairly sure she would have ended her own life. There literally was nothing left to live for.

Matt watched Grace's face after her answer about the idea of having a baby. He was sure he saw sorrow and regret pass through her eyes again. His heart hurt at the thought of her going through the abortion and recovery all alone. Then, he remembered the week she suddenly went to spend with her sister. Of course, it all made sense now. He wanted to reach out and comfort her, but he didn't want to invade her privacy.

Grace didn't know if she would ever be able to tell Matt about the abortion. What would he think of her, killing her own child? It's not like she had a choice in the matter though. It was handled very quickly. Still, how could she tell him she allowed someone else to kill her own baby?

Grace wondered if she could have any more children because of the abortion. The doctor who examined her after she came to the Garrison ranch said the abortion doctor had done a pretty hacked up job on her. He told her she had about a 20 percent chance of ever getting pregnant and an even lesser chance of carrying a baby to term and delivering normally.

Now, suddenly, all these mattered. She had Matt, and she didn't want to lose him. By the look on his face, he definitely wanted children. How could she tell him that probably wasn't going to happen with her? She bit her lip and fought back tears.

Matt saw Grace bite her lip that way she did when she was tormented. He pulled her close and whispered in her ear, "We have all the time in the world, baby. There's no rush." And he kissed her temple.

That night, Grace crawled in bed while Matt was still in the shower. When he came to bed, she was curled up on her side facing away from him. He knew she was still very troubled by the conversation about starting a family. He turned toward her and snuggled up behind her, pulling her into his arms. As he held her, he could feel the quiet sobs coming from her chest. He didn't say a word; he just held her until she fell asleep.

37

THE DECISION HAD BEEN MADE to change Matt's and Grace's last name from Wilson to Adams. It didn't take more than a week to get all the new identification documents in order—driver's licenses, birth certificates, passports, and health records.

It took another week to erase the deep web part of Matt's background and replace it with Matt Adams. Now if anyone tried to find Matt Wilson on the deep web, they would come up with zero information about him specifically. That Matt Wilson had been erased.

The next decision to make would be where they would live. They decided to travel to a few places and explore. New York City was out. They visited Washington, DC, and the Virginia area. They loved the ambiance and age of the area but not the humidity.

Next, they visited Chicago. It was a beautiful city, unlike any other they had visited or worked in, but the extreme cold winters and wind were not for them. From Chicago, they traveled to St. Louis, another city with beautiful summers but very cold winters.

Texas was too humid, and the southern part was prone to hurricanes. Montana was big sky country for sure but felt too remote. Wyoming and Idaho fit the same category as Montana. Los Angeles was, way too big and spread out. They hated the traffic. They finally settled on San Francisco, California. It had mild summers and winters, rain mostly in the winter and not that cold. San Francisco had the beach and the feel of a European city. It was perfect for them.

After six weeks of traveling around the United States, Grace felt like she had a good feel for her new country. Her French accent was barely detectible. But she was still working hard on getting rid of it completely.

They returned to the Garrison's ranch to get their things and say good-bye. Mitch and Marty had been such great friends, Matt and Grace hoped they would remain so.

They planned a farewell barbeque the afternoon before Matt and Grace would fly out to California. The food was amazing, the temperature was in the midseventies and perfect for one last ride. All four of them set off for the river valley. When they arrived, Mitch and Marty dismounted, and Matt and Grace followed.

Mitch cleared his throat and began, "Grace, I want to tell you that Marty and I have decided that we will not be handling any more witness protection. We feel that you are the high note we want to go out on. You have blown us away with your poise, the way you have handled the toughest of tough situations. You have set your standards high and maintained them. You have been true to yourself. We could not be more proud of you than if you were our own flesh and blood daughter."

As Mitch finished, he had tears in his eyes. Marty picked up where Mitch left off. "Grace, I have never seen a more broken human being as you were when you arrived here. And I have never seen anyone embrace therapy with the energy you have. You have stood tall and acknowledged your mistakes, and those that others forced upon you. You have come to understand the difference and start living in a new normal. You are no longer a slave to fear and regret. You are a free woman, married to an amazing man who loves you dearly.

"I know that you are and will continue to be an amazing woman, wife, and hopefully someday have the courage to be a mother. Like Mitch said, we love you guys like you were our own children."

Mitch chimed in again, "We want you to know that our door is always open to you both. You are welcome here anytime. We hope you come and visit often."

Grace was speechless, so Matt replied, "We feel the same about you both. I don't think we could've gotten through any of this past year without you. Thank you so very much for opening your home and your hearts to us."

Grace had tears sliding down her cheeks as she went to Marty and gave her a big hug. "You are the mother I wished for growing up." Matt and Mitch shook hands at first; then, Mitch pulled him into a huge bear hug. Before long, the four of them were in one big embrace.

They mounted back onto their horses and road back toward the house as the sun was setting in the west. It had been a beautiful day with the Garrisons. Grace felt like she had experienced what a real mother should be like.

The next morning, Mitch and Marty drove Matt and Grace to Casper to catch the first leg of their flight to Salt Lake City and then onto San Francisco. They shared another tearful good-bye and boarded the plane.

Fifteen minutes later, they were airborne and on their way to their new life. There was a lot to be done once they got to San Francisco. They had secured an apartment with a garage while they were visiting but still needed to get a car and some furnishings. They had left everything behind from their old lives. Now they would shop for everything together for their new life. Grace was quite excited at the prospects of shopping again.

They landed in Salt Lake City just before the airport shut down all outgoing flights due to a freak early snowstorm. Matt and Grace were able to find a Windham hotel near the airport and settled in for the night.

The next morning, the airport was still closed. Matt and Grace decided to enjoy a leisurely breakfast, then walked the airport and shopped. Matt purchased a new leather aviator's jacket. Grace found a fine leather Louis Vuitton handbag in the same store and purchased it for herself.

By noon, the snow had stopped, and the airport was working on clearing the runways. It would be 3:00 p.m. before Matt and Grace were able to get a flight out. They landed in San Francisco after 6:30 local time. Since it was getting late, they rented a car and made their way into the city. Both had been to San Francisco many times for work and knew their way around the city a little bit enough to find a good restaurant and have a nice meal together. They rented a room at the Marriott near the Moscone Center for the night. They didn't have any bedding yet for their new apartment. Grace was having a difficult time with the terminology; she kept calling it a flat and would stop short and correct herself.

The Marriott was beautiful and comfortable for the night. Both Matt and Grace were used to nights in a hotel from their years of work in the fashion industry. Well, those days were over. Grace would not be going anywhere near the fashion industry, and Matt wanted to take his photography in a new direction.

The following morning, they took their luggage to the new apartment and dropped it off. They stayed long enough to make a list of essentials that needed to be acquired. At the top of the list, of course, was sheets, pillows, towels, dishes, and utensils, as well as a car. They decided to tackle the housewares first. Matt said buying a car could become an all-day affair if they went there first.

Grace got to see a great deal more of the city by shopping at Macy's and Sacs Fifth Avenue. She thought the stores were high class until she went into Neiman Marcus. She fell in love with the store. It was here that they bought most of the housewares they needed. Grace even found a few new outfits for herself. She tried to get Matt to shop for some clothes for himself, but he said a man doesn't need a vast wardrobe like a woman does.

After lunch, they dropped all their purchases off at the new apartment; then, they started the search for a car. They settled on a BMW M850i. It was beautiful, and Matt had secured the garage under their apartment as part of the rent. Grace drove the rental back to the airport while Matt followed in the new BMW. It was fun driving it for the first time. He picked up Grace after she turned in the rental, and they headed for home.

When they arrived home, they had several more packages and boxes to carry up the stairs, but Matt insisted that he would haul the stuff up, and Grace would stay inside and begin unpacking things. It was a good thing they had stopped and picked up a pizza because by the time they got everything into the apartment, they were both exhausted and starving.

They ate their pizza on their new dishes. Only then did they realize they had forgotten to purchase any glassware. After the meal, Grace hand washed the dishes and put them away with the others in the cupboard.

Grace followed Matt into the bedroom, and together, they made the bed with the new sheets they bought. Grace started pulling Matt toward the bathroom. "Let's take a shower, so we don't get the new sheets all dirty on the first night."

Matt laughed out loud and asked Grace, "Have you seen the tiny shower in this place?" There's barely room for one in there. I don't think we will be taking any showers together in this place.

Grace gave Matt a pouty face and said, "We'll have to start looking for a bigger place then, won't we?"

Matt let Grace take the first shower; then, he followed suit. They were tired, and they were happy. They christened their new bed and bedroom appropriately that night. After the love making, Matt held Grace in his arms until she fell asleep. She was getting better; she was sleeping better and having fewer nightmares. All in all, Matt was pleased with the healing process so far for Grace. He prayed it would continue.

Matt spoke often of his parents who lived in the state of Washington. They had never visited them because of the witness security program.

When Matt and Grace got settled in their new home, Matt bought two burner phones. He mailed one to his parents in Washington with instructions of how they would use them. A week later, Matt called his parents' burner phone from his own. It was the first they had talked to each other since he had set up all his royalties from his photographs to go to his parents.

Matt had all his income go to his parents in Washington. They in turn would convert half of it into gold and silver and send the remaining half in the form of a cashier's check to a PO box in San Francisco where Matt lived.

His parents knew that he had gotten married but didn't know anything else. They followed the Farini trial because they knew that

Matt did some photography for them. They had no idea of how involved Matt was in bringing the organization down.

Roger Wilson's burner phone rang right when Matt's note said that it would. He answered it after the first ring. It was Matt, of course.

"How are you doing, Dad?"

"We're doing real good, son. We sure miss you."

"Well, that's why I am calling. Grace and I are going to take a trip up to the Napa area to tour some of the wineries, and I've made all the arrangements for you and mom to do the same thing. We will end up in the same place at the same time. I can't wait for you two to meet Grace. You guys are gonna love her."

"How will you get all the information to us, son?"

"I rented you guys a PO box at the post office there in La Conner. You should get the key in the mail in a day or two. I will send all the information to the PO box. Okay, Dad?"

"Sure, son, that sounds good. Now talk to your Mom before she hits me with her rolling pin."

"Hi, Mom."

"Hi, son, are you eating well? Does your new wife cook?"

"Yes, mom. She is a great cook. I'm eating just fine. I've even had to loosen my belt a notch."

"Well, that's good. I can't wait to meet her. We are going to meet her sometime, aren't we?"

"Yes, Mom, you're gonna meet her in July in Napa. Dad will tell you all about it."

38

. . . .

IN SYDNEY, A LETTER ARRIVED postmarked from New Orleans, Louisiana, USA with no other return address. Kaelynn opened the envelope. It was a very short note from Matt. It read:

> *Package for you in PO Box*
>
> *Matt*

Kaelynn loaded Addie in the car and drove to the post office. She opened the PO box and retrieved the package. She drove directly home and then opened the package. Inside was another note and a cell phone. The note read:

> *This is a burner phone with a secure connection. In simple terms, it will allow you and Grace to communicate at least once a month. Wait for Grace to call you in a couple of days. Then you will be able to log her burner number in your phone. When she calls you or you here, you will each know who's calling. Grace's number is 555-548-1212. For security purposes, do not answer any other phone number.*
>
> *Matt*

Kae was ecstatic that Grace and Matt had found a way for them to communicate. Kae could hardly wait for Grace to call her. Three days later, the burner phone rang. She looked at the number, and it was indeed Grace. Kae answered the call, and she and Grace were connected.

"Kaelynn, hi, it's Grace. How have you been? I have missed talking to you so much."

"Grace! Hello. It's so good to hear you. How in the world did Matt come up with this idea?"

"We use it for emergencies with his parents, so I asked him if we could do the same thing between us."

"That is so great. But can we really only talk once a month?"

"The nature of a burner phone is that it stays out of the mainstream phone pathways. So it is best if we use it sparingly. And yes, once a month would probably be the most we should use them."

"Okay, we can make that work, can't we?"

"Yes, we can!"

* * * * *

Matt wanted to try some new directions with his photography. He and Grace decided to take in all the scenes around San Francisco and get to know the place. Matt photographed everything and made sure that Grace was in 90 percent of the photos. She was so darned photogenic and beautiful that he couldn't help himself.

Grace didn't mind. She was so used to being in front of the camera. She asked Matt to teach her about photography. So he began to train her on the camera, its features, and how to use them. He taught her that light is the single most important element to any good photograph.

Grace tried to take pictures and was doing pretty well. When they got home and brought up the photos in the editing studio, she could see that her photos didn't hold a candle to Matt's. True to her nature, she was very critical of her own work. She wanted it to be perfect right off the bat. Matt assured her that it was an acquired talent and took lots of practice.

Matt explained that each photo shoot was an opportunity to learn something new about the craft. Grace asked, "Do you still learn something new every time?"

"Most of the time I do," replied Matt. "You know that you expect perfection out of yourself in whatever you are doing. You just happen to be a natural model, so you think everything should come that easy. I get it."

"I'll have you know that modeling is very hard work, buster. It does not come that easily. There is an art to it."

"I didn't mean it wasn't hard work, Grace. What I meant is that you are very good at modeling, so good that it looks like a walk in the park. Don't forget that I've worked with you on some really long, hot, sweaty shoots, some of them sixteen-hour days. I know how hard you work. You have an amazing work ethic."

"Matt, I was teasing you."

"Oh, okay," he said as he blushed.

It was decided that Sunday would be their weekly "day of rest." They found a television network that played nothing but old classic movies. They bought a popcorn maker so they could have fresh popcorn to go with the movies.

One Sunday, Grace found Matt sitting out on their tiny little balcony with his feet propped up on the railing reading an old, leather-bound book. She brought him a cup of coffee and asked him what he was reading.

"The Bible," he responded. "I feel like I need to get back to my roots a bit."

"What roots are those?" Grace asked.

"Well, my parents took me to church every Sunday growing up. I learned a lot about God and how He loves us so much and wants to participate in our lives. You know? Not just sit up on his mountain and watch us like little ants. He really wants to have a personal relationship with each of us.

"This past year with all the legal stuff we've been mired in, I have gotten away from that part of my life, and I miss the closeness I had with God before this all started happening."

Grace scoffed, "Personal relationship? Are you serious? If God is so personal, where was he when I needed him? Where was he when I was being forced to do unspeakable things for the Farinis? I can hear that you are very serious about this. I'm not trying to pick an argument with you, Matt, I just don't see it."

"I can understand that. You have legitimate questions, and I don't have the answers to them. I could tell you he was right there with you, but what good would that do for you? I could tell you that he was there too and protected you form far worse things, but why didn't he protect you from all of it? I don't have the answers to those questions."

"I don't see it, Matty. I can see that you believe in God very deeply, but I just can't. I hope you understand. This is not something we're ever going to see eye to eye on."

"I get it, Grace. It will be a subject that we agree to disagree on."

"Ya, kind of a topic we choose to avoid. I think that would be agreeable."

So the subject of God and religion was avoided in their relationship. This didn't stop Matt from praying for Grace or asking God for himself, where was he when all these horrible things were happening to her.

For Grace's part, she left Matt alone while he read his Bible on Sundays. She brought him coffee and sometimes sat with him on the balcony and looked through her fashion magazines while he read. It was an amicable solution. They could still enjoy each other's company without having to agree on everything. Grace felt like it was a healthy balance for them both.

Matt joined up with a local photographer's group to see what the art world was like in the Bay Area. He met some other very good photographers; some did mostly portraits, others were magazine photogs and some were landscape photographers. Matt enjoyed his time with his new friends. They shared a common occupation and passion.

Each month, one of the group's members would bring a bunch of their own work and put it on display for the others. It was sort of like a gallery showing but on a private scale.

The month came for Matt to showcase his work, and he labored over which shots to take with him. He finally selected twenty-five of what he thought was his best work and took those. After he set up his display, he sat down and had the strangest sense that he had forgotten to put his pants on or something. He was so nervous. He couldn't understand why. His work had been published in fashion magazines all over the world, and he had never felt this nervous.

The other photographers from the group came in and began to look over Matt's work. His hands were sweaty. He felt like a schoolboy at his high school prom. Then it hit him. He realized that he was nervous because he cared what his friends thought of his work. It mattered to him.

When Matt shot photos for agencies and magazines, they had chosen him because they liked his work. His new friends had never seen his work.

After ten minutes or so, Matt stood up and paced back and forth wanting someone to say something, anything. He was dying here, waiting.

Finally one of the guys, Tim, said, "Matt, these are amazing, man. I mean some really good work, bro."

Matt thanked him. Soon all the others were commenting as well and congratulating Matt on outstanding shots.

"Who's the babe?" asked Tim.

"Oh, that's my wife," said Matt.

"Shut up! You dog, you've been holding out on us on every level. Where in the world did you meet such a beautiful woman and what does she see in you?" asked Tim.

"We met at work about four years ago. I have no idea what she sees in me. But she loves me, and I'm just fine with that."

"How long have you been married, bro?"

"Just over a year."

"Newlyweds, congratulations!"

"Thank you."

The rest of the evening went better than Matt had anticipated. The other photographers wanted to know about his light metering and how he got such amazing light and shadows in his pictures. Matt had no problem sharing his routine and knowledge with the others. That's what the group was all about.

Matt drove home after the meeting feeling relaxed and happy. He was excited to share the events of the evening with Grace.

When Matt arrived home, he found Grace curled up on the bathroom floor. She had been vomiting.

"Baby, what's wrong?" he asked Grace.

"I'm not sure. I've got bad cramps, and they're making me sick to my stomach."

"Has this ever happened before?" Matt asked.

"Not like this," Grace replied.

Matt helped Grace to the bedroom, but just as soon as he got her settled in bed, she bolted for the bathroom again.

"Baby, I think I should take you to emergency. This could be an appendicitis or something serious like that."

Grace objected to going to hospital. She assured him she was on her monthly cycle and would probably be better in the morning. But within the hour, she vomited again, and this time, it contained blood.

Matt drove Grace to University of San Francisco Medical Center. The emergency room was packed. Matt waited in line for the triage nurse as Grace sat in a rolling chair and continued to throw up blood.

When Matt was still four people away from the triage nurse, Grace passed out and fell out of the chair. Medical people came out of everywhere and took Grace and Matt back into the belly of the emergency department. They put Grace in a small room and closed the door giving her and Matt some privacy. The ED was noisy with people crying out in pain and screaming at nurses and doctors.

A doctor came into the room and began to examine Grace. He asked her a lot of questions. At one point, he asked if Grace had ever been pregnant or had a baby or abortion. She quickly asked Matt if he would get her some water. The doctor understood that Grace didn't want Matt to hear the answer to this question.

As soon as Matt was out of the room, Grace quickly told the doctor about the quick drive-through abortion.

Matt returned with the water, but the doctor wouldn't let Grace have any of it. He declared that she might need surgery, and if this was her appendix, she could not eat or drink anything until that was determined. The doctor ordered X-rays and an ultrasound and left the room.

Matt leaned over Grace and kissed her cheek. He spoke in a low voice so as not to be heard outside the room.

"You know you can tell me anything. I know you've been through unthinkable things, but I promise I won't judge you for anything."

Grace turned her face away from Matt and said, "Thank you."

Matt noticed a tear trickle down her cheek as Grace doubled over in pain. Matt stepped out of the room into the hall right across from a nurse's station. The doctor was still there making notes in Grace's chart. Matt asked him if he could give her anything for the pain. The doctor instructed a nurse to give Grace fifty milligrams of Demerol for pain and to repeat it again in thirty minutes if pain persisted. Matt thanked him and went back to Grace.

"They're going to give you something for pain," Matt stated. Just then, the nurse arrived with an IV setup and inserted it into Grace's arm. Then she gave her some fluids on the drip and injected the Demerol. Within seconds, Grace felt the relief.

"Oh thank you," she said to the nurse.

Fifteen minutes later, a young man came to take Grace for the X-rays and ultrasound. She was gone for thirty minutes. Matt waited. When Grace arrived back to the room, she was in a lot of pain again. Matt looked for the nurse who had been given the order to give her more Demerol but couldn't find her. He asked at the desk, but everyone was busy. He was told the nurse would be by as soon as she could. An hour later, Matt stepped out of the room and saw the nurse. He asked her about another dose of pain medicine and was promised she would be in as soon as possible.

Four hours later, the doctor returned with news that Grace's appendix had ruptured, and they would be taking her up to the OR in a few minutes for surgery. Grace's eyes widened with fear and concern. Matt held her hand and assured her that he would be right here and that he would pray for her while she was in surgery.

Another young man came to take Grace and Matt up to the OR. He stopped at the waiting room and told Matt that he would wait here while Grace was in surgery. Matt leaned down and kissed Grace and told her he loved her. Then he let go of her hand as she was wheeled away down a hall. He stood and watched her go until the OR doors closed and he couldn't see her.

The surgery went well. Grace was taken from the OR recovery room to a regular room where she would stay for a couple of days. The doctor was concerned about infection due to the length of time the appendix had been ruptured before they got in there to clean everything up. He told Matt to go home because Grace would be out and sleeping until late tomorrow morning. They would make sure she was comfortable.

Matt opted to sleep on the little chair bed that was in Grace's room. It was probably a mistake, but he didn't want to leave Grace alone. While he tried to sleep, the realization that he could have lost her set in. She had not been feeling well for several days but kept pushing forward. At first, they both thought it was just simple monthly cramps, but the vomiting and blood was scary.

Matt realized that the appendix had probably ruptured several days ago. By the time Grace was vomiting blood, infection had already set in according to the doctor. Now they had Grace on an IV drip of antibiotics.

The understanding that she could have died and still had a long road to recovery made Matt start thinking about Grace's soul. He knew she didn't believe in God, and he understood why. But in his heart, he knew that she needed to hear the truth about God and his overwhelming love for her. He just didn't know how to start this conversation. Matt prayed for help from God. He knew the Holy Spirit would give him the words when the time was right.

39

SATURDAY MORNING AROUND 11:00 A.M., Grace began to wake up. She was groggy and didn't know where she was at first. She started saying, "Don't take my baby," over and over. Matt went to her and helped calm her down. He told her they were in the hospital and that she had just had surgery.

"Where's my baby?" she asked him. Grace could see Matt's face, but everything was a blur and as if she were looking at him down a long tunnel. Matt kept soothing her and caressing her hair.

A nurse came in to see what the commotion was and saw that Grace was awake. She left the room and came back quickly with a syringe of something.

Matt asked, "What is that?"

The nurse responded, "It helps with agitation." The antibiotics can cause agitation, and agitation needs to be managed as much as possible to keep her still and able to heal without ripping open stitches.

"Okay," said Matt.

The medication worked within minutes, and Grace was calmer. The nurse told Matt to keep her calm as she left the room. Matt wanted to talk to Grace about her cry to keep her baby, but he thought it would just agitate her more. So he kept this information to himself. He promised himself that he would not invade her privacy until she was ready to talk to him about it.

Grace recovered quickly and was released the following Friday with orders for oral antibiotics and a follow-up appointment with her primary care doctor.

Matt took Grace home and walked with her every day to help her recover her strength and stamina. In a couple of days, they had mapped out a lovely one mile walk around their neighborhood and walked it every evening. Grace was getting stronger and feeling much better.

As they were walking one day, Matt asked Grace, "Have you ever wondered why there are so many species of trees? I mean why not just one kind of tree?"

"No, I can't say that I have given trees much thought."

"I wonder what God was thinking when he created so many different kinds of trees?"

"Matt, I believe there is a God. I just don't think He pays any attention to people."

"Why would a God pay so much attention to the details of trees and flowers and every other plant but not care about the people he created? Have you ever read the Bible for yourself?"

"No, actually I haven't."

"You should read the account of creation. It's very interesting."

And that was how their conversations about God and the Bible started. Grace was far more open than Matt had thought she would be. He thanked God for working on softening her heart.

40

....

MATT AND GRACE BEGAN THE search for a new larger home to live in. They had lived in the tiny apartment for a year now and were feeling quite crowded. They found and purchased a house on El Camino del Mar in Seacliff. Grace loved the house but thought it was a bit extravagant for the two of them.

"Then we will fill it with children," said Matt.

Grace couldn't take it anymore. "Matt, we need to talk," she began that evening before they went to sleep. Matt knew she was either very serious or angry.

"What is it?" he asked.

Grace turned on her side toward Matt.

"Here's the thing. My doctors don't think I can have children." There! She'd said it, out loud.

Matt turned on his side to face Grace.

"What makes them say that?"

"Examinations of course," she replied.

"What did they find?"

"Okay...listen...this isn't easy for me." After a long emotional pause, she continued, "While I was working for the Farinis, I got pregnant...and Megan made me get rid of the baby..."

"I am so sorry, Gracie," said Matt as he pulled her into his arms. "We can work thorough this. We will get through this. I promised you that I would never judge you, and I won't do it now. I want to be here with you for the rest of our lives, with or without kids. We can always adopt if we decide that's right for us."

Grace began to cry, "I don't want to adopt. I want to have your children. I want to give you children. I know you want them so badly."

"I will adjust, baby."

Later that night in the dark, Matt couldn't sleep. He got up and went to the living room and poured his heart out to God, laying all his hopes and dreams down on the floor in front of Jesus.

"God, help me adjust to this news. You know my heart. You know how much I want children, and you know there's no one else I want to have them with." He began to sob. "I need to be strong for Grace. She's been through so much, and she doesn't need to see me falling apart..." Matt couldn't speak; he was sobbing so hard.

Suddenly he felt Grace's arm come around him and hold him from behind. She was crying too. "You were right when you said we would get through this together." For several minutes, they held each other and cried. It was a huge loss to them both to know they might never have their own children.

The following morning, Matt was hopeful, but Grace was not. Matt was cheery and whistling; Grace was depressed and angry.

"How can you be so happy?" she snapped.

"Because I serve a God who caused Mary the mother of Jesus to conceive a child while she was still a virgin. You do still believe your Catholic upbringing, don't you?"

"Yes, I do, but what does that have to do with us?"

"Because if God can cause Mary to conceive as a virgin, then He may just have a miracle for us as well."

"Okay, Matty, don't go pinning all your hopes and dreams on a miracle. When is the last time you experienced or witnessed one of those?"

"When you agreed to marry me, and I was able to get you out of Europe and into the witness security program. That was a miracle!"

"I'll give you that one. There were some strange sensations happening during those first few days."

"That's the God I know!"

Grace was speechless; she didn't know what to say. She felt like Matt was pinning all his hopes on a cloud, but he was so serious that she didn't want to disappoint him or see him get disappointed when nothing happened. Or worse, she did get pregnant but lost the baby somewhere along the way.

"Well, I guess you're gonna be doing a lot of praying then, because the doctors aren't generally wrong about these things."

"Prayer is something I happen to be pretty good at. I will be talking to God about it every day."

Grace still didn't know what to say. She was afraid of poking fun at Matt's beliefs but seriously worried he was talking nonsense.

They didn't speak about babies or children again. Grace never knew if Matt was still praying for a baby or had given up. She, on the other hand, was absolutely convinced they would never have one.

July came, and Matt and Grace drove up to Napa, California, for a tour of the wineries. They met Matt's parents at one of the tours and stuck together for the rest of the vacation. Grace fell in love with Matt's parents. They were so cute together. She could tell they loved each other dearly, but they teased each other incessantly as well.

All too soon, the week was over, and they were each headed back to their respective homes.

"I loved meeting your parents, Matty," said Grace on the drive home. "They are so sweet. You must have had an amazing childhood."

"I have no complaints. I got in my fair share of trouble, and I know what the back of the woodshed looks like. That's for sure."

"What is the back of the woodshed?"

"It's where I got my whoopins."

"Whoopins?"

"Yes, ma'am, my dad believed if he spared the whoopin' rod that I would be a very spoiled child."

"So a whoopin' is a form of discipline?"

"Oh yes. A painful one."

"You aren't spoiled, so you must have gotten a whole lot of 'whoopins'"

"What kind of discipline did you have growing up?"

"We had so many chores to do that we didn't have time to get into too much trouble. But I do remember getting hit on the backside with a long wooden spoon now and then. One time, Kae and

I were supposed to be doing the dishes, and we got into this water fight and got water all over the kitchen. We thought sure Mum was going to use that spoon on us, but she decided that we had too much energy and time, so she gave us each a toothbrush and told us to clean every inch of the kitchen floors and countertops until there wasn't a speck of dirt or dust."

"How long did that take?"

"We started at 4:30 in the afternoon and worked until 4:00 the following morning."

"How old were you?"

"We were ten I think."

"Grace, that's child abuse."

"Probably, but it was normal for us. By the time Kae and I were twelve, we did all the cooking, laundry, and cleaning at home. All we had time for was school, homework, and chores."

"That's not right, Grace."

"Yes, it's the truth, I swear it."

"I don't mean you're lying. I mean it's wrong of your parents to treat you that way."

"Oh, well, it's all we ever knew."

"My whole life I've really only had two friends, my sister and you."

"We have Marty and Mitch. They're friends now."

"Yes, they are, but they are so far away."

They arrived in the city just as the sun was setting. Grace suggested they get a pizza before they got home so she wouldn't have to cook for dinner.

They curled up on the couch and turned on their favorite old movie channel while they ate their pizza.

41

MATT HAD BEEN DOING SOME arial photography over the Bay Area for a local firm. They paid well, and Matt was thrilled to be in a helicopter soaring over the area. He came home exhilarated and full of tales about his day.

On a Thursday afternoon, Matt's boss called Grace to come get Matt at work. He was seeing double and had a terrible headache. Grace called a Lyft and went directly to the office Matt was working at.

Matt didn't look good at all; in fact, his skin was a grayish color. Matt's boss asked Grace if she wanted to take him to the hospital. They agreed he didn't look well.

Just then, Matt collapsed to the floor and began to shake uncontrollably. Matt's boss pulled out his phone and dialed 911 immediately.

By the time they got to the hospital, the shaking had stopped, but Matt was still unconscious. It seemed like hours before the doctors sent for Grace to come back into the emergency department.

Dr. Swanson had a lot of questions about Matt's medical history that Grace didn't have the answers to. Did he have a history of seizures? Was he on any medication for seizures? Grace's head was swimming.

"No, there was no history of seizures, no medications at all," overall Matt was a very healthy twenty-five-year-old male.

Then Dr. Swanson explained that Matt had a grand mal seizure, caused by abnormal electrical activity throughout the brain. They would be keeping him overnight for observation. She was welcome to stay with him.

Grace was glad that she had followed the ambulance in their BMW. Having the car with her was one less thing she had to worry about.

Once they moved Matt into his own room, things began to settle down around her. But Grace was a bundle of nervousness. Why wasn't Matt waking up? What in the world was a grand mal seizure all about and what did it mean for Matt?

Dr. Swanson came in the room later in the evening. He pulled up a chair and began to explain to Grace what was happening with Matt.

"Usually, a grand mal seizure is caused by epilepsy. But sometimes, this type of seizure can be triggered by other health problems, such as extremely low blood sugar, a high fever, or a stroke.

"Many people who have a grand mal seizure never have another one and don't need treatment. But someone who has recurrent seizures may need treatment with daily antiseizure medications to control and prevent future grand mal seizures."

"Which is the case with Matt?" Grace asked.

"We have to wait and see. That's why we are keeping him for another couple of days to watch him."

Later that evening, Matt began to wake up. Grace called for the nurse as she had been instructed.

"Oh, God, my head hurts. Where am I?"

"You're in hospital," said Grace. "You had a seizure."

"It feels like someone beat me in the head with a baseball bat."

Matt tried to sit up and grabbed his head.

"Don't try to sit up, baby, just lay back and rest."

The nurse came quickly into the room with Dr. Swanson who examined Matt and explained again what had happened to him.

"You're going to have to take it easy for a month or two. We don't know what brought the seizure on, and we don't know what might trigger another one. At this time, there is no evidence of a stroke."

The following afternoon, they released Matt to go home and rest there. He slept a lot the first couple of days. But he began to get restless very quickly. He grabbed his camera and laid on the couch taking photos of Grace whenever she was within shot. After a few hours of that, it began to get annoying to Grace.

"Will you stop that, please? You're driving me crazy."

"I'm bored, and I'm tired of watching TV and just laying around. I need to work."

"Why don't you go sit in your office at your computer and try to edit some photos? Maybe you can do that without stressing your brain."

"Ouch! That hurt. Editing photos is no day at the beach. It's hard work and lots of concentration you know."

"I didn't mean it that way. Just don't edit so long that you get too tired. Take breaks in between."

Matt tried to edit, but in less than an hour, he had a splitting headache, and back to the couch he went. He put an ice pack on his forehead and slept the rest of the afternoon.

Grace felt so bad for him. He was going stir crazy but wasn't well enough to do much. She decided to see if he was up to going out to dinner tonight. That would get him out of the house, get some fresh air, and they could relax together at a nice restaurant.

Grace made a reservation at Gary Danko, an upscale French restaurant. Matt was feeling a little better, the headache was gone, and he got out of his sweats and into a pair of jeans, a white button-down shirt, and a navy blazer. Grace put on a chic silver romper-style sleeveless jumpsuit. She looked stunning.

They enjoyed their meal and the evening out immensely. When they arrived home, Matt was exhausted. He got back into his sweats and laid down on the bed. Within minutes, he was asleep.

Grace was a little worried; it seemed Matt was not bouncing back as quickly as the doctor had hoped. Dr. Swanson wanted to run some more tests on Matt to see how he was progressing.

The medical tests all came back in the normal range, so Dr. Swanson cleared Matt to go back to work two days a week but not consecutively. He thought that might pick Matt's spirits up a bit.

That night, Matt reached for Grace to make love, and she pushed him away, saying she was nervous that it might cause another seizure. Matt was frustrated, but he understood.

Matt went to work the next morning and made it until lunchtime. Then he came home and slept for the afternoon. The next evening, he caught Grace in an embrace that led to the bedroom and love making. He was fine afterward, but Grace was a nervous wreck. She was just sure that he would have a seizure during the night. She didn't sleep at all. She just laid there and watched his every move.

This went on for the next few times they made love. But slowly, their lives got back to a somewhat normal routine. It had been three months since the seizure, and they were both feeling like they were on the other side of the critical zone.

42

MATT WAS BACK TO WORK three days a week with a day to rest in between. On the days when he was home, he would spend a few hours editing with breaks in between. He started working on compiling his favorite photos for a book. With the extra time he had at home, he found the idea fun. He would title the book Matthew Adams: Anthology. Everything was getting back to normal.

The twins call that week was full of hope and great expectations.

Kaelynn had a lot to tell Grace about Addie. She was crawling all over the place and pulling herself up onto furniture. She hadn't mastered moving around the furniture yet, but Jon-Pierre and Kaelynn were in the process of babyproofing everything.

Kae said every time she turned around, Addie had opened another cabinet or drawer and was pulling stuff out of them. She said she spent half of her day running behind Addie and putting things away.

Grace laughed and could imagine Addie keeping her parents on the run all over the house cleaning up after her. Grace said, "If she is doing all these now, what is she going to be like when she takes off walking?"

Kaelynn said, "We already call her the human hurricane. But besides that, she is such a joy. I never knew I could love another human being like this. It is amazing."

Grace needed to wrap up the call; they had been talking for over thirty minutes. "Say hello to Jon-Pierre for us and give him our love," said Grace.

"I will. You do the same to Matt from us."

"I will," said Grace. "I love you, sis. Talk to you next month."

"Love you too." And they hung up.

One afternoon, Grace went out to do some marketing. When she returned, she found Matt on the floor of their bedroom having another seizure. She quickly called 911, and they kept her on the phone with them. They told her what to do to keep Matt from swallowing his tongue until the paramedics arrived and took over.

At the hospital again, Dr. Swanson wanted to keep Matt for at least three days. So Grace decided to go home for the night knowing now that Matt would not be waking up until sometime tomorrow. She was feeling a bit more tired than usual and figured it was from the stress of the last few months.

Grace arrived at the hospital the next morning around 10:00 just in time to see Dr. Swanson. Matt was awake and eating. He was feeling much better and wanted to go home. But Dr. Swanson wasn't releasing him. These were two large seizures way too close together for his comfort.

Grace sat all day with Matt. They talked about where they would like to travel and places they would like to see. Grace wouldn't let go of Matt's hand. She had a very bad feeling about this second seizure.

"What do you have planned for tomorrow?" Matt asked.

"I have my annual physical in the morning, and then I'll be here with you."

That night, Grace spent three hours on the phone with her sister. She talked into the wee hours of the morning with Kaelynn. She poured her heart out to her sister about Matt's seizures and not being able to get pregnant or have a baby and how much Matt wanted a family.

Kaelynn said, "Matt adores you, Grace, he's not going anywhere. I would be more worried about these seizures than I would about a baby."

Morning came very quickly after falling asleep at 3:30. Grace made it to her doctor's appointment for the physical on time but very tired. The physical exam went the same as usual with all the same results for the most part. It would be next to impossible for Grace to every conceive a child let alone carry to full term.

It wasn't anything new, but the news always depressed her. So much for a God of miracles. If God would listen to anyone in the world, it would be Matt. He was such a good person, a great husband, and he would make an outstanding father too.

Grace left the doctor's office and stopped by home to repair the mess of her make-up the tears of regret had caused. She pulled herself together enough to head back to the hospital to spend the rest of the day with Matt. As she was driving, she decided to try a little prayer of her own.

"Please, God, if you're there and you care even a little bit for us down here, let me give Matt a baby. I know he wants to be a father, and you'd have to admit, of all your children, he'd make a great one. Amen." It was Grace's first prayer since her catechism.

Grace parked the car at the hospital and was just getting out when her regular cell phone rang. She looked at the screen; it was her doctor.

"Hello?" she answered.

"Hi, Grace, this is Dr. Avilla. We ran a test on your urine sample this morning because of your recent fatigue. It came back positive. You are pregnant. Congratulations! I know you've been wanting a baby for some time."

Grace could not believe the timing of her first prayer in a long time and the phone call from her doctor. She couldn't wait to tell Matt.

Grace rushed into the hospital and up to the fourteenth floor to his room. As she rounded the corner of the wing, she saw a lot of commotion down the hall. As she got closer, she realized the activity was in Matt's room. She entered the room to see Matt experiencing another seizure. The nurses and doctors were trying to hold him down on the bed. He was having seizures so bad that they couldn't get the syringe of medication into his IV port.

Finally the medicine went into Matt, and he began to settle down. Dr. Swanson told the staff around the bed, "That's the worst one I've ever seen." He didn't see Grace standing in the doorway. When he did, he moved toward her and ushered her into the hallway.

"That was a bad one. I don't have any idea what is causing the seizures, but as you know, they can just happen with no cause or warning. I'm afraid that's what is happening to Matt. I would encourage you to call the family together. The next twenty-four hours are going to be critical."

Grace couldn't believe what she was hearing. Suddenly everything seemed to be moving in slow motion. Her ears began to ring and the room to spin; then, everything went black.

When Grace awoke, she was lying on a gurney in the hallway outside of Matt's room. Dr. Swanson was there with her.

"What happened?" she asked.

"You fainted," he replied. "Lay still until you know you're okay to sit up."

Grace's head was spinning. What had the doctor told her? Call Matt's family he might not make it in another twenty-four hours. That couldn't be right. Matt was just fine when she left last night. In fact, he was joking about coming home today.

Grace began to sit up. Dr. Swanson helped her.

Are you dizzy or lightheaded at all? Is there any chance that you're pregnant?

"No, yes, I'm fine," stuttered Grace. She asked, "Did you tell me to call Matt's family?"

"I said that it would be a good idea. Matt has had three grand mal seizures in rapid succession with no prior history. It's unprecedented. I think you should let his family know."

"Okay, I'll do that. Can I see him?"

"We have him sedated. He should wake up in a couple of hours."

Grace walked into Matt's hospital room and sat in the reclining chair. She pulled out her phone and searched for Matt's parents' number. Then she remembered she didn't have it in this phone. She would have to go home to call them. She went out to the nurse's station and talked to the nurse there. She let her know that she had to run home for a little bit, but if Matt woke up, please tell him she would be back soon.

When Grace arrived home, she sat and contemplated for a moment how to break the news to his parents. She settled on the direct approach and would fill in the gaps when they got here. Witness security be damned. His parents would be staying with her at their home.

The burner phone in Roger Wilson's pocket vibrated just as he and Mary Wilson were sitting down for lunch.

"It's Matt," he announced as he answered the phone. "Hi, son!"

"Hi, Dad, it's Grace."

"Oh, Grace, honey, how are you?"

"I'm afraid I have some bad news. Matt has had a series of seizures and is in the hospital in critical condition. His doctor thinks you guys should come soon. He doesn't know…"

Grace choked up and couldn't get the last part out.

Roger said, "Grace, we will be there as soon as possible. We'll get a flight right away and let you know when we arrive. We'll take a cab to the hospital."

Grace gave them the name of the hospital but not the room number because they were moving Matt into the ICU. She would let them know when they landed where to come.

43

....

THERE WAS A FLIGHT OUT of Tacoma in less than two hours, and the Wilsons made sure they were on it. They landed at San Francisco International Airport two hours later. Within five hours from Grace's call, they were at UCSF Medical Center. They had called Grace from the cab and got the room number.

Roger and Mary went straight to ICU and asked to see their son, Matt Wilson. But there was no Matt Wilson in ICU. Grace saw them at the nurse's station just outside ICU and went out to get them. They shared an emotional embrace. Grace walked Roger and Mary into the ICU.

"Prepare yourself. They just intubated him because he wasn't breathing very well."

When they entered the room, Mary lost it and buried her head into Roger's chest. Roger looked at his son and nearly lost it himself. He pulled Grace into his other arm and held both of them close. Grace felt love, acceptance, and comfort form Matt's dad.

They all sat down, and Grace filled them in on the past three seizures. She apologized for not calling them when Matt had the first seizure. But Matt didn't want to worry them if it was going to be a one-and-done as he called it.

Roger said that sounded like Matt. He never wanted to worry them.

The three of them sat and chatted for an hour while Matt slept, the breathing tube working rhythmically in the background. Roger told Grace how Matt called them the day he and Grace got married.

"Dad, it's me. Guess what?"

"What's up, son?"

"I'm getting married tonight. Before you get all upset because you're not here, let me explain."

"I'm listening."

"There's this woman I work with, one of the models, and she is being forced to do awful things with the company's clients. If she doesn't comply, they have threatened to kill her family. If she tries to escape, they will kill her."

"Son, this sounds like a serious situation. You should let the authorities handle this and don't get all tangled up and get yourself killed too."

"That's just it, Dad, I am working with the authorities. We're getting married tonight, then taking the Concord to New York City where US witness security will take over. I won't be able to contact you or talk to you for a long while. I wanted to let you know that I'm okay, and everything is going to be fine."

"Son, do you love her?"

"She's my best friend, Dad. I gotta go. I'll call as soon as I can."

"That was a whirlwind couple of days," said Grace. "It was over six months before I saw Matt again."

Grace called her twin, Kae. "Matt has had two more seizures, and the last one he hasn't woken up from. His doctors think that the seizures have been related to a stroke or something. It's been five days, and he hasn't woken up yet. I'm really scared, Kae."

"Oh, Grace, I am so sorry. Do you want me to come be with you?"

"I would love to have you here, but it's not possible. You have Addie to take care of, and Jon-Pierre has the studio to run. I'm just freakin' out. I'm completely scared I'm going to lose Matt. I have a very bad feeling about this."

"I can hear it in your voice. Really, I can get Jon-Pierre's parents to watch Addie during the day, and I can come to wherever you are now."

"Let me see how things go this next week. I'll give you a call next week."

"What are the doctors saying now?"

"They say that whatever has happened, Matt's brain is fighting to recover. That's why he is in the coma. His brain isn't well enough to allow him to be conscious. They put a breathing tube in because he wasn't breathing well."

"This sounds like a wait-and-see situation for sure. Listen, Jon-Pierre and I will say a prayer for Matt tonight."

"What, have you guys gotten religion or something?" Grace said sarcastically.

"Not exactly, we decided to go to church while Addie is growing up because we think it would be good for her."

"A lot of good it did us," Grace muttered.

"Ya, I know," said Kae, "but we found a church that is different than what we went to at the Catholic church. It is much more modern. The pastor uses English, and everything is easier to understand. They have an excellent band and what they call a worship team. I mean it is really great. We love going now."

"Well, good luck with all that. After everything I've been through, I find it very hard to believe there is a God who gives a hoot about people. If he is there, then where was he when I was going through hell on earth with the Farinis?" Grace asked.

"I don't know enough to even try to answer that. All I know is that we feel really good when we've gone to church."

"Like I said, good luck with that. If you believe God gives a hoot about Matt, then by all means say a prayer for him. I know that Matt would appreciate it."

"On a happier note," said Kae, "I'm pregnant! I just found out last week. We're due in September. Addie will be eighteen months old by the time this one is born.

"Congratulations! Guess what?"

"What? Are you pregnant too?"

"As a matter of fact, yes, I am. I found out at the same time Matt was having this last seizure that put him in a coma. I haven't even been able to tell him. I know he will be so excited."

"Congratulations to you too then. When are you due?"

"September 9th."

"Oh wow, I'm due September 10th."

"We're going to have our kids grow up together."

"Speaking of that, I want to ask you, if something were to happen to me and Jon-Pierre, would you and Matt take our children and raise them?"

"Of course! You don't even have to ask me that. You know we will."

"Actually, I do have to ask because we have to put it into our written wills."

"Oh, okay. Ya, we would be honored. Can I count on you guys for the same thing?"

"Of course. Hey, I've got someone knocking at my door. I've got to go. Love you, 'bye."

And that ended that conversation.

44

· ·

WHEN JON-PIERRE ARRIVED HOME FROM work, he spent twenty minutes playing with Addie so Kae could finish dinner preparation. They sat down to eat as a family. Kaelynn fed Addie while trying to eat her own meal.

Kae brought up the conversation she had today with Grace. It was still so hard to call her twin by the new name. She started, "I got a phone call from Grace today. Matt has had two more seizures, and he is in a coma. It doesn't look to good," Kae said with emotion in her voice.

"Oh, no," replied Jon-Pierre. "Do we need to go to...ah... wherever they are and be with her? I could get my parents to watch Addie."

"I was wondering the same thing, but Grace said she wanted to wait another week to see how things went. She didn't sound good at all, Jon-Pierre. I mean, I know she is strong and all, but she has already been through so much, and now this."

"Oh, and guess what," she continued. "She's pregnant too."

"What do you mean too?"

"I mean, we are both pregnant! Our babies are due one day apart, hers on September 9th and ours on September 10th."

"How long have you known you are pregnant?"

"Since yesterday. Are you mad?"

"No, it just seems like a funny way of telling me, that's all."

Jon-Pierre finished his meal and took his dishes to the kitchen. He rinsed them and placed them in the dishwasher, then went to the living room and turned on the TV.

Kaelynn could tell that he was agitated. She just didn't know if it was about Matt being in a coma or her being pregnant.

Kae cleaned up the baby and took her into the living room to play. She returned to the kitchen to begin cleaning up the dishes, something Jon-Pierre usually helped with. She finished the dishes and went into the laundry room to continue folding a load she had taken out of the dryer before dinner.

After Kae finished folding the laundry and putting it away, she went to get Addie for her bath. Jon-Pierre didn't say a word to her; he just kept watching TV. Kae looked at him while she picked up Addie. It seemed he wasn't really watching the TV but rather just looking at the screen.

Addie's bath was usually a quick affair, but tonight, Kae took her time in order to give Jon-Pierre space to process his feelings. Whatever he was brooding about, she didn't want to interrupt until he was ready to talk. She had made that mistake before, and it always led to a fight, something she wasn't interested in tonight.

Addie went down easily. Kaelynn was glad of that. Then she went to take her own shower. Jon-Pierre new she was avoiding conversation with him. He couldn't blame her. He needed some time to process the two bombs she had dropped at dinner: Matt in a coma and her pregnant. He wondered if she had planned to gloss over the fact that she was pregnant again like it sounded. And now she was in the shower.

Jon-Pierre knew they needed to talk through this tonight before they went to sleep. He wondered if Kaelynn was scared to tell him she was pregnant. Addie was nine months old now. They had agreed to wait for a year to get pregnant again to allow the studio to become more stable.

Jon-Pierre turned off the TV and went to their bedroom. Kaelynn was just getting out of the shower. He started the conversation by saying, "So, you're pregnant."

"Yes, I know it's sooner than we had planned."

"Ya, quite a bit sooner. I thought we had agreed on waiting for the studio to be at least a year old before we had another baby."

"Yes, we did. But that's only three months away. Don't you think the studio is solid enough yet?"

"Yes, I do. It's standing solidly on its own. But it would have been nice if we had talked about that before you got pregnant."

"You make it sound like I did this on purpose." Kaelynn was towel-drying her hair. "I promise you I did not."

"You mean you didn't stop using birth control or decide not to use it a couple of times?"

"No! Of course not!" Kaelynn sounded hurt.

"You mean this is another surprise pregnancy for both of us."

"Do you really think I would do this behind your back on purpose?"

"I don't know, I guess I'm just shocked at the timing...and at the news about Matt. That was two big whoppers at dinner."

"I'm sorry. I have my hands so full with Addie these days, it's hard to find a good time to really talk anymore."

"And yet we have another one on the way now. It doesn't look like it's going to get much better any time soon, does it?"

"You're unhappy that I am pregnant."

"No, I wouldn't say unhappy. I'm not ecstatic about it."

"We don't have a choice now."

"You promise you didn't do this on purpose?"

"No! Jon-Pierre, I did not."

Jon-Pierre knew he had struck a nerve with Kae because she called him by his given name.

"Well, then, I guess this is God's timing for us, just like Addie was definitely God's timing."

"I'll be honest, baby, I was very nervous telling you about it. I was afraid you would be mad."

"Come here," he said as he pulled her into his arms. "I'm not mad at you. I'm just in a little bit of shock." He ran his hands through her damp hair. He looked at her face and kissed her on the lips. "I love you so much. If this is God's timing for us, then I will adjust and eventually be able to be happy. Are you happy about it?"

"To be honest, I was shocked too. It doesn't make any sense to me. If birth control isn't going to work like it should, we could end up with a whole bunch of babies."

"I suppose I will have to start using condoms as well. We're zero for two, aren't we?"

"I wouldn't say that. I wouldn't trade Addie for anything in the world."

"Neither would I," said Jon-Pierre. "What about Grace and Matt? That doesn't sound good at all. Do you want to go be with her for a week or so?"

"Yes, I would. But with the witness security, it might be the exact wrong thing to do. I would hate to lead an assassin right to her."

"Good point. Let's wait until Grace calls again in a week like she said."

"I agree."

"Can you feel her emotions?"

"Yes, I can feel distress. She told me today she's very scared that she might lose him."

"Not good timing, is it?"

"I don't think any time would be."

Jon-Pierre hugged Kaelynn tighter and apologized for his reaction earlier to the news about the baby.

* * * * *

Dr. Swanson came by on his rounds and greeted Matt's parents. He gave them all an update on Matt's condition. He said the breathing tube ensured that Matt would make it through the night. He said that it was a mild form of life support at the moment. He encouraged them all to go home and get some rest tonight.

Roger, Mary, and Grace thanked the doctor. But no one would be going home tonight. If something happened or Matt woke up, they wanted to be here.

Matt's room had a comfortable recliner and a fold-out futon. Roger took the recliner, Mary the futon, and Grace curled up on the bed with Matt. It wasn't a restful night. The nurses came in every hour and took Matt's vital signs even though they were being monitored nonstop at the nurse's station.

Grace dozed in and out of sleep all night. Morning came streaming through the window and woke Grace, Roger, and Mary. They were stiff and sore from the night.

At 7:00 a.m., Dr. Swanson came in to check on Matt. He was stable but not improved.

"What does that mean, Doctor?" Grace asked.

"It means he's stable enough to move out of ICU, but he will be staying in the hospital obviously until he regains consciousness."

That was some good news anyway. Grace talked Matt's parents into going downstairs to the cafeteria to get something to eat. They hadn't eaten dinner last night, and she could hear stomachs growling, hers included.

It was then that she remembered the baby. Should she tell Roger and Mary? No, not yet. Matt deserved to know first. For now, it would be her own private miracle.

Days went by, and Matt didn't wake up. After a week, Roger and Mary had to return home to La Conner, Washington, leaving Grace alone.

Grace drove them to the airport. They shared a tearful good-bye. Grace watched their plane take off until it was out of site. Then she drove back to the hospital.

Weeks went by, and there was no change. Matt was officially in a coma with a machine helping him to breathe.

In an attempt to become even closer to Matt, Grace brought his Bible to the hospital and read to him every day. She had no idea where to start, so she started where you start every book, at the beginning.

* * * * *

One morning while going through the mail at the house, she saw a postcard from the church Matt had started going to. She picked it up. It was an invitation to a Sunday service. It even had a convenient map on it to show how to get there. Grace started to throw it away but had that same strange feeling she had when she left her handbag and keys at her flat in London the night she and Matt got married. She set it aside.

The following Sunday, Grace Adams went to church for the first time in fifteen years. It wasn't a large church, maybe two hundred people. It was quite different from Catholic mass. Everyone sang the same songs together. The priest didn't wear robes or even a collar. He spoke in plain English, not Latin. She actually understood what he was talking about.

After service, Pastor Bill Charmaine introduced himself to Grace. She introduced herself back in her now perfect English accent.

"Oh, so you are Matt Adam's Grace?"

"Yes, that would be me."

"Where is Matt? Is he off working on an exotic location somewhere?"

Grace swallowed hard. It had never occurred to her to let the people at Matt's church know about his seizures.

Grace started, "Did you know that Matt had a seizure a few months back?"

Pastor Bill turned suddenly serious. "Yes, he came by, and we talked at length about it. He was very concerned that it might happen again. Mostly he was concerned about you and what would happen to you if something happened to him."

"Matt has had three grand mal seizures, and he is in a coma. I'm sorry that I didn't think to let you know here at the church."

"That's understandable. I'm sure you have had your hands full. What hospital is he in? If you don't mind, I would like to visit and pray with him."

"I'm sure that Matt would like that." Grace gave him the details and said that she enjoyed the service today, unlike any other she had ever been to.

That afternoon, Grace called Matt's parents to tell them they were going to be grandparents. They were ecstatic. They wanted to help get ready for the baby in any way they could. Mary planned to come to the city and help Grace shop for a crib and changing table and all the other necessary things for the coming baby. But still there was no change with Matt.

Matt had been in a coma for four months. Every day Grace sat at his bedside talking and reading to him. She told him about the baby, of course. She asked him about baby names for a girl or a boy. She talked about what she had been reading in the Bible to him. It was all quite strange and awkward to her.

Pastor Bill started coming by once a week on a regular basis. He would talk with Grace, and she would ask him questions about what she was reading in the Bible or about something from last Sunday's service. Grace realized she had a lot to learn about Matt's God. She told Pastor Bill that Matt's God was quite different from the God she was taught about growing up.

Pastor Bill always prayed with Grace and Matt at each visit, always asking for God to heal Matt and bring him back to consciousness. But each week passed with no change.

Matt was a mess of tubes. He had a tube to help him breathe, another to feed him, and others that fed medicine into him. Grace was used to it by now. Roger and Mary came down as often as they could. When they did, Grace made sure that she went home those nights so the Wilsons could get some real rest.

At the end of the fifth month of Matt being in a coma and Grace's pregnancy, Dr. Swanson told Grace that Matt might never wake up, and she should prepare herself for that possibility. Grace was five months pregnant and showing by now. All the hospital staff knew she was pregnant, and their hearts went out to her. Would her husband ever wake up and know that he was going to be a father? They all thought her situation was so tragic.

Grace tried to stay positive and upbeat every day when she came to the hospital. But she had started to notice that Matt wasn't looking as good. He had lost so much weight. The daily physical therapy kept his muscles from atrophy, but Grace was wondering if he would ever use them again. She hated these thoughts, but they were pressing in on her more and more.

Grace told Pastor Bill what Dr. Swanson had said about preparing for the worst. She asked him how preparing for the worst worked with faith?

"That is a really tough question," he said, "one that I don't have a very good answer for. Faith is believing in something that we cannot see. But here in the natural world, we do have to face some facts.

Will Matt wake up? I don't know. In the meantime, you have to prepare to bring this child into the world, that's a fact. And you have to prepare to be a single mother if Matt continues in the coma, that is another fact. Matt may wake up and be able to come home and be a fantastic father. But I don't know that for a fact. Does that even make any sense to you?"

"Yes, actually it makes a whole lot of sense. I never planned to be a single parent."

"I'm sure you didn't. How long did you and Matt know you were expecting when he went into the coma?"

"I never got the chance to tell him. He was having the seizure at the same time I found out I was pregnant. I still don't know if he's aware. You know he had been praying for a baby for over a year."

"Oh, Grace, I'm sorry."

45

A WEEK AND A HALF went by before Kaelynn heard from Grace again. Kae's burner phone rang while she was feeding Addie lunch. Grace told Kae that Matt wasn't any better. She said that Matt's parents had just left after staying a week.

"How was it to have them there with you?"

"Great. They are both so nice. And as an only child, they of course dote on Matt."

"Did you tell them you are pregnant?"

"Of course. I wanted to wait until I could tell Matt first, but I don't know if that's going to happen." Grace's voice cracked with emotion.

"Oh, honey." Kae said. "Are you sure I can't come be with you?"

"I wish you could, witness security be damned. I miss you so much."

"You send me the place, and I'll be on the next plane."

"I can't, Kae. It's too risky. I'm sure Farini has people watching you just waiting for something like this. I can't risk it."

"I'm so sorry, Grace. This whole nightmare is just not fair."

"Tell me about it. And now Matt...I can't lose him now, Kaelynn. I need him."

* * * * *

Addie's one-year-old birthday was a joyous occasion for the Laurents. They invited several young families they had met at their new church. All the couples had small children like them, so they had a lot in common.

Kaelynn had joined a morning ladies' Bible study at the church. It was great because they had childcare for any of the ladies who had children. Kae was one of the youngest moms at twenty-one.

Kaelynn was learning a lot about the Bible that she had never heard growing up in the Catholic church. She knew the basics—Jesus was God's son, and his mother, Mary, was a virgin who conceived him by the Holy Spirit—but she never ever thought about what that actually meant nor had any priest expounded on it either.

At this new church, Kae was hearing words like "salvation" and "baptism." Well, she and Grace had been baptized as babies, so that part was covered, but she had no idea what salvation was. One morning at the Bible study, they read a verse from Romans 10:9 that read, "If you confess with your mouth that Jesus is Lord and believe in your heart that God raised him from the dead, you will be saved" (NLT).

Kaelynn was finally able to ask what it meant to be saved and why is it important. The leader at their table explained the Gospel to Kae in its simplicity. Kae replied that she had never heard of this at her Catholic church. But it sounded really important, so she wanted to be *saved* too. The leader helped Kae pray a simple prayer to confess that she had sinned in her life and needed Jesus to save her from her sin and eternal death and give her the gift of eternal life.

Kaelynn meant the words as she prayed them. Then the leader asked Kae if she had a Bible of her own. She did not. So the leader got one for her to have of her very own. Kaelynn took the Bible as the group's time ended. She picked up Addie and headed for home.

Once Kae got Addie down for her afternoon nap, she opened up the Bible and began to read in the book of Luke chapter 8 where Jesus was asked to pray for the little girl who had died. After he commanded the little girl to wake up, she opened her eyes and was alive again.

The passage made her think of Matt who was still in a coma wherever he and Grace were living. She didn't even know where in the world her own sister was living because of witness protection.

Kae bowed her head and asked Jesus if he would command Matt to wake up and heal him.

Kae's and Grace's phone calls escalated to once a week. Grace would call Kae just to talk. It was usually around 11:00 p.m. Australia time. Kae could tell how lonely Grace was. After all, she had only one or two friends locally besides Matt. Matt had become her life.

With a baby on the way, Kae realized that she needed to keep Grace focused on that. Matt may very well not wake up, but this baby was coming whether he did or not. Grace was ecstatic about the baby. From the time she was a little girl, she had always wanted children of her own, as did Matt. If he were conscious, he would be overjoyed.

But the coma didn't seem to want to let go of Matt. It had been five months already with no signs of improvement.

Grace called Kae one night. "Damn it, Kae, I just wish he would wake up! I want him to get better. Instead I feel him slipping away."

"I'm so sorry, honey. Please just tell me where you are, and I'll be there in fourteen hours."

"You know I can't do that."

"Maybe you could call the guy that brought us to the other place, and he could work something out?"

"Keith, no, we don't have contact with him anymore. We're on our own now."

"Unless your cover gets blown, right?"

"Well, yes. But I would probably be dead before they could hide me again. Kae, I don't think you understand what my life is like. I have to watch over my shoulder every minute of every day. I have to take one of eight different routes to the hospital every day just be sure I am not being followed."

"I'm sorry, sis. I feel so desperate to be with you right now."

"I know. I feel it too."

"And I feel your depression and sorrow."

"Do you still go to that church you were telling me about?"

"Yes, we do, why?"

"I've been going to Matt's church for a couple of months now. His pastor comes once a week to check in on Matt and pray with us both."

"And you don't object?"

"No actually, I've been going to Matt's church on Sundays myself. I understand what you've been saying about the pastor talking and explaining things in plain English."

Grace could feel the tug at her heart to make Jesus her Lord. She had been coming to church for several months. Sure she still had a lot of questions, but in her heart, she knew this was right. There is a God, and He does care about people. She prayed at church the following Sunday morning and asked Jesus to come into her life and be her Lord. She sat for a long time and confessed all the terrible things the Farinis and their clients made her do. She confessed and asked forgiveness for allowing her own baby to be ripped from inside her womb, limb from limb, and thrown aside like trash.

When Grace had confessed everything she could think of, she heard the sweetest voice from inside her say, *My child, none of those things were your fault. You had no control over any of those situations. I absolve you of any wrongdoing. I am so happy to finally hold you in my arms and call you my child.*

Grace felt such a huge weight lift off her shoulders. She thought she probably lost literal pounds today by unloading all those heavy burdens and leaving them with Jesus. Now she understood what Matt meant when he talked about a relationship with God. It seemed impossible, but it clearly was true.

Later that day at the hospital, she told Matt what she had done at church that morning, and his heart rate went way up and stayed elevated for several minutes. The nurses rushed in and checked all the machines and the connections trying to fix whatever had made his heart rate rise. Finally, they were satisfied that the machines and settings were functioning properly when his heart rate returned to its normal resting rate.

Grace understood that Matt was using his heart rate to communicate with her. It was the only function he had any control over. She wondered if he would be able to answer a question. She asked him, "Matty, can you squeeze my hand?"

She felt the slightest of pressure from his thumb on her hand.

"Can you move your thumb up and down?"

He was able to move it back and forth but not up and down.

"Matty, say yes by moving your thumb and no by squeezing, okay?"

Matt moved his thumb back and forth.

Grace was ecstatic, but she kept this all to herself because she knew the nurses wouldn't believe her.

"Matty, I have an ultrasound tomorrow. Do you want to know if our baby is a boy or a girl?"

Matt moved his thumb signifying yes.

Grace tried to ask him more questions, but he appeared weaker and stopped responding as if he had drifted off to sleep.

On their next phone call, Grace told Kae, "I asked Jesus to save me and forgive my sins last Sunday. Have you ever done that?"

"Yes, I have! I am so happy for you, Grace! Did you feel a huge weight lift off you?"

"I did, gigantic. All the things that I had to do for the Farinis, I thought were my own sins to carry forever. But I felt like I heard Jesus say that none of that was my fault, that I was a victim of those circumstances. He forgave me! Kaelynn, isn't that amazing?"

"Yes, it is. And think about this, our sins are gone forever, like they have been magically painted over."

"No, it's better than that. It's as if our sins never happened at all!"

"Isn't it wonderful?"

"It is. Now if God would just heal Matt, I feel like our lives would be complete again."

"How is your pregnancy going?"

"Perfect, which is a miracle in itself. I wish I had a way for Matt to know about the baby. Maybe that would give him a reason to wake up."

"Honey, Matt absolutely adores you. You are enough reason for him to wake up, believe me."

"Ugh, I am so exhausted, Kae. I could sleep for twenty hours and still not be rested."

"You need to go home tonight and sleep in your own bed."

"I hate sleeping in our bed alone. I miss him, Kae..."

"I know you do. But think of the baby too. You both need real rest. It will help with the depression too. You know there are some studies that suggest that people in comas are aware of what's going on around them. They just aren't able to interact or respond. Tell Matt you're going home tonight to get some rest for yourself and the baby's sake. Tell him you love him and kiss him good night. You *need* to get some rest."

"Okay, I'll take your advice and go home tonight."

"I will be praying for you."

"Thank you. I love you, sis."

"Me too, good night."

"'Bye."

And they hung up. That evening at 8:00 p.m. West Coast time, Grace held Matt's hand and told him again about the baby. She told him she loved him, but she was exhausted and was going to go home tonight so that she and the baby could get some good rest. Then she kissed him, stroked her hand through his hair, and left for the night.

46

....

THE NEXT DAY, GRACE FELT the baby move and actually saw her belly bulge and move along with the baby. She sat down on the side of Matt's bed and picked up his hand. She laid his hand on her belly, and the baby moved again. At the same time, Matt's heart monitor beeped faster and continued at a faster pace for a minute or two.

The nurse from the station outside the door came into the room quickly to see what had happened. She also saw Matt's heart rate increase.

"What just happened?" she asked. "Did he open his eyes?"

"No, actually, I put his hand on my belly, and the baby moved."

"Oh, that was probably just a coincidence, honey. He doesn't know what's going on."

"Well, then what made his heart rate increase if not the baby moving? That's the only thing different?"

The day nurse placated Grace a moment longer, then went back to her station. That night, it all happened again. Grace put Matt's hand on her belly while the baby had hiccups, and his heart rate increased again. This time, the night nurse came in. Grace told her the baby had the hiccups, and she had put Matt's hand on her belly to feel it.

The night nurse winked at Grace and whispered, "He's there, Gracie, keep talking to him. He hears you, and he is aware of his surroundings."

"Then why won't he wake up already?" asked Grace in frustration.

"Because his brain is still trying to heal. His brain and his body have to be on the same page before he can wake up."

"This is all so frustrating." Grace broke and began to cry. It was the first time the night nurse had seen her crack in five months. She went to Grace and wrapped her in her big, loving arms.

"Honey child, you know the Lord works in mysterious ways, His wonders to perform. When your husband is ready to wake up, he will."

"What if he never wakes up?" Grace asked. "What if all these tubes are just keeping him trapped inside there? I just want my husband to wake up and share in the wonder and miracle of this new life growing inside me."

"I know you do. You just keep praying and don't give up."

After the night nurse went back to her station, Grace curled up beside Matt.

"I know you can hear me. I know you felt our baby move today. I miss you so much. I wish you would wake up, and I could take you home. It feels like you're slowly dying right before my eyes. I want you to know our child. I want to grow old with you. I know we said our wedding vows quickly and for another purpose entirely, but I mean every word of them now. I hope you know that. I need you to know that."

Matt's heartbeat remained solid and steady. Grace laid next to him and cried for a long time. She finally fell asleep and slept until 4:00 a.m. She woke up and went home to shower and change. Now that she knew he could understand some of what was happening around him, she wanted to be there as much as possible.

On the following week's phone call, Grace called Kae all excited.

"You'll never guess what happened."

"What?"

"The baby had started moving so much that I can see it on the outside. So I put Matt's hand on my belly, and the baby moved again. Matt's heart rate increased so much that the nurse came rushing in to see what happened."

"Oh my goodness! That's amazing!"

"Ya, the baby moved again about an hour later, and his heart rate went up again. He knows, Kaelynn. He knows we're having a baby. I'm sure of it now."

"That is so wonderful, Grace. I am so happy for you."

"I wonder what else he can do. I am praying too that he will find some way to communicate with me. I know he is still here, trapped inside his body, but he is still with me."

"He is, honey. That is so great!"

Two weeks later, Grace could see that Matt had lost more weight and didn't look as well as he had. His color was gone, and he was sort of ashen looking.

Dr. Swanson came by for his daily rounds about 4:00 p.m. He noted the same changes in Matt.

"He's not looking too good today, Grace."

"I know, Dr. Swanson. What does it mean?"

"It might mean that it's time to remove the breathing tube and see if he can breathe on his own. If he can't, well, then it's time to make a decision."

"You mean the life or death decision?"

"Unfortunately, yes."

Grace put her hand to her mouth to stifle a sob. She sat down in the recliner chair, and Dr. Swanson sat on the futon.

"We've known that this was a possibility all along. If Matt can breathe on his own, then we continue the feeding and the medication. Does Matt have an advance directive? Or did you two ever talk about what you would want in this type of situation?"

"No, we never had that conversation. But I think Matt would want to live if he could breathe on his own. I don't think he would want to be kept alive on machines forever."

"We don't have to make this decision today. Take all the time you need over the next few weeks. Talk to your pastor about it, and come to a decision you can make peace with."

47

....

AFTER THE ULTRASOUND, GRACE WENT to the hospital. Matt was having his daily physical therapy. She stepped outside and called Roger and Mary, Matt's parents. She told them about accepting Jesus and starting her new life as a believer. She also told them about Matt's ability to communicate for a short period. She asked if Matt had ever talked with them about final wishes and life support. He hadn't. She told them about the ultrasound and that she would soon give them a baby granddaughter.

After the physical therapy was completed, Grace told Matt the news that their baby was a girl. She told him she wanted to name her after Matt. Matt squeezed her hand to indicate no. She went on to propose they name her Madeline but call her Maddie for short. Matt rubbed her hand, yes, this time. He approved of her name.

Later that week, Grace invited Matt's parents to come down. She told them she didn't think he would last much longer and that the doctors were talking about removing the life support to see if he could continue on his own. Grace could hardly talk. She was crying and sobbing between sentences.

Roger and Mary hung up from talking to Grace and began packing immediately. They didn't know how long they would be staying but planned to stay as long as they were needed. And it was clear that Grace needed them more than she had let on in the past.

When they landed in San Francisco, they rented a car rather than having to depend on Grace for transportation. They went straight to the hospital. They stopped at the nurse's station to make sure that Matt was in the same room. He had been moved to a corner room with more windows.

They ask the nurse if Grace was here often. The nurse replied, "All day, every day. We have to make her go home and get some rest. She never wants to leave his side. It just breaks our hearts."

Roger and Mary made their way to the end of the hall to the corner room. There was Grace holding Matt's hand to her cheek and talking softly to him. They almost felt like they were intruding on a private moment. They knocked on the open door.

When Grace saw them in the doorway, she jumped up and went to them. The three of them wrapped in a big hug all crying together. After a moment or two, they moved on into the room.

"Matt, your parents are here, baby."

Matt's heart rate picked up a little bit. Grace explained quickly that meant he was aware of them and excited they were here. She stepped back to sit in the recliner while Roger and Mary went to Matt's bedside. The talked to him and told him he looked good and how excited they were about the grandbaby coming soon.

Matt's heart rate remained elevated while they talked about the baby and how proud they were of Grace and how well she was holding up with everything that was going on.

A couple of hours later, Matt looked exhausted again and had drifted off as Grace called it. Roger and Mary took this opportunity to get Grace out of the hospital and home to get some rest.

"Let's go over to your house, and you let me cook you a good old-fashioned country meal tonight. Then you sleep in your own bed, and we'll come back tomorrow. It seems like this way of communicating wears Matt out pretty quickly."

"Yes, it does," said Grace. "How about I cook you a good authentic French meal instead?" she asked."

"Okay," said Mary, "I'll cook country tonight, and you cook French tomorrow night, deal?"

"Deal," Grace replied.

The following week, the twins talked again. That night when Jon-Pierre got home, Kaelynn was chattering all about the events of the day with Grace and Matt. Jon-Pierre listened patiently and played with Addie. He knew that when Kae got excited like this, it was best to just let her get it all out. Then ask questions later.

Later that night when they had gotten Addie to bed and they were in bed themselves, Kae reached for Jon-Pierre's hand and put it on her belly. She asked, "Can you feel that?"

"The baby is moving!" he exclaimed. "That is so great. Life growing inside your own body. Amazing!"

"Yes, it is. I can't wait to see if this one is a boy or a girl."

"I thought you said this one behaved just like Addie and wouldn't let the ultrasound technician get a good look."

"Yes, but that doesn't mean 100 percent that it's a girl."

"Well you know my theory. Boys are proud and girls are modest."

"We'll see. I have another ultrasound in three weeks."

"Let's see, you'll be just about six months then, right?"

"Yep. How is work going?"

"Good, Lacy is catching on very quickly to the business side. We have doubled the amount of portraits we are doing each week, and we even had our first repeat customer two weeks ago. It's a husband and wife. They came back to get pregnancy portraits. That reminds me. We need to get some photos of you pregnant like we did with Addie."

"I don't know about that. It sounds like you are booked and may not have a slot to squeeze me in."

"Oh, baby, I always have time for you. You name the day, and I'll make a time for you."

"I wish Grace and I could get a twin portrait while we are both pregnant."

"That is a fantastic idea. It would be so cool."

"Ya, but it can't happen."

"What a shame."

48

....

ROGER AND MARY STAYED FOR three weeks then had to return home. Grace was sad and relieved all at the same time. She loved them dearly but was worn out when they left. She thought it might be the feeling of having to fill the silence with conversation while they were at the house, when usually there was no one there and Grace could completely relax. She didn't know. But she was sad to see them go.

That week, Grace had a heart to heart with Matt. She told him, "Matty, I'm going to be okay. I'm going to have our baby girl, and I'm going to be okay. I have our church family now and your parents too."

Grace cried softly, letting the tears drip down on their hands. "I don't want to raise our daughter by myself. I would rather you jump up out of this bed and get back to living with me again. But I know you're going downhill. You are looking more and more ashen each day."

More tears were shed. Matt tried to squeeze Grace's hand, but she stopped him.

"No, please let me just get through this. Please. I love you so much, but if you're ready to go home to heaven, I understand. I will be okay, I promise. Do you want me to let them remove the breathing tube?"

Matt rubbed her hand with his thumb *yes*.

"Do you want to try to breathe on your own?"

He rubbed her hand again *yes*.

"If you can't breathe on your own, do you want to put the tube back in?"

Matt squeezed her hand *no*.

By now, Grace had no control over the tears that were spilling from her eyes. She didn't want to lose Matt, but she didn't want this to be his life either.

Grace informed Dr. Swanson of their decision, and he made arrangements for her to talk to a hospice counselor before they would set the time for removing the tube.

The hospice counselor began to explain the emotional and spiritual end-of-life signs, which was fine, but not many of them applied to Grace and Matt.

Grace explained that Matt had a grand mal seizure and went into a coma immediately following and that he had been there for almost six months. The counselor asked Grace how far along she was, referring to her pregnancy. Grace explained that she found out she was pregnant at the same time Matt was having the seizure that put him in the coma.

When the counselor got to the "saying good-bye" stage, Grace told her that was where she and Matt were. She explained that most people scoff at her when she tells them that she and Matt communicate by him squeezing her hand in answer to yes or no questions. The counselor said she believed that to be possible especially when two people are extremely close.

When the counselor finished with the interview, she asked Grace if she had any questions. Grace wanted to know if there would be any pain in the process if Matt couldn't breathe on his own.

"No, what we use will make Matt calm and pain-free. He will eventually fall asleep and just won't wake up. In your specific case, Matt's heart will slowly stop beating. But we will keep him very comfortable. Does Matt believe in an afterlife like heaven?"

"Yes, we both do," replied Grace.

"Then he will most likely step through whatever portal there is between this life and the afterlife very peacefully."

Grace left the meeting feeling a lot better about letting Matt go. Now that she knew how it would all take place, she felt more ready to move forward. She didn't want to rush anything, of course. She would call Matt's parents and let them know when the doctor would be removing the breathing tube.

The end process could take a couple of hours to a couple of days depending on Matt and how much strength he had and will to live.

Grace called Kae two weeks later with the news that Matt was in decline.

"Kae, he's losing weight, and he looks almost gray. I don't think he's going to make it much longer."

"Have you been able to communicate anymore with him?"

"Yes, we had the life-or-death conversation. He wants to have the breathing tube removed. He says he's tired of fighting and just wants to go home to heaven."

"He said all that with a yes or no answer?"

"Ya, actually, I could sense he was getting tired, and I asked him if he was getting weary of fighting to breathe and live, and he answered yes. I asked him if he wanted to have the tube removed, and he said yes."

"What if you remove the tube, but he can't breathe on his own?"

"I asked him that too and asked if he would want the tube reinserted, and he said no."

"Oh, Grace, I am so sorry, honey. Are you sure I can't come?"

"I'm sure. I wish you could. I would kill to have you here. But you know what? Since I accepted Jesus, I don't feel so alone anymore."

"Isn't that something? I know exactly what you mean."

"I feel like I have a really close friend with me all the time now."

"Me too! When do you think you will remove the breathing tube?"

"I have to call Matt's parents first. I know they will want to be here to say a possible good-bye."

"You sound like you're sure he isn't going to live after the tube is removed."

"I don't think he will. He looks so tired and worn out, Kae. His skin is actually a gray color. Did I tell you that already? I'm sorry. I am so tired myself."

"It's okay. I understand. Well, actually I don't really understand, but I can feel your fatigue."

Grace began to cry softly over the phone. "I feel in some ways that I've already lost him, you know? I haven't had a husband for almost six months. But my best friend is dying right before my eyes, and I can barely stand it. I feel so selfish right now."

"Do you remember your wedding vows? Well, in your case, maybe you don't. It was in such a rush. But part of the vows are—"

"In sickness and in health, I know," cut in Grace.

"No, I was going to say the part about the two are now one! You and Matt are one now, and you are feeling that being torn apart. This has got to be worse than what I went through when you were missing and then they found your body. I can't imagine what you're going through. I wish I could be there even if just to hold you right now."

"Me too." Grace sobbed. "Listen, we've been talking way too often on these phones. I am in the process of getting two new burners for us. So I won't talk to you again until I get a new phone to you. Give me a week. Then, you know what to do, right?"

"Right. I'll check on it in a week. Will we have new numbers too?"

"Yes. I better go. The doctor is here now. Good-bye, Kae, I love you."

"Love you too, 'bye."

49

....

MATT'S PARENTS ARRIVED ON A Monday morning flight, and they insisted on renting a car again. They did not want Grace driving herself around during this emotional time especially being very pregnant.

The time was set for Wednesday morning at 10:00 to remove the breathing tube. That would give Matt's parents a full day to see him and to say a possible good-bye. Grace, of course, would be there as well. She had rarely left Matt's side since the morning he went into the coma.

Grace started to wonder what in the world she would do with herself if Matt didn't survive and instead passed away. She had not given much thought to a funeral or burial, or maybe even cremation, which was a popular choice from her French culture.

She talked with the doctor about it, and he referred her to the hospice nurse who had come in to work with the family. Grace found out that Matt's parents had purchased burial plots for themselves several years ago. They could see if there was a plot nearby for Matt if that is what Grace wanted.

Grace gave the idea serious thought throughout that night and the following day. She gave Roger and Mary plenty of space with Matt while she sat in the recliner. She was glad to have them here for this crucial time.

After careful thought, Grace called Marty and Mitch Garrison. She caught them up on everything that had happened in the past several months. She asked them if it would be okay to spread Matt's ashes over some of their property because it was there that she and Matt really started their married life together. Marty and Mitch were very gracious in saying yes to her request. Again, their hearts ached for this young woman who had already been through so much.

* * * * *

A week later, there was a package in the PO box. Kae brought the package home and opened it. It was a new burner phone with a new number. Grace had included a small note that contained her new phone number as well as Kae's.

Kae dialed Grace's new number, and she picked up on the third ring.

"Hi, Kae. I see you got the phone."

"Yes, how are things going now?"

"Well, I have decided to remove the tube. That's what Matt wants. His parents are here now. They got to spend most of the day with him yesterday while I stayed home and rested. This morning, it's just me and Matty—" She broke down again and continued through her tears. "The doctors will be here at 10:00 a.m. our time to remove the tube."

"Jon-Pierre and I are both right here with you, honey."

Jon-Pierre got on the line. "Hey, Gracie, we are praying for you all there. I truly hope Matt pulls through. But if he doesn't, at least we all have the assurance that we will see him again when we get to heaven."

"I know, that gives me great hope."

* * * * *

On Wednesday morning, Roger and Mary told Grace to go ahead of them to the hospital. They wanted to allow Grace some private time to say her last good-byes to Matt. None of them knew for sure that Matt would pass quickly or more slowly. But they wanted to be prepared anyway.

Grace arrived at the hospital at 8:30 a.m. and went into Matt's room and closed the door. She wanted to be completely alone with Matt. She sat down on his bed, and he physically stirred, something she had never seen before, but he looked like he was in pain at the same time. So she pulled a chair over instead.

She held his hand while she told him how much he meant to her. She thanked him again for saving her life and ultimately introducing her to Jesus. She put his hand on her belly and told her daughter, "This is your papa, and he loves you more than you'll ever know." A tear slid down Matt's cheek. Grace kissed his lips and told him again she loved him.

It was 10:03, and Matt's door opened slowly. Dr. Swanson and a couple of nurses came in the room wanting to respect Grace's last few moments before they pulled the tube out.

Right behind Dr. Swanson were Matt's parents. They were all there and ready for whatever would happen once the tube was removed. Mary stepped up to the bed and kissed Matt on his cheek as she whispered, "I love you, son."

Roger stepped in next and kissed his son on the forehead and said, "I love you, and I am so proud of the man you have become, son."

Then they all stepped out of the way while the doctor removed the breathing tube. At first, Matt sputtered and gagged a bit. The doctor said this was a normal response. Matt seemed to gulp for air but slowly began to breathe on his own in a slow, rhythmic pattern. It wasn't a steady pattern; it was sort of start and stop and gulp and breathe for a beat or two and then repeat.

"What's happening, Dr. Swanson?" Grace asked.

"He's trying to breathe on his own. He's a bit of a fighter, isn't he?"

Roger replied, "Yes, he is. He's never been one to give up easily, has he, Grace?"

Grace let out a small chuckle and agreed with Roger, "No, he has always been a fighter."

"Well, let's let him settle into a pace, and we will see how it goes. The nurses will stay here and watch him with you guys for a little bit. I'm going to step out in the hall and make some notes in the chart."

Matt finally did settle into a pattern, but it wasn't good. His oxygenation was low, and his heart rate was dropping little by little. The doctor came back into the room to check on Matt and asked if they wanted him to reinsert the breathing tube because Matt wouldn't make it through the night at the rate he was breathing on his own.

Grace said no. She and Matt had talked about it, and that's not what Matt wanted. This was new information to Roger and Mary, but they respected Grace and Matt's relationship enough to honor Grace's answer. "Matt said if he couldn't breathe on his own, to let him go home…" Grace broke down. "He's so tired of fighting…he just wants to rest in the arms of Jesus…"

Roger pulled Grace into his embrace and held her. In a little under an hour, Matt took his last breath and was gone. His heart rate flattened, and his chest relaxed. Grace commented that he looked so peaceful. Mary and Roger were weeping, but for now, Grace's tears were done.

Dr. Swanson called the time of death and began the paperwork for a death certificate. The nurses patiently waited for Roger and Mary to clear the room so they could prepare Matt's body for transport to the morgue.

The nurses removed all the IV lines and tubes. They removed Matt's hospital gown and washed his body. They put him in an inner bag and tagged his toe with his name and date of death. Then they sealed it shut and put him into an outer black bag that was heavier material.

Dr. Swanson offered a clipboard with some papers to sign and also his condolences to Grace and then to Roger and Mary. It seemed odd to him that such a man wouldn't have had more friends who would want to be here. But there was only his wife and his parents.

Grace signed all the papers and gave the clipboard to the nurse. She pulled out her phone and called the crematorium she had selected and made all the arrangements for Matt's body. Between the hospital and the cremation services, everything would be handled. She would get a call in a few weeks telling her where she could pick up the ashes.

Next, Grace called Matt's closest friend, Tim, from the photography group and let him know that Matt had passed. Tim asked if he could helped plan a memorial for Matt. Grace said that would be fine. She could use the help. Tim said he would call her again in a few days.

50

GRACE HAD CALLED KAE EARLIER that morning and told her today was the day that Matt's breathing tube would be removed.

"Kae, if he can't breathe on his own, he'll die. And he doesn't want the tube reinserted no matter what. I'm afraid I'm going to lose him today."

"Hang in there, Grace. We are praying for you."

A few short hours after they hung up, Kaelynn felt an intense surge of sorrow and knew that Matt had passed away. He was in the arms of Jesus now, but she could feel Grace's sorrow.

A week later, Jon-Pierre decided to scour the Internet until he found a small obituary for Matt Wilson. It listed his current home as San Francisco, California. With a little more digging, he found a memorial service planned for a Saturday two weeks past Matt Wilson's death but for a Matt Adams, also a photographer from San Francisco.

Jon-Pierre called the church in San Francisco where the memorial would be held and asked the receptionist if this was the Matt Adams married to Grace Adams. Bingo. He had found Grace. He wondered if Farini's people could find her that easily too. He prayed for Grace's safety. He asked God to blind the Farinis to the Matt Adams information.

Kae wanted to go to the memorial service, but Jon-Pierre wouldn't hear of it. "You are not flying anywhere at seven months pregnant. I will go by myself. No one will follow me, not like they would follow you. So no, you're not going, and that's final."

Kae new he was right, that his reasoning made perfect sense, but his use of the words "and that's final" absolutely infuriated her. Who was he to tell her what she could and couldn't do? And that started the biggest fight of their four years of marriage.

"You don't own me, Jon-Pierre Laurent! You don't have the right to tell me what I can and cannot do! I am still an individual with my own thoughts and rights. Just because we are married and I am not working to bring in money doesn't mean you own me!"

"Making money and being married doesn't have anything to do with it. You're pregnant! For Pete's sake, and that's my baby you're carrying. I won't have you putting our child in jeopardy just so you can prove that I don't own you! Of course, I don't own you."

Kae stomped out of the room into their bedroom and slammed the door. The raised voices, and the door slamming woke their sleeping daughter. Kae opened the bedroom door and yelled at Jon-Pierre.

"Take care of your crying daughter!" And she slammed the door shut again.

Jon-Pierre went to Addie and rocked her back to sleep. He knew Kaelynn was very angry and thought it would be best to leave her alone for a while. Being pregnant sure made women emotional. But he had learned the hard way when Kae was pregnant with Addie not to bring that subject up. Whew, that was another big fight they'd had.

Jon-Pierre got on the Internet and purchased a roundtrip ticket from Sydney to San Francisco. He hoped he would be able to get Kae to drive him to the airport next Friday. "Maybe she'll have calmed down by then," he muttered.

"I heard that!" Kae called out to him. "You can just get your own damn ride to the airport. Since it's become very clear where I stand in this house."

"Honey, I'm sorry, I made a bad choice of words. I shouldn't have said 'that's final.' I should have let us talk about it. I know this is your sister we're talking about."

"My twin sister! There's a huge difference that you can't seem to get through your thick, dense skull!"

"Ouch!" he said. "Let's not escalate to berating each other, okay?"

"Why? Don't you like feeling like you mean absolutely nothing in this house?"

"Okay! I said I'm sorry."

"Well, 'I'm sorry' isn't going to get you out off the hook that easily, mister."

Oh, boy, thought Jon-Pierre, *she is beyond angry to furious.* He was in serious trouble here. He decided to take a ride for a while on his BMW motorcycle. He rode around for about an hour and decided to buy Kae a dozen red roses. He stopped at a flower shop and told the clerk what he was looking to buy.

The flower shop clerk came out with thirteen long stem red roses. She explained to Jon-Pierre that a dozen was just too easy of a way to say you're sorry. But thirteen roses said, "I've really thought this through, and I am truly sorry." Jon-Pierre bought the flowers.

At the same time, he ordered a large spray of flowers to be delivered to the church on the morning of Matt's memorial service. He ordered another beautiful planter to be delivered to Grace personally that same day at the church. He still didn't know her home address.

Jon-Pierre strapped the box of flowers onto the back of his bike and rode home, the long way. When he got home, he had been gone for over three hours. When he walked into the house from the garage with the flower box, Kae threw her arms around Jon-Pierre's neck and said, "Thank God you're okay! The news just reported a motorcycle-involved accident on the freeway, and the bike looked just like yours! I'm sorry I got so angry."

"No, baby, I'm sorry I was so insensitive to you. Here"—he handed her the box—"I brought you some flowers that are not even close to as beautiful as you are."

Kaelynn sat the box on the kitchen table and put her arms back around Jon-Pierre's neck, and they kissed.

"I forgive you," she said to Jon-Pierre. "Will you forgive me?"

"I forgive you," he said, and they kissed again.

Just then, they heard something fall from the table to the floor, and Addie began to cry. She had reached up to the box on the table and got her fingers inside it. As she went to pull the box toward her, her fingers caught a thorn on one of the roses, and the box came crashing to the floor and Addie crying big crocodile tears from the thorn.

Both parents went to her immediately, Kae pulling Addie into her arms to comfort her and Jon-Pierre picking up the roses which had scattered on the floor.

When they both stood up, Jon-Pierre took Addie and kissed her boo-boo while Kae put the flowers into a vase with some water. She asked Jon-Pierre over her shoulder, "Why did you buy thirteen flowers instead of a dozen?"

Jon-Pierre replied, "Well, a dozen says, 'I'm sorry,' but thirteen says, 'I've really thought about this, and I am truly sorry for the pain and hurt I caused you.'"

With that, Kae put the vase in the center of the kitchen table and went into Jon-Pierre's arms again and kissed him.

"I love you," she said and kissed him again.

"I love you too," he said and pulled both of his girls close.

51

THE FIRST FEW DAYS AFTER Matt passed were a blur for Grace. She didn't know what to do or where to turn. She finally called Pastor Bill to see if they could get together to talk. He came over to her home and met Matt's parents. They talked for a while about Matt and their best memories. Pastor Bill suggested that Grace have a memorial service for Matt so those who had gotten to know him over the past year would be able to gather and pay their respects.

Grace wasn't sure what the difference was between a funeral and a memorial. Pastor Bill said it was really a formality and suggested they call it a celebration of life instead.

That sounded much better to Grace. She found out from Pastor Bill that the church would help put the whole thing together. All Grace had to do was set a date and a time and help him with putting together some memories to share about Matt.

Grace was beyond relieved. She didn't know the first thing about funerals in this culture, and she wanted to honor Matt's memory in the best way possible. Roger and Mary agreed with Grace's plans for the service.

Jon-Pierre landed at San Francisco International Airport at noon Friday. He had left Sydney at 9:00 a.m. Friday morning, but with more than a fourteen-hour flight and the seventeen-hour time difference, only three hours had passed on the clock. It made the body feel very strange.

Jon-Pierre's body clock said it was 2:00 a.m. instead of noon the day before. He grabbed his carryon bag and went to retrieve his car rental. He called Grace's burner phone from Kae's burner that he had brought with him. Grace answered thinking it was Kae.

"Hi, Kae."

"Hi, Grace, it's me. I am in San Francisco. Would you text your address to me so I can come by the house while I'm here, please?"

Grace said, "I'm not sure that's a good idea. How do I know you're alone and not being forced to make this call?"

"I'm sorry. I didn't think of that when I left Sydney. I wanted to be here for the memorial."

"Is your wife with you?"

"No, we agreed she's too far along to travel this far. She stayed at home. Not without a fight, mind you."

"That sounds about right. Let me direct you to a hotel instead."

Grace gave Jon-Pierre directions to the San Francisco Marriott at Moscone Center. She then called Tim, Matt's photography friend, and asked if he would scope things out for her. She gave Tim a photo of Jon-Pierre and told him she wanted to make sure he was alone. If Tim was sure Jon-Pierre was alone, then he could have him follow Tim back to the house.

Jon-Pierre completely understood Grace's caution, but Tim did not.

When Tim spotted Jon-Pierre, he was entering the Marriott alone. He took a seat in the lobby that was in plain view from any entrance. Tim watched Jon-Pierre for about thirty minutes before calling Grace to ensure her he was in fact alone.

Grace asked Tim to hold the line for a moment. She called Jon-Pierre's burner phone and told him to sit where he was, that a friend of hers and Matt's would approach in just a moment. She then instructed Tim to go over to Jon-Pierre and introduce himself and say he was a friend of theirs.

Tim did exactly as he was asked. Grace told Jon-Pierre to describe Tim to her, which he did. When she was sure that Jon-Pierre was alone and that Tim in fact was the man introducing himself, she relaxed and told Jon-Pierre to follow Tim back to the house.

When they all hung up, Tim Said, "I've never seen Grace so paranoid. I wonder what has gotten into her?"

Jon-Pierre explained, "Grace has some pretty horrible exes in her past. She's very cautious to stay well away from them."

"Oh," said Tim. "I had no idea."

"Let's keep that between us, okay, buddy?" Jon-Pierre asked. "It would embarrass her to no end if she knew I told you that. Not to mention how furious she would be with me."

Jon-Pierre followed Tim through the city until they got to Grace and Matt's home. It was a beautiful home in a very nice neighborhood. Jon-Pierre would be glad to let Kae know that Grace was in a very safe place. After all, they only visited San Francisco for photo shoots, and the garment district of SF was not a good place one would want to live.

When they entered the house, Grace flew into Jon-Pierre's arms.

"I am so glad you're here. I could kill you, but I am glad you came. I told Kae not to come."

"I know, and I am so glad that you did. But you never told me not to, and here I am."

They hugged again, and Tim could see Grace visibly relax. He wasn't sure who this Jon-Pierre was, but he was glad he was here.

Then Grace introduced him. "Tim, this is my brother-in-law, Jon-Pierre Laurent, from Sydney."

"Oh my gosh!" exclaimed Tim. "You're the famous portrait photographer, aren't you? I thought you looked familiar."

"Wait, you know who I am here in San Francisco?"

"Oh ya, we can't wait until you open a studio here. Are you planning to?"

"Well, perhaps one day. But this trip is about being with Grace and paying my last respects to one of my closest friends."

"You're right. I'm sorry. I lost myself there for a moment."

"No, It's all right. I can see your passion. Maybe we will have an opportunity to talk before I leave."

"That would be awesome," said Tim. Then he excused himself and left.

Grace led Jon-Pierre to the editing studio where Matt did his work. There was a very comfortable futon in there where Jon-Pierre could sleep.

"Grace, I don't want to put you out. Please tell me, and I will get a hotel."

"Nonsense, you're family! Besides Matt told me all about how you and Kae embraced him as family at my memorial. God rest my soul," she joked.

They both shared a chuckle over that. Jon-Pierre started looking over some other work Matt had in process. "He sure had great subject matter, Grace."

"Thank you. I love his shots of the city. You know Tim, who met you at the Marriott? Matt was in a photography group with Tim. He was having so much fun sharing tips and tricks, as he called it, with them."

"Matt was never afraid to help a fellow photographer get better at the craft, that was for sure. I am the photographer I am today because of Matt. Would you mind if I said a few words at the memorial tomorrow?"

"No, I wouldn't mind. But for the sake of witness security, I will ask you not to please."

"Yep, for sure. I keep forgetting about that. I'm sort of caught up in the moment here. I apologize."

"No need to apologize, Jon-Pierre. It's my concern, not yours."

"Well, it is ours as well because you and Kaelynn are so very close. Do you know she knew exactly when Matt passed because she said she could feel your deep sorrow and pain?"

"I don't doubt it. Do you know that I know that you and Kaelynn had a huge fight about a week ago? I don't know what it was about, but it was a big one. I could feel her fury."

"How do you know she was mad at me?"

"She told me." And they both laughed again.

"Do you think there is time to make a photography slide thingy for the service tomorrow?"

"I will stay up all night for you, Grace. Anything you want that I can help with. That is why I am here."

"Thank you, Jon-Pierre."

52

THE MEMORIAL SERVICE FOR MATT Adams began at 10:00 a.m. Saturday morning. Grace had no idea how many people Matt had come to know in the year and a half they had been in San Francisco.

All eighteen of his photography group friends were there. Plus there were quite a few people form the church too. All the church staff were in attendance.

Grace was astounded to find out how many people in the church Matt had helped out financially. She had no idea he had been so generous. She realized there was a precious part of his life that he did not feel he could share with her because of their philosophical differences.

It was another aspect to mourn. Oh, how she wished she had come to know Jesus before Matt had the seizures. Why hadn't she listened closer to him?

Because your heart wasn't ready, my child. She heard the now familiar voice of the Holy Spirit.

The photography montage was well received, and it highlighted the gift Matt had for imagery. Jon-Pierre had snuck in a lot of pictures with Grace in them. She had asked him to exclude them. When they came on the screen, she elbowed him in the ribs.

"I couldn't resist," he said. "They show how magnificent a photographer he was. It's not my fault you were his favorite subject."

The pastor got up and talked about Matt's generosity and his giving heart with his time, money, and talent as represented today by the photography club's presence. He tied that into the generosity of a God who was exuberant to share his time, money, and talent as well.

How God had even gone so far as to give the life of his only son so that we could become sons and daughters too.

He also shared a story about how Matt had come by his office one day after he had the first seizure wanting to talk. Pastor Bill said he had a very full schedule that day, but he could see the weight in Matt's eyes and told his secretary to clear his calendar for the afternoon.

Pastor Bill said that Matt wanted to talk about his wife and his possible death from another possible seizure.

"*That sounds like a lot of possibles, Matt. What has you so concerned?*"

"*My wife doesn't now the Lord. She couldn't care any less about Jesus and God. She's been through a lot of pain in her life and can't wrap her head around a loving God allowing all those terrible things to happen. Frankly, I don't know how to answer her.*"

"*Those are tough questions. To be honest, sitting here with you, I don't know what I would say to her. I pray if that opportunity ever comes that the Holy Spirit will give me the words to say like he did for Paul about the temple to the unknown God.*"

"*It breaks my heart, Pastor, to think that if something were ever to happen to her that she wouldn't go to heaven. It's killing me.*"

"*You know, the Bible tells us to not be unequally yoked with an unbeliever for this very reason, Matt.*"

"*Pastor, I can tell you unequivocally that I was supposed to marry Grace. I can't go into all the details, but rest assured, I spent six months praying about it.*"

"*I didn't say that to reprimand you, Matt. I said it to explain that I too married a woman who claimed to be an atheist. My circumstances, like yours, aren't at issue here. I am telling you this because I understand how your heart is breaking for your wife. I can tell you that I love my wife with all my heart. I would give my life for my wife. But we were married for twelve years before she came to know Jesus the way I do.*"

"*I don't know when your wife will come to know Jesus or if she will, to be honest. But I do know the power of prayer. And I do know that it is God's will that she come to know him as Lord and Savior. What you and I don't know is if Grace will respond to the call of Jesus in her heart.*"

"I am happy to report to you this morning that Grace Adams gave her heart to Jesus and accepted his gift of eternal life two months ago in this very room."

The room erupted in applause.

"There was another reason for Matt's visit to my office that day," Pastor continued. He was scared that he was going to have another seizure and that it would take his life. He was scared of leaving his young wife alone in this horrible world. He felt a great need to protect her.

"Now I've come to know Grace, and she is not a damsel in distress by any stretch of the imagination. Grace Adams is wise beyond her years and a very strong woman. I don't know what Matt was afraid of or why, but his fear was very real. I could feel it in my office, and I could see it on his countenance.

"We did some powerful praying that day. We prayed for you, Grace, that you would come to know Jesus the way Matt did. And that prayer has been answered. We also prayed for Matt to begin to have peace, to put Grace into God's hands and trust him with her life.

"Grace told me that toward the end of Matt's life, they had found a way to communicate. That Matt could use his thumb to answer yes and no questions. She told me that she spent several days telling Matt that she would be okay if he was ready to go home. She told him that she had accepted Jesus, to which his heart rate skyrocketed and brought several nurses running into the room.

"Grace was able to tell Matt about their unborn child and even test some names with him. And she said he still had very strong opinions about what names he liked and those he did not. Didn't he, Grace?"

Grace nodded yes.

"But Grace also knows that Matt was not scared anymore when he made the decision to remove the breathing tube. And it was Matt's decision, make no mistake about that. Grace only fulfilled what Matt wanted. She asked him if he wanted the tube removed, and he signified yes. She asked him that if he couldn't breathe well enough, did he want her to have the tube put back in? And Matt signified clearly *no*. That is not what he wanted.

"I don't want anyone here today to tell Grace she made a mistake or she misunderstood Matt or that she was simply imagining Matt's ability to signify his answers. You weren't there, and you have no idea how hard this decision was for her. Grace could have ignored Matt's wishes, and he might still be alive today but only by machines breathing for him. But that isn't what Matt wanted. He was at peace, and he was ready to go home to be with Jesus in heaven."

At the end of the service, the pastor gave an opportunity for anyone who didn't know Matt's God the way he did to meet him today. He led a simple prayer of confessing sins and receiving the salvation of Jesus. After the prayer, he encouraged anyone who had prayed the prayer with sincerity to let Grace know during the reception.

The reception was held on the same campus as the church in a large room for that type of gatherings. The pastor made sure there was a stool for Grace to sit on during the reception line. He wanted to make her as comfortable as possible in her expectant condition.

Almost everyone stayed for the reception. There was even a couple from the photography group who whispered to Grace that they had received Jesus today. Grace was so very happy. She knew that Matt would be happy too.

While she was greeting people after the service, she got very lightheaded and passed out. Fortunately, Roger, Matt's dad, was there to catch her before she hit the floor. He had seen her sway a couple of times out of the corner of his eye and was ready to catch her.

That was the end of the reception line for Grace. They sat her down at a table and got her some food and water. She didn't feel much like eating. The water was quite helpful.

Roger and Mary let Grace stay at the reception for another hour, then insisted that she leave with them. They drove home and put her to bed to rest. It was a very stressful day for Grace, but somehow, she felt closure. She was sure she wasn't through grieving; she doubted she ever would be. But the service today seemed to close a chapter for her. She wondered if her own memorial service was as helpful for Kaelynn.

53

ROGER AND MARY STAYED FOR another week, then went back home to Washington. Grace was now truly alone. There was no Matt to visit every day, no Roger and Mary to share memories with. She had her unborn baby to talk to, and that was all.

Jon-Pierre flew home to Sydney and had to take two days off work to recuperate. The stress of the trip, the service, and now the jet lag had caught up to him and wiped him out.

Kaelynn and Addie were thrilled to have him home. Kae made sure he was left alone to rest. Jon-Pierre had videoed the celebration of life service on his phone so Kae could watch it.

Kaelynn watched the video of the service several times over the first week. It made her feel like she was able to be there. She was not happy about Grace collapsing at the reception though. But Jon-Pierre assured her that they kept a very close eye on her and that it was Grace who wanted to stay longer. She said she felt closer to Matt than ever before.

Grace called her sister, Kae, on the burner phone and talked once a week. They stayed closely connected. Kaelynn was a life saver through these beginning weeks after Matt's passing. Kae suggested that Grace go through Matt's things that it might be therapeutic for her. Having remembered her old journal from the beginning weeks after entering the witness security program, she knew Kae was right.

Grace began to organize all of Matt's photos into groupings. She thought she would put together a nice big photo album to honor his work. She had no idea how to get to his photos on the computer; she worked with only what he had printed out.

One evening, Tim and his wife, Lucy, stopped in to check on Grace and see if she needed anything. Grace asked Tim if he could get into Matt's computer and print out some more of his work. Tim agreed and actually helped Grace arrange them for the photo book. Tim suggested that Grace publish a book of Matt's photography someday. He said the world would enjoy seeing Matt's work.

Tim and Lucy became good friends with Grace. They got together often for dinner. Grace asked Lucy if she would be her birth coach when it was time to give birth. Lucy was honored that Grace would ask her. She and Tim had three children of their own. She knew exactly what Grace would likely go through and wanted to be there to support her. At first, it felt odd taking Matt's rightful place. But in truth, it was a joy to step into such an important role.

There was still four weeks until Grace's due date, but she started having Braxton-Hicks contractions, practice contractions where the muscles of the uterus tighten for approximately thirty to sixty seconds, and sometimes as long as two minutes. It wasn't unusual, but Grace was having them for long periods.

Because Grace had been having these contractions for six straight hours, Lucy urged her to go ahead and go to the hospital just to be sure something else wasn't happening. Lucy and Tim came over to Grace's house to drive her.

When they arrived at the hospital and went to check in, the nurse told her to just go on home. It was only Braxton-Hicks contractions. Lucy stepped in and asked for the head nurse. Suddenly the nurse had a wheelchair and was getting all of Grace's paperwork in order.

In thirty minutes, they had her up to the maternity ward. Before they could get her into a room, they attached a fetal monitor to track the baby's heartbeat. The floor nurse recognized fetal distress right away and called for a doctor, *stat*.

Within minutes, they had Grace prepped and ready for an emergency C-section to remove the baby. When they got inside, they found the umbilical cord was wrapped around the baby's neck. Thankfully the doctor was able to cut the cord and deliver the baby before it was too late.

As soon as they got the baby safe, Grace's own heart started showing signs of distress. The doctors and OR nurses worked fast and got Grace stabilized. Then they were able to close.

With the extra complication Grace experienced during the surgery, she didn't get to see or hold her baby girl until the following morning. A nurse came to get Grace with a wheelchair and rolled her down to the neonatal ICU. Grace's baby was doing fine but was in the ICU because she was born four weeks early.

Grace got to hold and feed her baby girl, Madeline, for the first time. It was love at first site. She had Matt's little dimpled chin but Grace's nose and eyes. She held her baby and cried, cried for her loss of Matt and for her beautiful little Madeline in whom Matt's legacy would live on.

Jon-Pierre called Grace to let her know that on the exact same day, September 9, Kaelynn had their baby by natural birth at home because they couldn't make it to the hospital as planned.

Grace named her baby girl Madeline and would call her Maddie after Matt.

Kaelynn and Jon-Pierre named their second daughter Jaelynn after her auntie who had died a few years ago.

The babies looked like they could be twins, which made both mothers very happy. Jon-Pierre started talking about another baby immediately, but this time a boy.

"Whoa, slow down, mister," said Kae. "Let me recuperate from this one first, please?"

"I won't have to wait. The way you smile at me and get pregnant like that." He snapped his fingers. "We'll be expecting by the end of the year I bet!"

54

GRACE ADAMS LANDED AT CASPER, Wyoming, airport at 9:25 a.m. She rented a car and drove the now familiar drive to the Garrison's ranch in Worland.

Marty and Mitch were expecting her. They had flown out to California for Matt's memorial service and were such a blessing to have during that time. Mitch was like her father now, and Marty had taken the place of her mother a few years ago while Grace lived here in the early days of the witness security program.

Grace was caring two precious cargos on this trip: her daughter, Maddie, and Matt's ashes. She planned to spread his ashes across the beautiful Garrison ranch. It was here that Matt and Grace had truly begun their lives as husband and wife.

Grace didn't know if she had been a great wife, but she knew that Matt was a fantastic husband. She had tried her best to be a good wife, but her own mother's model was lacking. Her mother was self-seeking and self-centered, qualities that Grace did not want to aspire to.

The turn into the long drive up to the ranch came, and Grace turned the vehicle onto the dirt road. She remembered the long drive to the house with fondness. She was scared and uncertain the first time she made this trip, but now knowing the outcome, she knew the memory was a good one.

Mitch and Marty were out on the front porch when Grace drove into the circular drive. They welcomed her like the daughter she had become.

Grace stayed in the same room she had two years ago during her witness security time. It had become her room.

That night at dinner, Mitch and Marty were a welcome and comforting presence for Grace. Her in-laws had been with her through much of Matt's illness following his grand mal seizure and subsequent coma. When they left, the quietness and stillness of her home was deafening.

The following morning, Grace saddled a horse and started out for her main purpose, to scatter Matt's ashes. Marty was thrilled to take care of baby Maddie for a while. After riding for thirty-five minutes, she came up over the rise that led down to the stream. This place had become Grace and Matt's favorite on the ranch.

Grace stopped at the clearing that she and Matt had picnicked at so many times. She spread out a blanket and sat down in the shade. The horse was free to drink from the stream and nibble on the spring grass.

Grace sat the urn of ashes on the blanket. She pulled out her journal from the time spent here at the ranch. She recognized that almost every entry wound its way back to Matt. He had been such a good friend. Looking back, she could see what an invaluable part of her life he was even before they got married and came to the United States.

Now Grace could understand what others saw between them. Neither of them saw it back then. But Grace was grateful for every moment they had together before he passed away.

It was Matt who introduced her to Jesus. She had always focused more on God. God was a mean creator who didn't care about what happened to humanity after he created them. Matt had asked her once, *Have you ever thought about how many different species of trees and plants there are? If God cared that much about them to make no two alike, and he has made no two human beings alike, why would he do that and not care about them?*

Grace did not have an answer then. But it did make her begin to think.

And that same God sent his only son to earth to live and walk among humanity, to grow up and teach us the way to God, and finally allowed him to die the most agonizing death, crucifixion, all so that humanity could have a chance to be with him in heaven.

Grace now had a personal relationship with Jesus because of Matt. She was so sorry that she didn't get a chance to share her new life with him. She longed to have him sit beside her at church, to hear his rich baritone voice as they sang, to have him explain and answer questions she had from the sermon. But Matt was gone.

Grace thanked God that she knew she would see Matt again one day when she went on to heaven. But for now, she was here to scatter his ashes.

Grace opened her leather-bound journal to a fresh page.

Oh God, I miss Matt so much, sometimes it's hard to breathe. We didn't get to have very much time together, only two and a half years. I don't understand why you allowed him to die so young. It's just not fair, God. Why couldn't you heal him the way you did that little girl in the Bible and Lazarus too? Lazarus had been in the grave for three days, and you brought him back to life. Why do I have to live without Matt? Why does our child never get to know what a wonderful, amazing father she had?

A tear dripped onto the page and smeared some of the writing, almost as if to say that there weren't going to be any answers to these questions, at least not today.

Grace opened the urn and scooped out a portion of Matt's ashes and sprinkled them all around the picnic area they had shared on many occasions. She loaded everything back onto the horse and mounted to ride to the next location.

There was a jagged, rocky outcropping that they had ridden to often to watch the sunset. Grace scattered some ashes there as well as over on the other side of the ranch where the lake was.

It was after 3:00 p.m. when Grace rode back into the barn that day. She was emotionally exhausted and physically tired.

The scattering of Matt's ashes was complete. Grace had left a small portion in the urn to keep for herself. She would take them home and keep them with her wherever she lived for as long as she lived.

55

GRACE BROUGHT HER NEW BABY girl home to an empty house. Her in-laws, Roger and Mary, had stayed with her for a week after little Maddie was born. "She certainly looks like her daddy," said Mary, Matt's mother.

Even a short trip to the local market was a huge ordeal. Grace had to pack the diaper bag and get Maddie secured into her car seat, then drive seven blocks to the market to buy two bags of groceries. It would make a fine walk, but she hadn't got the whole stroller and groceries balancing thing down.

Grace unpacked the groceries and put them away. Maddie was such a joy. She kept Grace busy during the day, and when she slept, Grace would do cleaning around the house.

With Matt gone, there wasn't a lot of cleaning to do. Grace had been taught to clean as you go while growing up, so the house was always tidy.

It was at night that Grace felt lonely. Her bed was empty, and the night would close in around her. Most nights, she cried herself to sleep. She missed Matt so much it hurt.

Grace realized that she had never in her twenty-two years been truly alone. Growing up as a twin, you're never alone. When she was modeling and hosting guests, there was always someone around.

When Grace entered the witness security program in the United States after leaving England, she lived with Marty and Mitch in Wyoming. Then Matt joined her there, and they had been together since.

At night, the silence was deafening. She could hear street noise and occasionally a boat. There were the summertime crickets. But it was the silence that hounded her.

In the silence, her mind would race with thoughts from her past—guests that she was made to host for the Farinis, modeling jobs with her twin sister, the vacation on St. Croix that seemed like a lifetime ago, and the months of sitting in the hospital with Matt, praying that he would recover.

Often Grace would lie awake, tossing and turning, until Maddie woke up for her feeding. Even though she had a king-sized bed, she never brought Maddie into it with her. She used the gliding rocker that Marty had bought her. It was comfortable and perfect for feeding.

Maddie was an easy baby, until she started teething; then, she wanted to bite everything, including Grace. In a few brief months, Maddie was being fed by bottle.

At five months, Maddie couldn't get enough to eat and was waking up every hour and a half. Grace decided to start her on a thin cereal mix. Soon Maddie was sleeping through the night.

Roger and Mary came for a weeklong visit when Maddie was six months. Mary had a strong opinion about Grace feeding Maddie cereal so soon. But she warmed up to the idea when she realized how healthy Maddie was and how well she was sleeping.

56

GRACE SENT A NEW APPLE iPad to Kaelynn. This would allow them to FaceTime video chat. They would actually be able to see each other. Grace sent the iPad to the confidential PO box they communicated through.

Kaelynn got the iPad and turned it on. Grace had already set up her own contact info in Kae's iPad. She tapped on Grace's name and hit the camera icon. The tablet dialed Grace's number.

Grace answered on the second ring tone. Like magic, the twins were face-to-face for the first time in twenty-three months. The last time they had seen each other, Grace and Matt were still in Wyoming at the Garrison's ranch.

"It's so good to see you," said Grace.

"You too," said Kaelynn with excitement.

They spent forty-five minutes talking and catching up with each other's lives. Grace showed Kae around her home and vice versa. Kae's eldest daughter, Addie, who was now two and a half was so excited to see her aunt Grace.

Grace and Kae also got to see each other's babies for the first time. The girls, Maddie and Jaelynn, were born on the same day only a few hours apart.

After what seemed like ten minutes, it was time to end the video call. Grace said, "Let's do this again next week. Are you up for that?"

"For sure," said Kae. And they ended the call.

Grace had also sent an iPad to her in-laws in Washington State. They loved being able to see Grace and Maddie.

All too soon, Maddie and Jaelynn celebrated their first birthdays. Roger and Mary came down to San Francisco for the event. Grace thought she could feel Matt smiling down from heaven on this momentous day.

That night was especially difficult for Grace. Her heart ached for Matt; she missed him so much. And Maddie had so many behaviors that were all Matt. She was happy and sad all at the same time.

* * * * *

Time, it seemed to fly by for Grace and Maddie. It seemed that she blinked, and Maddie was three years old.

It had been three years since Matt had passed. There wasn't a day that went by that Grace didn't think of him. How could she help it, Maddie was a mini Matt, her natural behaviors, the little faces she made, even the way she objected when Grace told her to do something her three-year-old mind objected to. She was all Matt, and Grace loved it.

Grace was still attending the church that was Matt's before Grace gave her life to Jesus. She had met a lot of new friends there. Recently she had been invited to go to a singles' outing. Grace was nervous. She wasn't sure she was ready to call herself single. Widowed was one thing. It indicated that you had been married and were still off limits. Single meant you were open to dating relationships. Grace wasn't sure she was ready for that.

The singles' activity was a picnic at a local park. Grace decided that she would go just to see what the scene was like. Tim and Lucy, friends from Matt's photography group, agreed to watch Maddie while she went. They prayed she would have a good time. They had hoped she would start getting out there again and meet someone. She was far too young at twenty-four to decide to stay single the rest of her life.

Grace enjoyed the picnic. She played some volleyball, which she was familiar with from her school days. Then she watched as a bunch of people played a game she wasn't familiar with—softball. They were all having a good time. Grace couldn't figure the game out. Just when she thought she might be understanding some of it, the game was over.

She had noticed an attractive man playing, and he was very good at it. Whenever a person hit the ball with the bat, he turned up wherever the ball went and stopped it. The players kept referring to him as a pro, but Grace didn't understand why.

The following week, Grace decided to go to the singles' regular weekly meeting. The softball guy was there too. Suddenly Grace felt self-conscious about her looks, where she sat, how she behaved, everything. She felt like a silly schoolgirl.

When the meeting was over, the cute guy introduced himself.

"Hi, my name is Justin. Are you new here?"

"Yes, I'm Grace. I went to the picnic last Sunday, but tonight is my first meeting."

"Me too," he said. "Hey, would you like to get a cup of coffee before you go home? I know a great little coffee shop nearby."

Grace followed Justin in her own car to the little coffee shop. It was so close they could've walked. But Grace felt safer this way. She wasn't ready for a relationship yet, but a new friend, she could handle. They got their coffee and sat at a small bistro table outside. Grace found Justin easy to talk to.

Justin asked Grace how she came to try the singles' group. She told him that she was a widow with a three-year-old daughter. She told him she was tired of going out with couples and being the odd ball single one. She was looking for some new friends that could better understand her situation.

Justin told Grace that he too was widowed. His wife and two children had been killed in a car accident involving a drunk driver four years ago. Thus, he didn't drink and was a big supporter of anti "drinking and driving" campaigns.

Before she knew it, an hour passed, and Grace realized that she needed to pick up Maddie and get her home to bed. Justin completely understood and asked if maybe they could get together sometime again. Grace said she would like that, and they texted their numbers to each other.

When Grace picked up Maddie, she must have been glowing because Lucy said, "Oh my goodness! You met someone!"

Grace blushed and replied, "Yes, I met a whole bunch of new people, and I had fun."

"We're so happy for you, Grace. You deserve to be happy and have some fun."

Grace drove a very sleepy Maddie home and found herself humming along with a song on the radio. She hadn't been this happy in four years.

57

GRACE CONTINUED TO GO TO the singles' group at church. Each time that Justin was there, they would talk and end up out for coffee afterward.

Grace asked Justin, "What do you do for a living?"

"I'm a professional baseball player."

"Is that the game you were playing at the picnic?" asked Grace.

Justin chuckled and said, "No, that was softball. They're closely related, but softball has a soft ball that's larger than the smaller hard ball used in baseball."

Grace was completely confused and embarrassed that she didn't know more about the American game. Justin, seeing her confusion, jumped in and said, "I will be heading to spring training soon. My job takes me out of town a lot."

Grace could relate because of modeling but couldn't say so because of witness security. "My husband was a photographer, and he had to travel a lot also. I understand."

The following Friday night, Justin was not at the singles' group. He hadn't called her all week either. She hoped everything was okay. She texted him to see. Three days later, she got a reply.

"At spring training. Intense days and night scrimmages."

That was it. Grace didn't know what any of it meant. She finally Googled "baseball" and "spring training." The Wikipedia page was very insightful, but Grace didn't understand any of it.

Finally, she swallowed her pride and asked Tim if he would explain it in plain English for her. He did, then asked her why she was suddenly interested in American baseball.

"Justin, the guy I have been spending more time with, is a professional baseball player."

"You mean you've been dating Justin Jureau?"

"Well, we have been having coffee and occasionally brunch after Sunday service."

"Grace! That's dating! Justin Jureau is a shortstop for the San Francisco Giants. He is a big deal in major league baseball!"

"See, I still don't have a clue what you're talking about or saying."

"We need to get you to a game."

So Tim and Lucy bought season home opener tickets for the SF Giants versus Tampa Bay Devil Rays. They selected seats that would allow Grace to get a good feel for the game, one where she wouldn't get hit by a foul ball but could see the players up close.

Opening day came, and they made their way to Oracle Park. The traffic was usual for a baseball game day, but Grace had never seen it so congested.

"My goodness! Look at the traffic! Is it always like this on a game day?"

"Oh yes," replied Tim. "It gets worse when the game is over."

"Why is that?" asked Grace.

"Because coming to the game, people can get here an hour to an hour and a half before the game starts. They get some food and find their seats and watch batting practice and stuff."

"Oh," was all Grace could say. It sounded like a foreign language to her. Grace spoke French, Italian, German, Portuguese, and English. But she didn't speak baseball. She was about to start learning a whole new language.

The game started, and Tim basically talked Grace through the whole process for the first two innings. She was sort of catching on.

When Justin came up to bat, she recognized him right away. He hit a double according to Tim.

"What is a double?" asked Grace.

"It's when the batter hits the ball far enough to make it to second base, that's two bases, or a double."

"Oh, I see," said Grace. This game was very confusing.

By the end of the game, Grace's head was spinning. She asked Tim, "Will we be able to see Justin and talk to him?"

"It's doubtful," said Tim. "Unless he knew you were coming and wanted to talk to you. Otherwise, they players are carefully guarded for their security."

Grace hadn't even talked to Justin other than brief texts for over a month. She hadn't told him she was coming to the game.

Grace sent a quick text to Justin, "Was at the game today, my first American baseball game ever! Saw you play. Quite impressive."

She got a text back almost immediately. "You're here? Right now? Where are you? I'll come out and say hi."

"We are walking through a sea of people to the parking garage. I feel like I'm in a herd of cattle. Better that we talk later."

"Can I call you tonight?"

"Sure. Maddie is already in bed so call any time."

58

∙∙

JUSTIN PUT HIS PHONE DOWN with a big grin. He was going to talk to Grace tonight. He hadn't had the time to even text her lately. Spring training had been intense, and he was exhausted at the end of every day.

As Justin grew older, he was twenty-eight now, it took him longer to recover from intense training. He vowed not to take any more time off between seasons. He would work out, run, and take batting practice through the winter break.

He toweled off from his shower and got dressed. It was 11:00 p.m. He texted Grace, "Is it too late to call?"

"No, why don't you come over. I have coffee."

Justin's heart skipped a beat with excitement. He really liked this girl. She was beautiful, smart, a little reserved, but classy. He couldn't control his heart. He admitted to himself that he was smitten. Then his brain kicked in and cautioned him to take things slow.

A lot of good that had done him with Cassandra, his first wife. They were high school sweethearts who got married right after graduation. They had taken things slowly and carefully. Justin had a scholarship that he needed to maintain a B average to keep. So he worked hard at his studies and played ball the rest of the time.

Cassandra was on a cheer scholarship. Her grades were As and Bs, and it seemed she barely studied at all.

Just after their one-year anniversary, they welcomed their first child, a girl, named Cassandra after Cassie. By the end of their third year, they welcomed Justin, their second, a little boy.

During their fourth year, Cassie and their two children were killed by a drunk driver. It was a great tragedy. Justin lost his wife and two kids all in one day.

What nobody else knew is that Cassie was leaving Justin for another man, and she was carrying the other man's child. Justin was shattered. He didn't even know Cassie was having an affair, but he had been gone a lot and training quite heavily.

Playing in the big leagues was much more work and pressure than college ball had been. When Justin was drafted by the SF Giants, he and Cassie were so happy.

Apparently, Cassie couldn't handle the schedule of major league baseball. Or perhaps, she had always had a wandering eye. Justin didn't know for sure. But now, he second-guessed everything. What he did know for sure was that he really liked Grace Adams.

At 11:35 p.m., Justin arrived at Grace's home. She opened the door at this knock and welcomed him in. It was the first time he had been inside her house.

Grace showed him around the kitchen, dining and living rooms, then pointed out Maddie's room and her room. She passed right by another room.

Justin asked, "What's in this room?"

"Um, that was my husband's office. He did all his editing in there. I don't go in there very often."

"Oh," said Justin. "I would love to see some of his work sometime, if it's not too painful for you."

"Look around," she said and swept her arm around the walls of her home. "Almost everything on the walls is Matt's work."

Justin looked around at all the photographs on the walls. They were all stunning. Several of them had Grace in them as well. There was one photograph of Grace and a man Justin presumed was Matt. They were both smiling ear to ear and taking a selfie of themselves with the Golden Gate Bridge in the background.

Justin studied this photo. "Finally," he said, "I can see that you guys were very much in love."

"Yes," said Grace. She was a little emotional. She asked Justin, "Do you still get choked up when you think of your wife and children?"

"I do when I think of our kids, yes, but not Cassie."

"Why not Cassie? If I'm not being too personal."

"No, not at all. I will tell you, but you need to know that me and my parents and sister are the only other people who know this."

"Okay," Grace said hesitantly.

"Cassie was pregnant with another man's baby, and she was taking our kids and leaving me the day she was killed."

Grace's hand flew over her mouth. "Oh, Justin, I am so sorry! That must have been even more heartbreaking."

"I have to admit I'm still angry at Cassie. She didn't even have the guts to tell me to my face. She left a note on the kitchen table."

"Wow," said Grace.

"But my kids, yes, I get choked up when I think of them or talk about them. I miss them so much."

"Oh, of course," said Grace. "I'm so sorry for your loss."

"Ya, me too. And I am sorry for yours as well. How did Matt die?"

Grace told Justin about Matt's seizures and the six months in a coma.

"How old was Maddie when he passed?" asked Justin.

"She was born two and a half months after he passed away."

"Oh, wow, I am sorry."

"I found out I was pregnant at the exact time he was having the seizure that put him into the coma."

Grace told Justin the rest of the details about how they found a way to communicate at the end, how she had come to know Jesus because of Matt's personal relationship.

She told him how she wished she had come to Jesus sooner and had time to live together as believers. Grace said that was her only regret.

Justin could see the pain in her eyes. He heard that familiar voice in his head telling him to be careful and take things slow with this girl. She was fragile and still grieving.

Grace and Justin had coffee, and then he left. But just before he went out the door, he kissed Grace for the first time.

Grace was surprised by the feelings the kiss stirred in her. She didn't think she could ever have these feelings for another man.

But she did. Her brain sent up warning flags to be careful and take things slowly.

The next morning, Grace texted Justin asking how she could buy tickets to every home game. He told her he would take care of getting her a season pass and let her know the price before game time tonight.

Grace called her regular sitter to see if she was available. She was. Grace was all set to go to another game.

As the season progressed, Grace began to catch on to the game of baseball. There were still some obscure things she didn't understand, like how the umpire could throw the team manager out of his own game. And more disturbing to her was the flexibility of the strike zone. She noticed that the umpire would call a ball, but the next pitch would be in the exact same location, and he would call it a strike.

59

....

LATE IN THE SEASON, SF Giants were at home playing Miami. During the game, Justin hit a home run with two runners on base. Grace now knew the significance of this and cheered as loudly as the other fans.

In the last inning, SF was up by two runs. There were already two outs, and the batter came to the box. Everyone in the stands stood to their feet cheering for the pitcher to throw three strikes and end the game.

It was an exciting game, and Grace had enjoyed it. She texted a smiley face and two thumbs up emojis to Justin. Then a coffee cup and a house with a question mark.

Justin texted back, "See you at your house?" To which Grace responded yes.

Justin came over about an hour after Grace had gotten home. It had been a 4:00 game today, so it was 8:30 when Justin arrived. Grace let him in. She was just getting Maddie down to sleep.

Maddie really liked Justin. She had been going to preschool the past three months and was learning all kinds of new words and phrases. Some of which Grace did not approve.

Tonight when Justin came in the house, Maddie jumped into his arms and said, "You da man!" Clearly something she had learned at preschool.

Justin laughed, and Grace blushed. "I'm sorry," she said as she took Maddie from Justin. "She is learning too many phrases at preschool I'm afraid."

"It's fine," said Justin. "I completely understand."

"Help yourself to coffee," said Grace. "It will only take me a few minutes to get her bathed and into bed."

"Take your time," said Justin. "I've got all night." And he winked at her.

Grace's heart did a somersault as she carried Maddie into the bathroom. She drew her bath and bathed her more quickly than she usually did.

Maddie loved to splash and dump cups of water over her head. Grace washed her and let her rinse with the cup then pulled the plug and got Maddie out and wrapped in a towel.

When Grace turned to take Maddie to her room to dress her for bed, she found Justin in the doorway of the bathroom.

His eyes were misty. "How long have you been standing there?" she asked.

"Just a couple of minutes," he said.

He moved aside and followed Grace into the bedroom where she dressed Maddie for bed. Justin asked, "Is she already potty trained?" A little shocked.

"Yes," replied Grace, "since she was two."

"That's great," said Justin.

Maddie crawled into her "big girl bed" and reached for Grace to give her a hug and a kiss. She did. Them Maddie reached for Justin and said, "Daddy give hug and kiss."

Grace was horrified and blushed in embarrassment. "I'm sorry, Justin. I don't know where she got that."

Maddie looked shyly at Grace, then pointed at her and said, "Mommy," then pointed at Justin and said, "Daddy."

Justin said it was okay and leaned down and gave Maddie a hug and a kiss good night. When he raised back up, there were tears in his eyes.

Grace turned off the light and closed Madeline's door. She looked back at Justin who was wiping his eyes and apologized again.

"She's been picking up so much stuff at daycare."

"It's okay," said Justin. "I understand."

Justin followed Grace to the kitchen where she poured two mugs of coffee. She pulled out the cream and sugar for Justin. Her coffee was way too strong for him.

"Where did you learn to make such strong coffee?" he asked.

"Oh, I guess I just learned it growing up in France. My parents liked French press, and it is quite strong."

"You never talk about your parents, why is that?"

Grace told Justin about how her parents left her and her sister when they were sixteen to live on their own and finish their last two years of high school. He was shocked as most people were when they heard this.

Grace wanted to change the subject quickly. She did not want to talk about her parents.

"By the way, Jill at Bible study asked me if I would be willing to give my testimony sometime. What do you think she means by that?"

"She wants you to tell the group how you came to know Christ, you know, how you got saved. What your life was like before and leading up to accepting Jesus."

"Oh, all I could think of was when someone testifies in court, and I was very confused."

"How long have you lived in the United States?" Justin asked.

"Why?" asked Grace cautiously.

"Because you don't have a hint of a French accent until you are very tired, but you struggle with some of the American idioms."

"I have a lot to learn about American culture, I will admit that."

"So? How long have you lived here?"

"Why do you need to know that?" Grace asked defensively.

"No reason, I'm just curious. I didn't mean to offend you."

"I've lived in the US for almost six years."

"Wow, that's not that long. Losing your French accent must have been hard work."

"Why are you so interested in this?"

"I just want to get to know you better. That's all. You intrigue me."

"I was born and raised in France. I moved to London for work when I was eighteen and moved to the US when I was twenty."

"What did you do in the UK?"

"That's classified, I'm afraid. I could tell you, but then I would have to kill you," Grace teased.

Justin got the message that most of her past was off limits and changed the subject. "What do you see for your future?" he asked.

"Well, I've been working on finishing a photography book that Matt started before he died. It's an anthology of his work. I'm told it would be a best seller."

"Has that been difficult to work on?"

"Yes, very. It seems that I am in most of the photos, and that's hard."

"Ah, you were his favorite subject then?"

"Well, I used to be a model, and he was the photog on the majority of the shoots. And he liked to have people in his shots, so ya, there are a lot of me. It feels narcissistic to me."

"I get it."

"Anyway."

"You don't model anymore?"

"No, now that I have Maddie, I want to be here for her, not flying off here and there and leaving her with babysitters."

"Have you ever thought of a nanny?"

"*No!* I will never do that to my daughter! I want her to know that I am here for her, and I'm not going anywhere."

Justin caught the juxtaposition of Grace being here for her daughter and her parents leaving them at sixteen.

"I'm sure as she grows up, she will really appreciate that."

"I hope so."

"She will."

"So how do you live these days?"

"What do you mean?"

"Well, you clearly don't have a job perse, so how do you make money?"

"Oh, Matt had a large life insurance policy. I have invested well, and I am able to manage. He also had a policy that paid off the house if he were to die. So I don't have a house payment. That helps a lot."

"Sounds like Matt had a very smart business head."

"He did. I'm sorry, can we not talk about Matt, please? It's awkward."

"Let's see, we can't talk about your past. We can't talk about Matt. Maybe you want to ask me some questions?"

"I'm sorry," she said. "When I stopped modeling, Matt became my life." Grace choked slightly. "Now that he is gone, it's been very difficult to find a real purpose outside of Madeline. So you tell me," started Grace, "how did you get through losing your wife and children?"

"I threw myself into my career. I work out four hours a day, I run, and I take batting practice every day. And that's on top of working out with the team on the field and playing."

"You know what they say? All work and no play makes JJ a dull boy."

"Ah, but you see, I do play." Justin moved closer to Grace.

"Would you like another cup of coffee? I can water it down for you," asked Grace.

"I will take you up on that, and please do half water and half coffee. I won't be able to sleep for a week otherwise," he joked.

When Grace brought his coffee over to the island, Justin pulled her into his arms and kissed her. She let him hold her and deepen the kiss for a few minutes. She found she was kissing him back.

The feeling between them were electric. She wanted him. He wanted her. Neither had been with anyone since their spouses had passed, and their hunger was palpable.

Justin picked Grace up into his arms and moved to the couch where he laid her down. He lowered himself to her and continued to kiss her. He slid his hand under her shirt.

Before either of them could fathom what had happened, they had both shed their clothes and made love on the couch. When they were done, Justin pulled back and apologized for letting things go this far.

Grace was confused. "Was it not good for you?" she asked.

"It's not that," he said. "It's that we aren't supposed to go that far unless we are married."

"I'm sorry, I didn't know that," apologized Grace.

"Ya, it's my fault," said Justin. "I know better. But I think I am in love with you, and I just couldn't stop myself."

"I think you are pretty special," said Grace "I didn't want you to stop."

Justin lowered his head and kissed her again. Then he said, "We can't let things go this far again. It's a sin?"

"I didn't know," said Grace.

They put their clothes back on, and Justin sat on the couch next to Grace.

"What kind of religious upbringing did you have?" he asked Grace, raking his hand through his hair.

"Not much of one, I'm afraid," she said. "We were Catholic but didn't go to church really. I have so much to learn about the Bible and Jesus. I'm sorry," she apologized again.

"No, Grace, this one is all on me. You acted in pure innocence. But I knew better. We should pray and ask for forgiveness though."

"Ask for forgiveness? That was amazing, and I thoroughly enjoyed being with you. Why would I ask for forgiveness? I want to make love again!"

"But it's not right if we aren't married. Don't you see?"

"I guess not. I don't know if I am ready to get married again. Are you?" she asked innocently.

"I could, I would. If you would have me, I would marry you tomorrow."

Grace pulled back out of his embrace. "I don't think I am ready for that." Grace still didn't fully understand what was so wrong with enjoying each other.

Grace asked Justin, "Can you show me in the Bible where it says we have to be married before we can have sex? I need to study on this."

Justin turned to 1 Thessalonians 4:2–8 (NLT) and read,

> God's will is for you to be holy, so stay away from all sexual sin. Then each of you will control his own body and live in holiness and honor, not in lustful passion like the pagans who do not

know God and his ways. Never harm or cheat a Christian brother in this matter by violating his wife, for the Lord avenges all such sins, as we have solemnly warned you before. God has called us to live holy lives, not impure lives. Therefore, anyone who refuses to live by these rules is not disobeying human teaching but is rejecting God, who gives his Holy Spirit to you.

"You see what we did?"

"I do now. So let's ask for forgiveness."

Justin pulled her close to him again and prayed, "Dear Jesus, Grace and I have just crossed a line in our relationship that we should not have. We are not married, but we do have strong feelings for each other. Please forgive us for our sin tonight. Help us to set healthy, godly boundaries from here on out. In Jesus's name, amen."

Grace had to admit that she did feel better after they prayed together. She asked, "How do we set these boundaries?"

"Well, it might mean that I don't come over to your house at night."

"That doesn't give us any time to be together though."

"I know...will you marry me?" he asked Grace.

"I can't. I'm not ready."

"I know that I love you. Do you love me?"

"I think I do...but I have a whole lot of baggage, Justin. Things that you don't know about me. Things I cannot tell you. I just don't think it would be a very good idea, not yet anyway."

"Do you see yourself married at some point in the future?"

"Yes, I think I could."

"Could you see yourself married to me?"

"Yes, I could see that."

"Okay, then I'll give you all the time you need."

60

JUSTIN TRIED TO MAKE TIME during the day for Grace. He started coming over at lunchtime and eating with her and Maddie. They went to church together, and they continued going to the singles' group together. If they went out for coffee, it was to a coffee shop and in separate cars.

They did very well for the first few months. But it was getting harder and harder. Once they had tasted the fruit from the now forbidden tree, it loomed in front of them, beaconing them to partake again.

Grace decided one evening after taking a shower that it was time to stop wearing her wedding rings. Matt was never coming back, and it was time to move on.

This turn of events was not lost on Justin. He noticed it immediately. One afternoon while Grace was getting Maddie down for a nap, he snuck into her bedroom and took the set, putting it in his pocket.

Later that week, he went by a jeweler and used Grace's wedding set as a jumping off point for a set he intended to purchase. Having her set allowed him to order the exact size she wore and help the jeweler understand her taste and style she liked.

Finally, on a Tuesday night when Justin had a day off from play, he asked Grace out to a nice dinner, a dress-up affair he called it.

He picked Grace up at 6:00. She was wearing a classic *little black dress* with black high heels and simple classy jewelry. She took Justin's breath away. They had never been out any place fancy and therefore had never dressed up like tonight.

Justin held the car door for Grace. He drove them to the Top of the Mark restaurant high atop the Intercontinental building. The place had spectacular 360-degree views of the city, the bay, and both bridges. Tonight, there was a live jazz band playing.

They ordered fruity nonalcoholic drinks and enjoyed the view for half an hour before they ordered their food.

Grace ordered beef tenderloin medallions, au poivre sauce, with caramelized root vegetables. Justin ordered salmon vera cruz, scallop scampi. They thoroughly enjoyed their meals and were getting ready for dessert.

Justin ordered a classic French opera cake. Prior to getting to the restaurant with Grace, Justin had brought the engagement ring he had purchased specifically for her. He had asked the chef to put the ring on the top of the cake so it would be the first thing Grace saw.

The dessert was brought to the table and placed in front of Grace. By the time she saw the ring and looked up, Justin had gotten down on one knee. He looked Grace in the eyes and said, "Grace, I never thought I would ever give my heart to another woman as long as I lived. But you, you take my breath away. And you stole my heart before I even knew to be on guard. I want to spend the rest of my life with you. Would you do me the honor of accepting my proposal of marriage?"

Grace was overwhelmed. She was not expecting Justin to propose tonight. She didn't know what she expected, but he had completely caught her off guard.

She said *yes* and flew into his open arms. They kissed, and then he pulled the ring off the cake top and dipped it into her water glass. Then he wiped it clean and put it on her finger. It fit perfectly.

Cell phones were out all over the restaurant snapping shots and video of San Francisco's own Justin Jureau proposing.

"It's beautiful!" she exclaimed. "I love it, Justin! And I love you."

The following morning, Justin left for a three-week road trip playing at the Cardinals, Dodgers, and Marlins.

Grace FaceTimed Kae as soon as she got up. "Kae, guess what? I'm engaged! Ah!"

"To Justin, he finally asked you?"

"What do you mean finally? I'm the one who's been hesitant."

"Congratulations. Although I must say, I am not surprised. I've seen this coming for several months now."

"What do you mean?"

"Look, sis, you're not the sharpest tool in the shed when it comes to matters of love."

"What do you mean!?"

"Look how long you and Matt were in love with each other before either of you would admit it?"

"Those were very different circumstances!"

"Honestly, I am so happy for you!"

"Happy about what?" interjected Jon-Pierre as his face popped onto the screen with Kae's.

"I'm getting married. Can you believe it?"

"Congratulations!"

"Thank you. I would love to have the girls involved as flower girls and ring bearer. What do you guys think?"

"That would be so great!" said Kae. Jon-Pierre agreed.

"I'll keep you updated on dates and stuff," said Grace before they hung up.

61

JUSTIN BEING GONE ON A road trip for three weeks gave Grace a lot of time to process what had happened. She was engaged. She had never been engaged before.

Matt had basically kidnapped her one night, they got married, and caught a plane from the United Kingdom to the United States. Of course, these were all details that she could never tell Justin.

The fact that Grace would have to keep all her past life before the witness security program a secret from Justin bothered her. But her handler, Keith Hartman, was adamant. "The rules are you can never tell anyone, ever."

"But my husband?" she asked. "That doesn't make a lot of sense."

Keith said, "We've had numerous marriages fall apart and an angry spouse go public with the secret identity of the witness putting them in grave danger."

"Justin would never do that!"

"Ask any of these other witnesses, and they will tell you that at the time they revealed their past to their current spouse, they swore he or she would never do that."

Immediately, Grace thought of how angry Justin still was at Cassie. She decided not to rock this boat. Maybe when they were old and gray, she might consider it.

Grace resolved that she would never lie to Justin but would rather tell him that there were things from her past that she just wouldn't ever be able to talk about and leave it at that. Hopefully Justin would understand.

They were able to talk each night over FaceTime before Justin went to sleep. He asked her all kinds of questions like "What kind of a wedding would you like to have?" and "Where would you like to go for a honeymoon?"

To which Grace had no solid answers. These were decisions they needed to make together.

Grace began to scour the Internet for ideas. There were plenty. She started a board on her Pinterest account titled "Wedding." She began to "pin" all the ideas she saw that she liked.

By the time Justin got back to town, she had a general idea of what she wanted for the wedding.

Justin liked most of her ideas. The ones he wasn't too excited about or had no opinion one way or another, she tossed.

Justin asked all kinds of questions about inviting her parents.

She finally said, "*No!* I wouldn't dream of inviting them. But I do want to invite my in-laws and my friends from Wyoming, oh, and of course my sister."

"That's it?" asked Justin.

"Yes, that's all the family I have. Everyone else we both know from church and some from the team."

"And you're definite you don't want to reach out to your parents?"

"I'm sure," she said. "I haven't heard from my parents in over six years. There's no point in trying to find them."

"What are they doing again?" asked Justin.

"They are sailing around the world on their big beautiful yacht for the umpteenth time. At least that's what I think they are still doing. Besides, they would never be able to find me. But they might be able to find my sister, and they haven't reached out to her either. They don't care about us, so why should we care about them?" Grace asked.

"Did your parents know Matt?"

"No. They don't even know about Madeline. They don't know about Kaelynn's family either. I'm telling you, they don't care about us."

"When was the last time you saw them?"

"Kaelynn, Jon-Pierre, and I saw them when we were vacationing on St. Croix once about six years ago, but we didn't say anything to them. They didn't see us either."

"You mean you were both on St. Croix in the US Virgin Islands at the same time?"

"Yes."

"Wow, and you don't get postcards or birthday cards or anything?"

"Nope."

"That is bizarre."

"It is what it is. Did I use that correctly?"

"Yes, you did." He laughed.

62

GRACE CALLED MITCH AND MARTY to tell them she was engaged. They were beyond excited for her. She spent twenty minutes on FaceTime with them. She told them Justin's name, and they knew exactly who he was.

The call to Matt's parents, Mary and Roger, was a little bit harder.

"Hi, Mom."

"Oh hello, Grace! How are you, dear?"

"I'm good, thanks."

"How is our little Maddie doing?"

"She is down for a nap right now. I wanted to call you without her getting in the way."

"What's going on, dear?"

"Is Dad nearby?"

"Yes, Roger! Come here. Grace is on the FaceTime."

Both Roger and Mary's faces appeared before Grace on the screen.

"Hi, Grace," said Roger.

"Hi, I wanted to talk to you both. I'm a little nervous to tell you this, but...I'm engaged."

"Congratulations!" they both said in unison.

"Who is the lucky fellow?" asked Roger.

"His name is Justin Jureau."

"You mean the shortstop for the Giants?"

"Yes, Dad, you know who he is?"

"Well, I'll be. We're so happy for you, Grace. You are way too young to stay single."

"Dad, would it be asking too much for you to give me away?"

"What about your own father, dear?" asked Mary.

"I haven't talked to my father in over six years. I don't even know where he is," said Grace. "Besides, my parents abandoned my sister and I when we were sixteen."

"Oh, dear, we didn't know that. I always wondered why they weren't involved in your life."

"I thought sure Matt had told you guys."

"No, dear, Matt didn't tell us anything about your background. What we know about you is what we've learned by knowing you. And that is as it should be."

"Thank you, I appreciate that. Dad? Will you give me away, please? I want it to be you because I feel like until I have your blessing, I still belong to Matt."

"Sweetheart, it would be my honor to give you away. When is the big day?"

"We haven't set a date just yet. I wanted to talk to you guys first. We are thinking around Thanksgiving if you are available then."

"Grace, that's only three months away. Is there something else you want to tell us?"

"No, Mom, I am not pregnant. We only have four months between seasons end and spring training. November is in the middle of Justin's break. Besides, I don't want an elaborate wedding. I just want to be able to have the people we love there and a meaningful ceremony."

"I would have thought you would want a big shindig since you and Matt never got to have a wedding," said Mary.

"I really want a small wedding, Mom."

Roger cut in with, "You name the date, and we'll be there, Gracie."

"Thank you. I'll call you as soon as we settle on an exact date, but right now, we are looking at November 15. We still have to talk to Justin's parents about the date too."

Mary said, "We'll be ready for any date in November, dear."

Grace talked a little longer about Maddie and how big she was getting, "She'll be four years old in May. I love you, Mom and Dad. I'll talk to you soon."

They hung up. Now for Justin's parents. Grace had met them at several Giant's games, and she and Justin had visited them at their home in Cupertino.

Justin and Grace were going to call his parents on Monday while he had a day off.

63

MONDAY MORNING CAME, AND JUSTIN was at Grace's house by 9:00. They made the FaceTime call to Justin's parents.

Justin's mother, Jane, answered on the third ring. She was thrilled to see Justin and Grace together.

"Hey, Mom, where's Dad? Can you get him, please?"

"Bob!" she yelled. "Get in here, honey. Justin and Grace have some news!"

Bob came in and sat next to Jane at the dining room table. "What's up, you guys?" asked Bob.

"We're engaged!" said Justin holding up Grace's left hand so they could see the ring.

"Ah!" screamed Jane.

"Congratulations!" said Bob. "When is the big day?"

"We are looking at November 15," said Justin

"Next year?" asked Jane.

"No. This year, Mom. We don't want a big, elaborate wedding."

"Is that true, Grace, you don't want a fancy wedding?"

"Yes, actually, I want to have family and friends there and a meaningful ceremony. I don't want a huge thing."

"Define small, dear," said Jane.

"Well, I'm thinking a maid of honor and a best man for a wedding party and only very close friends."

"Well, that will be the whole team and their plus ones. That's a large wedding, hun."

"Oh dear," said Grace. She looked at Justin for help. "Is that true, do we have to invite the entire team?"

"Kind of, if we don't, there will be hurt feelings."

"You see, this is why people elope. To avoid the unavoidable hurt feelings."

"Whoa, let's not start talking elopement. We can work this out, can't we, Justin?" said Jane.

"Oh, Mom, this is gonna be hard, but Grace wants a very small, intimate wedding. I've already had the big fancy party wedding. I want small too."

Jane could see the fear in Grace's eyes. She was terrified.

"How many people would you be inviting from your side?" Jane asked Grace.

"Only six from my family. My sister and her husband, my in-laws who are like parents to me, and some dear friends who are also like parents to me."

Jane made a strange face and started to ask about Grace's parents, but Justin cut in quickly with "Grace's parents are not in the picture and will not be at the wedding."

Justin stated this so matter-of-factly that there was no room to question it. Subject closed. It was then that Jane realized that the wedding really *needed* to be a small affair.

"If you want small, son," said Bob, "then it will be small."

"But," interjected Jane, "it will be classy too."

"Thank you," said Grace with visible relief as she leaned her head against Justin's shoulder.

Justin said, "So, November 15. Will that work for you guys?"

Bob said, "We will mark it on our calendars, and nothing will stop us from being there."

Jane asked, "Grace, would you like some company to go dress shopping? I would love to go with you."

"I have lots of friends in the fashion industry. I've got the dress handled. But I could use some help with the other things, like a good bakery for the cake and flowers and those sort of things. If you're still willing?"

"Are you sure about the dress, sweetie? You know your waistline can change quite a bit in three months."

"Mother!" said Justin. "Grace is not pregnant! That's enough of that!"

When it was all said and done, Jane was thrilled to help Grace with some of the planning.

There was a lot to schedule in a very short three months. There was the church, the pastor, the cake, the flowers, the reception location, the invitations, the wedding registries—it was all so overwhelming to Grace.

Jane came up to the city and worked tirelessly with Grace to get everything in order for their big day.

64

....

THE WEEK PRIOR TO THE wedding, Mitch and Marty flew in. Mitch felt like a father to Grace, and he wanted to take some time in getting to know Justin.

Justin met Mitch and Marty at the airport and drove them back to the house. They insisted on staying at a hotel; they didn't want to put any more pressure on the bride and groom.

After warm greetings and catching up on the wedding preparations, Mitch asked Justin to help him find a good hotel with not too much driving for Marty and him. Justin was happy to help.

They settled on the Marriott Moscone Center. It was central to San Francisco and a nice hotel. They always had rooms available. They used an app to get a good rate and booked a room.

Mitch and Justin took the couple's luggage over to the Marriott and settled them into their room. On the drive over, Marty asked, "How did you and Grace meet?"

Justin answered, "We met at our church's singles' group. We had both been to a picnic the week before. She caught my eye, and apparently, I caught hers. The next Friday, we were both at the singles' meeting and officially met. That was about a year ago."

"So was it love at first sight? Grace is a beautiful woman."

"She sure is. I wouldn't say it was love at first sight. We have some key things in common that made dating a little easier."

"Such as?"

"Such as we are both widowed. We both have children."

"Oh, I didn't realize you had children of your own."

"Had. My wife and both children were killed in a car accident by a drunk driver."

"Oh my goodness, I am so sorry to hear that. How long had you been married?"

"Five years, Cassandra was four, and Justin was two years old."

"That's a tough loss. As you know, Grace's husband, Matt, died from complications from a brain seizure."

"Ya, out-of-the-blue kind of seizures."

"Yes. It devastated her. She came out to the ranch to scatter some of his ashes. They spent over a year out there with us."

"Grace told me they spent a lot of time with you guys. You know there is a lot about her past that she doesn't talk about?"

"Yes, that's true. It's for the best that you don't pressure her about it. Nothing good can come of it."

"She says the exact same thing. I just wish I could help ease some of the pain from whatever it is. I know there is still issues from her parents abandoning her and her sister."

"Well, Justin, if you really want to help her heal, then don't pry, pray for her. This kind of healing is best left in God's hands."

They arrived at the hotel and got checked in. Mitch asked the concierge if she could assist with a rental car with GPS.

Justin offered to chauffeur them, but Mitch insisted there was far too much to do the week prior to the wedding. He told Justin this way he could help with picking things up and shuttling people around. Justin was thankful for the forethought.

"After all," Mitch said, "I like to think of myself as a father figure to Grace, which would make me a father-in-law to you."

"Yes, sir," said Justin. Suddenly, he knew they were having the "you're marrying my daughter" conversation.

"What do you think of little Maddie?" asked Mitch.

"Oh, she is something special. She calls me JJ."

Justin and Mitch both got a chuckle out of that.

"How do you plan on handling discipline with Maddie?"

"We've talked about that. At first, I didn't want to overstep any boundaries, and it was kind of awkward. Grace has an idea of how she wants to raise Maddie. I've been working on absorbing the full scope of her ideal. If I disagree with her, we talk it through before I do anything.

"I feel like we're getting to a comfortable place where we understand each other's hearts for Maddie. We both want the best for her. We want to do what is in her best interest. Grace isn't afraid to spank Maddie or slap her hand for instance. But she also uses timeout and taking a favorite toy away for a time. All in all, I think she has a pretty balanced approach."

"Grace's own upbringing was a strange mixture of being treated like a maid and adored by her father. It's good to hear that she is using balance with Maddie. As you know, we tend to gravitate to what we experienced. At least, Grace knows what she experienced wasn't good."

"If her father adored her so much, where has he been the last six years?"

"Good question. Grace will probably never have anything to do with her parents again, even if they do show up one day."

"I'd probably punch him if he showed up now."

Mitch and Justin had gotten off on a good foot. It was time to head back at the house with both cars.

65

MARTY ASKED GRACE, "HAVE YOU heard from your sister yet? Is she going to make it for the wedding?" Marty's voice was full of caution that Jane didn't miss and didn't understand, but Grace seemed to.

"We're still working on some of the finer details of them coming, but it looks promising."

"I hope they can make it."

Jane interjected, "You mean you're not sure your own sister is going to be able to come?"

"It's not so easy for them. They have a thriving business that depends on Jon-Pierre. Coming to the wedding might mean shutting down their business for a week if he can't get another photographer to fill in. Plus, they have two little girls to travel with. I offered to pay the airfare for them because I really want her to be here. But the issue isn't money. It's their business details."

Grace gave a pointed look toward Marty who understood the real issue was witness security's stand on her twin sister coming to her location. Nothing could be more dangerous than the two of them being in the same public location.

The business explanation seemed to satisfy Jane. "Well, I will certainly say a prayer that it all works out for them to come. Are they coming from France?" asked Jane.

"No, Australia," said Grace. It's a fourteen-hour flight with a four- and five-year-old. Plus it's a seventeen-hour time difference. I hope to know for sure tonight."

Just then, her iPad rang. Grace opened up FaceTime; it was Kae reporting that they had overcome all the obstacles to be able to come to the wedding.

They had their flights all arranged just like last time, she said, a code that witness security was involved, and they would travel under the radar. They also had hotel and rental car all locked in place and would be landing around 9:00 p.m. local time.

"I will text you all the numbers you need," said Grace. "I can't wait."

"Me either. I'm so excited."

Jane thought the girls had a very strange way of communicating. It was all so vague and cryptic. It almost sounded like a spy movie.

The next morning was the day before the wedding. Grace had a checklist of things to make sure were secured for tomorrow. She checked with the bakery, the florist, the church, and Pastor Bill.

Justin and Grace had agreed on who would be invited. There were a handful of people from the team, people he was close to. And there were about six couples from church they considered close friends, that included Tim and Lucy.

Then there were the families. Justin's side had about forty people that were close family. Grace's side had eight including the Laurent girls.

Addie Laurent would be the ring bearer and Maddie and Jaelynn would be flower girls. Grace was getting excited and nervous as the hours ticked by.

Before she knew it, it was time for the rehearsal. Everyone got to the church on time. The rehearsal only took forty minutes, and they ran through it twice mainly for the little girls.

Jon-Pierre, Mitch, and Justin's brother-in-law, Travis, agreed to be ushers and help get everyone seated. Justin had made arrangements for a private party for the rehearsal dinner at Top of the Mark where he had proposed to Grace.

Jane commented to Grace how beautiful she looked tonight, just radiant. She said, "I guess I didn't catch that you and your sister were twins. You two look exactly alike. Except that you are absolutely glowing tonight."

Grace blushed.

"Kaelynn, I couldn't help but notice that you travel with security. Why is that, dear?"

"I used to be a model, and I get too much attention when I go in public or travel. It's safer for our family if I travel with security. I hope it doesn't bother you."

"Oh, don't mind me," said Jane. "Bob is always telling me I stick my nose too far into other people's business. I'm just naturally a curious person. I hope I haven't offended you?"

"No, not at all. I am so used to them I hardly know they are there."

They had a wonderful time at dinner. Everyone got to know everyone else a little more and came to appreciate the mix and blend of backgrounds.

Toasts were made with sparkling cider, and everyone had warm wishes for the bride and groom. By 9:30, the evening was winding down.

Justin's friends from the team and his brother-in-law all wanted to take him out for a bachelor party. It all seemed relatively harmless since Justin didn't drink alcohol. So the guys all went out while the girls all went to Grace's house.

Kaelynn said she needed to get the girls back to the hotel and into bed or they would both be monsters tomorrow. Grace completely understood. She was having a difficult time getting Maddie in bed herself.

Just before Kaelynn left, Grace, Kae, and the security team got together on the back porch for a conversation about tomorrow. Jim, the main security man, began, "Grace, you have a limo ride to the church tomorrow. And, Kaelynn, you and Jon-Pierre and the girls also have a limo for tomorrow. I will be with Grace at all times, and my partner Geoff will be with you, Kaelynn. Neither of you will ever be out of sight.

"I need you two to promise you are going to stick to the plan at all times. No sneaking off or trying to ditch us. Remember, Grace, you have never been more exposed than you are right now and will be tomorrow. Kaelynn, any sniper would easily mistake you for Grace, so you are in just as much danger as Grace is. Am I making myself clear enough?"

"Yes," they both responded.

Grace asked, "Is there any way that we can make sure that Kaelynn is never in a place where a sniper could get to her?"

"We will do our best, but your cooperation is imperative."

"Grace, great call having your brother-in-law as photographer. That is making things much easier. Now the cake and flowers are all being delivered an hour before the wedding. We will be able to get those people in and out without a problem."

"The fact that you're not having a DJ or band for the reception is also a huge plus. We have been able to vet almost everyone who has been invited to the wedding."

"Who haven't you been able to clear yet?" Asked Grace.

"The caterer. They have been in business for two generations in San Francisco Bay Area, but we can't find anything on them prior to that. I don't think it is a problem, but I would feel much better if the proverbial loophole was closed. I'm waiting for one more confirmation from Washington, and I hope it comes in before tomorrow."

Jane had been reading Maddie a bedtime story as she nodded off to sleep. She was coming to tell Grace that she was asleep when she heard the last portion of the conversation out on the porch.

Why would Grace need to have the caterer background checked before the wedding and why would that need to come from Washington?

Jane had a strange feeling about Grace's obscure past life. Plus, she wasn't altogether buying her sister's bodyguard story either. But Grace had given her no reason to suspect any foul play.

Jane knew Grace genuinely loved her son. And her son adored Grace and Maddie. But Jane couldn't help but feel there were some missing pieces to the puzzle. She prayed that whatever Grace was hiding would not break her son's heart.

66

....

JANE DECIDED TO TALK TO Grace before returning to her own hotel for the night. When everyone had finally left and it was just Jane and Bob with Grace, Jane asked, "Grace, will you be okay here tonight by yourself?"

"Oh, sure. It's just me and Maddie all the time."

"Dear, I was coming to tell you that I got Maddie off to sleep, and I overheard Kaelynn's security guy talking about the caterer and their background check. Is there something we should know?"

"Oh, Mom, it's routine with Kaelynn. Even though she gave up modeling when she had her first baby, it's still rough for her when she goes out publicly."

"Okay, but why would that put you in possible danger?"

"We're identical twins. It would be easy for one of us to be mistaken for the other. It happens all the time. At least it used to when we both lived in France. There's a funny story about that…"

Grace rushed into the story of Jon-Pierre mistaking Grace for Kaelynn when Grace was recovering from surgery at Kaelynn's house.

She told them how he came home from working for a week in Australia and saw Grace asleep on the couch but thought she was Kaelynn. How he came over and kissed her neck and called her baby and told her how much he had missed her. And how Grace jumped up, shocked, and told Jon-Pierre that she was Grace not Kaelynn and how Kae came home at that exact moment.

They all got a big laugh and it effectively moved the conversation away from the security question. Jane offered to stay the night with Grace if she wanted her to. But Grace assured her she would be fine.

The guys stayed out well past midnight. They were quite the enigma at the pub they chose to celebrate at—a group of guys, obviously at a bachelor party, but no one was drinking alcohol.

They played pool and darts; they laughed and told jokes. All in all, it was the tamest bachelor party the pub owner had ever seen. Somehow it was refreshing.

Justin left the guys at 1:30 a.m. to head for home. He wondered how Grace was doing, so he texted her:

"Are you still up?"

"Yes."

"Can I come by?"

"I wish you would, please."

So Justin went straight over to Grace's house. He let himself in with his new key. The house was dark except for a night-light plugged into the living room wall.

As Justin's eyes adjusted, he could see Grace's silhouette as she sat on one of the sofas. He heard her sniffle.

He moved to the couch and took her into his arms.

"What's wrong, baby? Are you getting cold feet? Are you thinking about Matt? What is it? I'm right here for you."

"Justin, you have no idea how much baggage I am bringing into this marriage, and it's absolutely not fair to you."

"Now you hold it right there. We are going to make vows to each other tomorrow. We are going to promise to love each other no matter what comes against us. You know, good times or bad times, sickness or health, riches or poorness. We are in this for the long haul 'til death do us part."

"I know that. I know that you mean it too. But it's not fair to you because there are some things about me that you don't know. And I can't tell you."

"Why can't you tell me? You can tell me anything."

"No, I can't. And the reason I can't tell you goes against everything about our relationship that I hold sacred."

"I don't understand."

"I know you don't, and I am so sorry. Baby, I don't want to start our marriage with things hidden from each other."

"Then don't."

"But telling you could cost me my life."

"Look, I know you're under a lot of stress right now, but you don't need to be so dramatic about it. Say the word, and we will call the whole thing off and just get married by a justice of the peace."

"No, that's not it."

"Okay, why don't you give me a hypothetical situation?"

"Okay, what I'm about to tell you could very well cost me my life. Should you ever get mad enough or file for divorce and want to really hurt me, what I'm about to tell you would be catastrophic for me."

"But, Justin," Grace continued, "I want us to be one, like the Bible says, where the two become one. And I don't think I can do that with you and keep my past hidden from you."

There was a long pause, silence, Grace pulling herself together and Justin waiting in the dark patiently.

"I've been praying about this for months. My security contact tells me not to open up to you, but I feel God telling me to trust you with my life. So you need to understand that. I am trusting you with my life."

"I will do my best to understand. I've been praying too, asking God to help you feel like you could open up to me. So I believe we both have gotten answers to our prayers."

"Here it is…I am in the witness security program. I had to testify against an organized crime syndicate a few years ago. There are only a handful of people on this planet that know, Marty and Mitch, Mary and Roger, and Kaelynn and Jon-Pierre."

"So that's why there are so few of your family around."

"No, actually, that is all the family I have."

"Go on."

"This crime organization fronted as a legitimate modeling agency." Grace paused, biting her lip. "They were involved in sex slavery."

Grace buried her head in her hands and sobbed. Justin asked, "Did Matt know all about this?"

"Matt rescued me from it. He literally saved my life."

"Go on."

"It was my testimony that sealed the conviction and gave them all life in prison without the possibility of parole."

"Okay, done deal. You should be safe now, right?"

"No, they have a nonrevocable contract on me for 1.5 million dollars and hit contacts all over the world. Just having Kaelynn here for the wedding is a huge security nightmare."

"Oh, so the security isn't for Kaelynn. It's for you."

"Yes and no, remember we are identical. She could be taken out just because she looks like me."

Grace went on, "Justin, I've been through some unspeakable things. I have been made to do things that would make your skin crawl. I had no choice. If I messed up, I got a correctional visit from one of the owners. And believe me, he had a very physical way of persuading me to do as I was told. I was about to take my own life when Matt talked me into escaping with him."

Grace told Justin about the elopement, the immediate plane ride to the United States, the justice of the peace in New York City, the year spent with Mitch and Marty in Wyoming.

She told him about the nightmares, about being told she could never have a baby, and about Matt being instrumental in leading her to Christ. She told him about the forced abortion and the damage done to her body.

Justin pulled her tighter into his embrace and cried with her. He kept saying, "Baby, I am so sorry that all happened to you."

Finally, he pulled her away so he could look at her face. Her eyes were puffy like she had been crying for a couple of hours. She said, "I understand if you want to call the wedding off. I really should have told you all these a long time ago, but I was, I am still, so afraid of losing you. I know this is selfishness on my part. You deserve to be able to make your own decision."

"You think after telling me this about your past that I wouldn't want to marry you?"

"I'm damaged, can't you see that? I am broken and no good for you or possibly anyone. You deserve so much better than me. I had no right to keep all this from you. It's not fair to you."

"What I see is a beautiful woman, whom I love with all my heart, who is being beat up hideously by the enemy of God. When you came to Christ, all your past was washed away by the blood of the Lamb. Who am I not to accept you exactly the way you are today? I'm not perfect. And you are not damaged!"

"But I am. And I'm afraid you are going to regret this marriage."

"I'm not. I'm not afraid. I'm not scared. I want to marry you tomorrow, for better or worse, in sickness and health, for good times and bad, for richer or poorer as long as we both shall live. I want to marry *you*!"

"You say that now, but what about when we can't have a baby together? What about when I have a nightmare I can't shake and don't want to be touched for a month? Will you still want me then?"

"I said for better or worse, in sickness and health, for good times and bad, as long as we both shall live. You just put your life into my hands. God told you to trust me. Now trust me, please. I want to marry you today."

Justin slid off the couch and onto one knee. He took Grace's hands in his and asked, "Will you marry me today?"

Grace collapsed into his arms and sobbed. "Yes."

67

THE MORNING OF THE WEDDING arrived. Grace woke up and felt like her eyes were full of sandpaper. She showered and started working on her hair. There was a knock at her front door.

Grace went to open it, and there was Kaelynn.

"Hi, I'm here to help get the bride ready."

She took a good look at Grace and asked, "Honey, what's wrong? You've been crying your eyes out."

"Oh, ya, I decided to tell Justin about witness security. I couldn't go into this marriage with a lie between us."

"What? Did he call off the wedding?"

"No, he got down on one knee and asked me to marry him again."

The girls hugged each other and were both crying at how romantic a moment that must have been.

"Grace, he is your knight you always dreamed of when we were little girls, the one who knows the worst but loves you the most."

"I think you're right."

The girls started getting Grace all dolled up for the wedding. Each of the girls did the other one's hair and make-up. It was like old times.

Grace's dress was tulle and lace, with a fit and flare design, featuring a deep V-neckline, wide sheer lace straps, and a stunning V-back with covered buttons. The skirt had a scalloped lace hem and a chapel train. She looked amazing with her blonde hair down and curled softly. She wore a plain pearl bracelet and her engagement ring.

Kaelynn's dress was a sea-foam mint color with a halter top and empire waist. Her hair was a beautiful brown French braid cascading halfway down her back.

Just as they were finishing preparations, their limo pulled up. The driver, one of their security details for the day, got out and came to the door.

68

....

INSIDE THE LIMO WAS A bucket with a bottle of champagne and two flute glasses. Kaelynn opened the bottle and poured them each a glass.

"Oh, Kae, I don't drink anymore."

"Grace, you're a nervous wreck. Have a little to help you relax. Besides, you used to drink like a fish. What happened?"

"I have a daughter. I can't be inebriated anymore. Plus, Justin's wife and two children were killed by a drunk driver, so he doesn't drink either. It's just easier all around."

"I get it. But today is a little special, wouldn't you say?"

"Yes," she said as she took the flute and sipped.

"Ah, I forgot how good this stuff was."

"Okay, slow down now. You'll be tipsy before we get to the church. You're not having any second thoughts, are you?"

"No, this is right. I can feel it."

"From the little I've gotten to know Justin and what you've told me, I think it is too."

They arrived at the church and pulled into a special parking space at the back that led directly to the bride's room. It was raining when they arrived, and they were thankful for the parking structure. It shielded them from the moisture.

Once inside, Jon-Pierre wanted to stage some photos of the girls getting ready. He got one of Grace braiding Kae's hair and one of Kae curling Grace's. Then another of Grace putting on some pearl earrings her future mother-in-law had given her.

Jon-Pierre had already gotten shots of Justin shining his shoes and Travis, his brother-in-law and his best man, tying his tie.

Everyone was ready. Everyone was seated. Roger knocked on the bride's door and asked if Grace was ready. She opened the door, and Roger gasped. She was incredibly beautiful today.

"May I have the honor of walking you down the aisle?" Roger asked.

"Yes, you may." Grace kissed his cheek. There were tears welling in her eyes as she said, "This isn't an altogether easy day for us, is it?"

"No," he said. "It's not. But it is as it should be. Matt would have wanted you to go on, to find someone who could make you happy, that you could spend the rest of your life with. Someone who would love Maddie as if she were his own. And Justin is all those things, my dear."

A tear slid down Grace's cheek. Roger slipped his hanky from his pocket and gently dabbed at the tear careful not to mess up her make-up.

"Dad, I wanted you to give me away today. I wasn't thinking about how hard it would be for you and mom. I'm sorry. But I wanted to ask you if you two would mind if I still called you mom and dad? I feel so close to you, and we've been through so much together."

Now Roger was tearing up. "Of course, you can, dear. You are the daughter we always wanted."

They embraced and began their walk to the church door. The music changed to the wedding march. Roger and Grace began their walk down the center aisle. Grace saw Justin standing at the front by Pastor Bill. He looked so handsome.

Justin's eyes locked with Grace's as she walked with Roger. When they reached the front, Pastor Bill asked," Who gives this woman to be with this man?

Roger said loud and clear, "Her mother and I."

69

. . . .

THE REST OF THE CEREMONY was a blur to Justin and Grace. They had said their vows to each other and before God last night. As far as they were concerned, today was a mere formality for their friends and family.

"Justin, you may kiss your bride."

Justin took Grace in his arms and kissed her ever so gently on the lips, a kiss that promised so much more to come.

The reception was a wonderfully small affair. Grace had had her fill of large, expensive parties in her short life. All she cared about was that she and Justin would never have to say good-bye again. They would live in the same house forever.

The reception was winding down, and Grace still didn't know where they were going for their honeymoon. Justin had been very secretive about it.

He had given her an idea of what to pack for the weeklong getaway, but it didn't give anything away. They got into the limo at the church and got comfortable.

Their driver, yet another security handler, opened the window between the front and the back. He looked at Grace and said, "I know you have a destination selected, sir, but we are going to have to make some minor adjustments. We will be flying out of Oakland instead of San Francisco due to a security situation at San Francisco."

"Sorry for the last-minute change. We have all the arrangements made, and your flight will be ready when you arrive."

Justin said, "That's fine, Juan, thank you for your attention to the details."

The window closed just as the limo was merging onto the Bay Bridge. Grace turned to Justin and said, "Welcome to witness security. If there is even a hint of a problem, they swoop in and take over. Did you tell them where we are going for our honeymoon?"

"I did, I guess that's how they know what kind of arrangements needed to change."

"Well, don't be shocked if we pull up to a private jet and step out of the limo and onto the stairs."

"Wow, such VIP service. I'm gonna like traveling with you."

"Unfortunately, it probably means that we are not going to your selected location. Wherever you were planning for us to go has likely been compromised."

"So where would we be going then."

"I don't know! You're supposed to know that, remember? You wouldn't tell me anything."

"So witness security can change our plans at their whim and not tell us where we are going?"

"If it is vital to my security, yes."

"Oh."

"If that is the case," said Grace, "a number of things are about to happen. First, we won't know where we are going until we clear Oakland airspace. Second, depending on the breach of security, we may have to relocate."

Justin's eyes got huge. His whole career was in San Francisco.

"But," Grace interrupted Justin's panicked look, "we will find out a whole lot more when we get to the plane. Just relax, please."

The limo pulled up onto the tarmac next to a Gulf Stream G650. The stairs were down, and Keith Hartman was standing at the base.

Grace introduced Justin to Keith as they boarded the plane. They took their seats and buckled in. Justin asked Keith, "Where are we heading?"

Keith responded in unison with Grace, "I can't tell you anything until we leave Oakland airspace." They laughed together.

As soon as the plane had taken off and cleared Oakland, Keith unbuckled his seatbelt, signaling it was okay to do so.

"Nothing about your honeymoon plans have changed at this point except your mode of transportation. Of course, I will assume you don't mind the private jet?"

Grace asked, "What happened that we couldn't fly out of San Francisco?"

"There was a security breach with another witness, not you, but we absolutely couldn't walk you into that situation."

"Okay, so then would one of you kindly tell me where we are going?"

Justin jumped in, "A little birdie told me that you really enjoy St. Croix in the US Virgin Islands?"

"Yes, I love it there."

"Well, that is where we are going. I am so happy that Jon-Pierre and Kae are staying for a week to watch Maddie for us."

Grace asked, "Have you ever tried surfing? Because I'm going to teach you to surf."

The end.

CPSIA information can be obtained
at www.ICGtesting.com
Printed in the USA
LVHW030248250220
648116LV00001B/89